GREEN SOLUTIONS FOR LIVABLE CITIES

Sonia Chand Sandhu
Ramola Naik Singru
John Bachmann
Vaideeswaran Sankaran
Pierre Arnoux

ASIAN DEVELOPMENT BANK

ADB

© 2016 Asian Development Bank
6 ADB Avenue, Mandaluyong City, 1550 Metro Manila, Philippines
Tel +63 2 632 4444; Fax +63 2 636 2444
www.adb.org

Some rights reserved. Published in 2016.
Printed in the Philippines.

ISBN 978-92-9257-350-8 (Print), 978-92-9257-351-5 (e-ISBN)
Publication Stock No. BKK157697

Cataloging-In-Publication Data

Sandhu, Sonia Chand; Naik Singru, Ramola; Bachmann, John; Vaideeswaran, Sankaran; Arnoux, Pierre.
            GrEEEn Solutions for Livable Cities
Mandaluyong City, Philippines: Asian Development Bank, 2016.

1. Cities.   2. Urban development.   3. Environment.   4. Climate resilience. I. Asian Development Bank.

Notes:
In this publication, "$" refers to US dollars.
Corrigenda to ADB publications may be found at http://www.adb.org/publications/corrigenda

Contents

Figures, Tables, and Boxes

Boxes

Foreword

GrEEEn Cities: An Imperative for Asia's Future

Asia's cities are some of the biggest and most populous the world has ever seen. These megacities drive economic growth in a region that generates 40% of global gross domestic product, but which is also home to half the world's extreme poor. By 2050, 1.4 billion people will have moved to them, seeking better lives.[1]

To cope with this human influx, we need a new approach to designing urban space. Sustainable development cannot be achieved without transforming how we build and manage our cities.

Bold steps now can help our cities absorb the pressures of mass urbanization. Without such steps, inefficient land-use planning and natural resource management, limited community engagement and decision-making processes, and insufficient financing will expose our cities to risks. Climate change and natural disasters compound these risks, as most urban agglomerations in Asia are located on or near vulnerable coastal zones. This region accounts for more than half the world's disaster death toll and more than three-quarters of its damage bill from natural hazards.

Vancouver in Canada as well as Yokohama and Kitakyushu in Japan show that cities can thrive despite these pressures. All are economically prosperous, enjoying a world-class physical environment, infrastructure, and services. Of course, it takes time to reach these goals—between 20 and 40 years. But their example shows that urban transformation based on green principles and informed by integrated and collaborative approaches can balance the demands of the environment, infrastructure, and economic growth.

Can Asia's cities follow suit? They can, if they have the leadership, vision, broad community participation, and stakeholder ownership. We have the opportunity to learn from international best practice and leapfrog some of the difficulties experienced in other parts of the world.

Our efforts will support Goal 11 of the recently adopted Sustainable Development Goals, which marks a historic commitment to Sustainable Cities and Communities. Its stated aim is to "make cities inclusive, safe, resilient, and sustainable." This requires urban transformation on an unprecedented scale, to support the environmental, social, and economic well-being of future generations.

---

[1]   ADB. 2011. *Fast Facts: Urbanization in Asia.* http://www.adb.org/sites/default/files/Urbanization-fast-facts.pdf

This publication is authored by a multidisciplinary technical assistance team of experts. It shares solutions emerging from the GrEEEn Cities Initiative of the Asian Development Bank (ADB) in Southeast Asia and good practices that show the effectiveness of integrated approaches that reinforce each other, rather than work in isolation.

The authors have developed approaches to address varying urban contexts, which have been successfully piloted in seven Southeast Asian cities. This has led to the development of GrEEEn City Action Plans and road maps for investing in livable cities. Furthermore, the publication describes the value of developing consensus among stakeholders and investing in strong institutional Urban Management Partnerships to enable peer learning and capacity building.

ADB recognizes that urban transformation promotes broader sustainability. Our Urban Operational Plan 2012–2020 outlines strategies for economic competitiveness, environmental sustainability, and social equity. We will continue to support local governments as they invest in green infrastructure by providing technical assistance and financing that leverages additional resources from the public sector, the private sector, and other development partners.

ADB thanks the authors for their valuable contributions. The publication has also benefited from an external peer review by the LSE Cities, London School of Economics and Political Science. Further valuable contributions were made by ADB's developing member country counterparts in Indonesia, Malaysia, Myanmar, Thailand, and Viet Nam, which validated the GrEEEn City Action Plans at the Enabling GrEEEn Cities Regional Conference in May 2014.

GrEEEn Solutions for Livable Cities is a valuable guide for creating livable cities, not just in Asia and the Pacific, but in all parts of the world that face this defining challenge.

Stephen P. Groff
Vice-President (Operations 2)
Asian Development Bank

Integrated Solutions for GrEEEn Cities

Asia's urbanization is unprecedented and fast-paced. By 2050, two-thirds of Asia's population will be urban.[2] This makes Asia the most dynamic region in the world. While megacities continue to grow, the spatial trends indicate that urban growth is increasingly moving to medium-sized towns and secondary cities in Asia. Over the past decade, the world has witnessed a growing incidence of climate change-induced extreme weather events, increasing the vulnerability of people and infrastructure in these cities and towns. Informal settlements are often expanding into areas vulnerable to flooding, pollution, and other hazards, increasing the incidence of risk. Cities in Asia are facing growing environmental problems and infrastructure demand to meet the growing needs of citizens. Various studies estimate that almost 75% of all infrastructure investments will be needed in urban and peri-urban environments over the next 40 years.[3]

The urban challenge lies in meeting infrastructure and service delivery needs efficiently and effectively balancing environmental considerations and sustaining economic and inclusive growth. This is indeed a tall order for urban managers, practitioners, and citizens alike. *GrEEEn Solutions for Livable Cities* addresses some of these challenges facing the quality of life of urban dwellers today and provides solutions by capturing knowledge from field experience, including Asian Development Bank (ADB) operations, and demonstrating good practices relevant to ADB's developing member countries. It highlights the key role of leadership and a shared vision built through broad stakeholder participation and partnerships, which are prerequisites for the transformation of cities of today into livable cities of the future.

The book presents an integrated approach that breaks down sector silos, to show that a city is a complex space in which all sectors intersect and all disciplines interact. This is a critical and timely publication as ADB moves toward a "One ADB" approach to address the challenges of sustainable development. It provides solutions and conduits for leveraging finance through adaptive engineering design, planning, and innovative institutional partnerships.

This volume is forward-looking and is embedded in this emerging global context. 2015 was a watershed year for the world's future. Landmark events, including the adoption of the Sendai Framework for Disaster Risk Reduction 2015–2030 in March, the Third International Conference on Financing for Development in Addis Ababa in June, the United Nations Summit in September to finalize the post-2015 United Nations Sustainable Development Goals, and the Conference of the Parties (COP) gathering in Paris in December, have given us an unprecedented opportunity to shape this century's preeminent challenge—sustainable development. Recognizing that Asia and the Pacific is the key battleground in the global fight against climate change, the challenge is to translate policy into actions at the city level. This book sets down successful experiences and best practices to promote learning and sharing of knowledge on integrated urban development in making cities green, resilient, safe, competitive, and inclusive. I highly recommend it to all those interested in making cities around the world more livable.

Bambang Susantono
Vice-President for Knowledge Management and Sustainable Development
Asian Development Bank

---

[2]   ADB. 2012. *Key Indicators for Asia and the Pacific 2012: Green Urbanization in Asia.* Special chapter. Manila.

[3]   World Economic Forum and European Bank for Reconstruction and Development. 2014. *Accelerating Infrastructure Delivery: New Evidence from International Financial Institutions.* Geneva: World Economic Forum.

Message: ADB Southeast Asia Department

The Urban Development and Water Division of the Southeast Asia Department at the Asian Development Bank (ADB) has pioneered GrEEEn Cities toward sustainable urban development by embracing innovation. This paradigm shift of "doing things differently" combines the 3Es of economy, environment, and equity. The GrEEEn Cities Operational Framework thereby provides an integrated perspective in redefining the meaning of livability, particularly in the design of infrastructure investments and urban service delivery. It offers a flexible and scalable approach to address Asia's livability challenge in cities, which are embedded in different country contexts and which are at different development stages.

This publication combines the findings from completed and ongoing projects throughout Southeast Asia and also showcases some of the innovative multimedia elements that have been produced during the process. This new way of capturing and sharing knowledge underscores our commitment to change the way we think about green cities and supports our mutual efforts to extend the reach of our work to raise awareness of *GrEEEn Solutions for Livable Cities*. In addition to the conceptual framework, lessons learned, and good practices, this publication tackles the key enablers for actually achieving livable cities. It discusses the role of more effective asset management for achieving resilient cities, possibilities for GrEEEn City financing, the growing importance of key performance indicators in monitoring urban service delivery and sustainable development targets, and the application of decision support systems to make better decisions in the planning and management of our cities.

The first Enabling GrEEEn Cities Regional Conference in May 2014 brought together the public and the private sector as well as civil society to nurture existing and potential partnerships in urban development. This publication makes a valid claim for strengthening such Urban Management Partnerships, as the challenges city managers face today, and potentially even more so in the future, cannot be tackled by governments alone.

I am pleased to see how countries in the region have embraced the GrEEEn Cities Initiative and found exciting ways to pilot integrated urban development activities in a number of cities. From this cooperation, both the GrEEEn Cities team in the Urban Development and Water Division and our partners in developing member countries and the urban development profession have mutually gained further experience and expertise in translating knowledge into practice. We are looking forward to seeing this work accelerate sustainable investments and help forge new pathways and further partnerships for realizing livable cities across Asia.

James Nugent
Director General
Southeast Asia Department
Asian Development Bank

Message: Vision for GrEEEn Cities

I have a dream, which I believe we all share: It is to see the transformation of Asian cities into livable cities. Cities that are the future cities for our children and grandchildren. Cities that are climate and disaster resilient, resource efficient, economically vibrant and competitive, socially inclusive, equitable, tolerant, access-oriented, with good quality public open spaces, affordable, healthy, walkable, and amiable for different groups of people. Cities contain the vital ingredients to improve millions of people's lives in the region. They are the engines of growth that drive prosperity in Asia and lead to solutions. I am pleased that my dream is on its way to translation as we share this book on grEEEn solutions for making livable cities.

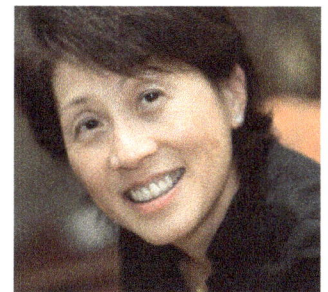

The GrEEEn Cities Initiative emerged as a response to the demands from developing member countries (DMCs) in Southeast Asia of the Asian Development Bank (ADB).[4] In December 2012, ADB approved a regional technical assistance on Green Cities: Toward a Sustainable Urban Future in Southeast Asia, led by the Urban Development and Water Division of the Southeast Asia Department. As the director of the division in 2012, I was keen to bring innovation to our urban operations. The innovative GrEEEn Cities Initiative puts into action the strategies under ADB's Urban Operational Plan 2012–2020 and the goals of ADB's Strategy 2020 of achieving environmental sustainability and inclusive growth.

Green urban infrastructure operations are expected to grow significantly in the next 15–20 years. Lending operations (sovereign and nonsovereign) are expected to increase in 2015 onward. Starting with Southeast Asia, ADB aims to provide support to its DMCs to move from green growth strategies to green city realities. Through the GrEEEn Cities Initiative, ADB is working with cities that commit to a long-term partnership (15–20 years) to make this happen. We have provided technical assistance in Indonesia, Malaysia, Myanmar, the Philippines, Thailand, and Viet Nam, to help cities develop GrEEEn City Action Plans. In this respect, *GrEEEn Solutions for Livable Cities* provides useful lessons learned, good practice, and operational guidance for DMCs on urban operations.

The percentage of Asia's population living in urban areas will increase to 55% by 2030 in countries such as the People's Republic of China, and urbanization policies suggest that almost 75% of the population will become urban.[5] Cities are the drivers of economic

---

[4] ADB. 2013. Greening Asia's Cities. Video: 16 September 2013. http://www.adb.org/news/videos/greening-asias-cities

[5] ADB. 2015. *Key Indicators for Asia and the Pacific 2015.* Manila.

growth, producing approximately 80% of a country's gross domestic product.[6] Asian urban productivity is more than 5.5 times higher than that of rural areas.[7] Cities have a high concentration of people and economic activities (commercial, industrial, services, etc.) but are resource intensive, accounting for 75% of both energy consumption and carbon emissions.[8] Many rapidly urbanizing Asian cities are threatened by excessive energy consumption, depreciating natural resources, and increasing floods and droughts caused by climate change. Asian cities are battling traffic congestion, air pollution, and water pollution. Most Asian cities lack effective wastewater treatment systems, and more than two-thirds of collected solid waste is not disposed of properly. These are just a few of the challenges.

ADB's Strategy 2020 states that to transform the archetypal chaotic, polluted, inequitable city of Asia into a competitive, equitable, and environmentally sustainable urban region—in short, a livable city—will require a new approach to city development and to ADB's support for that development. Core to the transformation is a new emphasis on the need for an integrated planning approach to the provision of environmental infrastructure and services and other public goods. As development professionals, with sound corporate strategies, we are still faced with daunting questions from an operational perspective on various aspects, such as incorporating efficiencies in resource management and infrastructure planning or whether decision support systems are in place that would lead to comprehensive and integrated urban management. To address such key questions and bridge this environmental quality and planning gap, there is an urgent need to break silos and recognize that environmental, economic, and social systems are complementary and not conflicting. What is needed is a paradigm shift. ADB introduced such a paradigm shift in Southeast Asia through the GrEEEn Cities Initiative.

GrEEEn Solutions for Livable Cities provides a road map for integrated urban development and environmental planning, using low-carbon technologies, innovative financing, enabling institutional structures, policy reform, and responsive governance. In the country context, there are several policy and strategy enablers; however, the key to translating strategies into actions is leadership and partnerships for improving competencies and capacities. GrEEEn Cities are about people. Making them work requires the engagement and involvement of a full cross section of society. To make this happen effectively, we need to strengthen the linkages that bind us and break down the silos that impede us from working together. We need a shared vision and a common approach. The GrEEEn Cities Initiative, through the Urban Management Partnership concept, has provided an institutional mechanism to bring together the cross-sector agencies involved in urban development. Urban Management Partnerships are built on the success of ADB's Water Operators Partnerships Program and expand across the urban sector to foster productive partnerships through peer-to-peer learning for urban transformation, improving efficiency in urban service delivery performance; strengthening institutions; and improving competency in integrated urban and environmental planning, climate resilience, energy efficiency, and project management through skills development and vocational training, innovative financing mechanisms for urban infrastructure, and developing decision support systems. Building a green future for our cities requires us to

---

[6]   M. Lindfield and F. Steinberg. 2012. *Green Cities.* Manila: ADB.

[7]   Asian Development Bank Institute. 2012. *Urbanization Can Be Good for the Environment.* www.asiapathways-adbi .org/2012/12/urbanization-can-be-good-for-the-environment/

[8]   F. Steinberg and M. Lindfield. 2012. Spatial Development and Technologies for Green Cities. In M. Lindfield and F. Steinberg, eds. *Green Cities.* Manila: ADB. pp. 23–107.

embrace a new paradigm: that the environment is essential to economic sustainability and prosperity—as reflected in policy making, land-use planning, and community engagement; accepting that good quality of life is good business. So let us start making things happen by "doing things differently," as the authors phrase it.

I would like to congratulate the authors on this landmark publication that is the first of its kind in providing solutions in an emerging area of interest for urban policy makers, city managers, and urban development professionals in addressing integrated urban development. I particularly thank Sonia and Ramola for their commitment and vision in taking forward the 3E strategies and moving them into urban operations and investments in Southeast Asia. The team has developed a series of publications starting with the working papers on "Enabling GrEEEn Cities: An Operational Framework for Integrated Urban Development in Southeast Asia," "Regional Balanced Urbanization for Inclusive Cities Development: Urban–Rural Poverty Linkages in Secondary Cities Development in Southeast Asia," and "Greenhouse Gas Inventories for Urban Operations in Southeast Asia: Challenges and Opportunities"; followed by the GrEEEn City Action Plans for the cities of Hue, Vinh Yen, and Ha Giang in Viet Nam, Melaka in Malaysia, and Songkhla and Hat Yai in Thailand; and culminating with this publication. I believe this timely publication will provide substantial guidance to urban managers and professionals in addressing the often conflicting challenges of urbanization, the environment, and inclusive economic growth.

Amy S.P. Leung
Deputy Director General
East Asia Department
Asian Development Bank

Messages: GrEEEn City Project Countries

**Ha Giang City,
Ha Giang Province (Viet Nam)**

Dam Van Bong, Chair of the Province People's Committee:

"I would like Ha Giang to be a sustainable tourism city that protects its natural environment and ensures social equity for all citizens."

**Hue City,
Thua Thien Hue Province (Viet Nam)**

Ngyuyen Van Thanh, Chair of the City People's Committee:

"We very appreciate the GrEEEn City approach—we embrace the idea and follow it in the development of Hue."

**Vinh Yen City,
Vinh Phuc Province (Viet Nam)**

Tran Ngoc Oanh, Chair of the City People's Committee:

"Under the leadership and the coordination of all parties, our cities can be improved in a grEEEn manner."

Photo Credits: Renard Teipelke

**Mandalay City,
Mandalay Region (Myanmar)**

Aye Aye Myint, Director, Urban and Regional
Planning Division, Department of Human
Settlements and Housing Development,
Ministry of Construction:

*"The GrEEEn Cities Operational Framework
is about doing things differently. And it is about
creating a livable city for the people."*

**Songkhla City,
Songkhla Province (Thailand)**

Vision exercise result:

*"We want to enhance our city's livability by
promoting economic growth in cultural and
natural tourism, particularly through a more
integrated development in our Old Town."*

**Hat Yai City,
Songkhla Province (Thailand)**

Vision exercise result:

*"We need to increase resilience to urban flooding
and continue our economic dominance in the
region, if we want to remain both a commercial
and educational hub, as well as a popular tourist
destination for entertainment and shopping."*

**Melaka City,
Melaka State (Malaysia)**

Datuk Seri Ir. Hj. Idris bin Hj. Haron, Chief Minister
of Melaka:

*"We want to make Melaka more environmental
friendly for all our residents and visitors.
We want to establish ourselves as one of the
leading green states in the region."*

Photo Credits (*from top to bottom*): Vaideeswaran Sankaran; Amit Prothi; Amit Prothi;
Melaka Ekocalendar

Preface

Background

The new 2030 Sustainable Development Agenda was adopted during the last weekend of September 2015 at the 193-member United Nations General Assembly, which included members of the Asian Development Bank (ADB). The Sustainable Development Goals (SDGs) will inform national action and development cooperation up to 2030 over the next 15 years. SDG11 is dedicated to cities and human settlements, covering the concerns addressed in this book. Many of the other SDGs are also highly relevant for the quality of urban life.[9] ADB too is starting work on a new long-term strategy, Strategy 2030, which is expected to help members respond to a rapidly urbanizing Asia and the Pacific. This publication contributes different options for the way forward through practice-proven examples of integrated urban development.

Objective

GrEEEn Solutions for Livable Cities is the result of a 2-year innovative, exploratory, and reflective study of cities as unique urban spaces that support life, work, and play. It responds to major issues that affect the quality of life of urban residents. This publication offers practical ways on how urban managers, urban practitioners, businesspeople, and citizens can engage to make our cities more livable by building on their distinctive physical, social, cultural, and economic characteristics.

The idea of this publication emerged from the work undertaken since 2012 through ADB's regional technical assistance (TA) Green Cities: A Sustainable Urban Future in Southeast Asia (GrEEEn Cities Initiative). It adopted a methodology for "doing things differently" and identified good practices that have demonstrated effectiveness in bringing about transformations toward livability in cities.[10]

It captures the lessons from the TA project and associated activities, including the first Enabling GrEEEn Cities Regional Conference, held at ADB headquarters in Manila on

9   United Nations Department of Economic and Social Affairs. 2015. Sustainable Development Goals. https://sustainabledevelopment.un.org/topics

10 ADB. 2012. Technical Assistance for Green Cities – A Sustainable Urban Future in Southeast Asia. Manila (TA 8314-REG).

13–14 May 2014.[11] The publication also incorporates findings from ADB's project preparatory TA to Viet Nam for the Secondary Cities Development Program (Green Cities); ADB's regional TA for Public–Private Partnership Development in Brunei Darussalam–Indonesia–Malaysia–Philippines East ASEAN Growth Area and Indonesia–Malaysia–Thailand Growth Triangle; ADB's small-scale capacity development TA to Malaysia for Sustainable Urban Management (Green Cities) Support for Follow-Up Activities in Melaka; and ADB's capacity development TA to Myanmar's Ministry of Construction.[12]

Scope

The scope of the publication is to take stock of ongoing urban, environment, and green growth practices and to identify shifts required for urban transformation based on good examples that have demonstrated successes, such as green infrastructure modifications to designs, urban planning, and public consultation processes. Anchored in ADB's Urban Operational Plan 2012–2020, the team articulated the term gr*EEE*n with the three Es (3Es) for economic competitiveness, environmental sustainability, and social equity for understanding of city managers and officials beyond their traditional perception of green cities as equivalent to cities with trees and flowers along the street landscape and green spaces.[13] In discussions with ADB's developing member countries (DMCs) and participating cities, an operational framework was developed, within which the 3E attributes were unbundled by articulating and detailing elements for consideration under the three pillars of economy, environment, and equity.

The Gr*EEE*n Cities Operational Framework (GCOF) was first conceptualized through the Gr*EEE*n Cities Initiative and described in the working paper "Enabling Gr*EEE*n Cities: An Operational Framework for Integrated Urban Development in Southeast Asia."[14] Simultaneous work in the field progressed to develop Gr*EEE*n City Action Plans (GCAPs) as investment programs according to the demand from DMCs and their cities throughout Southeast Asia. A strong demand from the DMCs, as expressed at the regional conference, was to capture and document this learning process. Additionally, there was express demand to share examples from across the world, which demonstrated good practices and had potential for replication in the Asian context.

---

[11] ADB. 2014. Enabling GrEEEn Cities: A Sustainable Urban Future in Southeast Asia, Regional Conference, Manila, Philippines, 13–14 May. http://www.adb.org/news/events/enabling-greeen-cities-sustainable-urban-future-southeast-asia

[12] ADB. 2014. Project Preparatory Technical Assistance to the Socialist Republic of Viet Nam for the Secondary Cities Development Program (Green Cities). Manila (TA 8671-VIE); ADB. 2010. Technical Assistance for Public–Private Partnership Development in the Brunei Darussalam–Indonesia–Malaysia–Philippines East ASEAN Growth Area and Indonesia–Malaysia–Thailand Growth Triangle. Manila (TA 7627-REG); ADB. 2014. Technical Assistance for Sustainable Urban Management (Green Cities) Support for Follow-Up Activities in Melaka, Malaysia. Manila (S-CDTA 8781-MAL); ADB. 2012. Capacity Development Technical Assistance to Myanmar for Capacity Development Support for Project Identification: Support to the Ministry of Construction, Union of Myanmar. Manila (CDTA 8251-MYA); ADB. 2012. Technical Assistance to the Union of Myanmar for Capacity Building Support for Project Identification. Manila (TA 8251-MYA).

[13] ADB. 2013. Urban Operational Plan 2012–2020. Manila.

[14] S. Sandhu and R. Naik Singru. 2014. Enabling GrEEEn Cities: An Operational Framework for Integrated Urban Development in Southeast Asia. SERD Working Paper Series. No. 9. Manila: Asian Development Bank.

Operations Impact

The GCOF was piloted in 11 cities in five countries with different growth trajectories and informed the development of integrated investment plans and projects in Southeast Asia:

- **Viet Nam:** The GCAPs prepared for the cities of Hue, Vinh Yen, and Ha Giang in Viet Nam are the basis of the ensuing investment Secondary Cities Development Program (Green Cities), which incorporates elements of environmental sustainability, climate change, and disaster resilience of ADB's Strategy 2020.[15] The provinces demonstrating significant ownership have endorsed the GCAPs as their cities' investment programs. The value added of this endorsement is that the institutionalization of the GCAPs will help operationalize the Vietnamese government's national urban development program and national green growth strategy. ADB's TA was the basis for the successful approval of funding from the Urban Climate Change Resilience Trust Fund for capacity building for the three cities in Viet Nam and from the Special Climate Change Fund of the Global Environment Facility for the project on Promoting Climate Resilience in Viet Nam Cities. The team also collaborated with ADB's Sustainable Development and Climate Change Department's Transport Advisory Group and the Ministry of Land, Infrastructure and Transport of the Republic of Korea to develop the Hue Urban Mobility Masterplan.

- **Viet Nam:** The Second Greater Mekong Subregion Corridor Towns Development Project is piloting a green city action plan for Sa Pa in Viet Nam as a specific output for urban regeneration and increasing economic competitiveness of the city through improved tourism.[16] This complements the planned investments for improving wastewater management, drainage, and transport mobility.

- **Malaysia:** The regional public–private partnership TA contributed extensively to regional cooperation and engagement with middle-income countries through improved knowledge solutions toward "finance ++" with the Indonesia–Malaysia–Thailand Growth Triangle (IMT-GT) and Brunei Darussalam–Indonesia–Malaysia–Philippines East ASEAN Growth Area (BIMP-EAGA).[17] The GCAP for Melaka was

---

[15] ADB. 2014. Project Preparatory Technical Assistance to the Socialist Republic of Viet Nam for the Secondary Cities Development Program (Green Cities). Manila (TA 8671-VIE); ADB. 2015. Enabling GrEEEn Cities: Hue GrEEEn City Action Plan. Manila; ADB. 2015. Enabling GrEEEn Cities: Vinh Yen GrEEEn City Action Plan. Manila; ADB. Forthcoming. Ha Giang GrEEEn City Action Plan. Final report of the Preparatory Technical Assistance to the Socialist Republic of Viet Nam for the Secondary Cities Development Program (Green Cities). Manila (TA 8671-VIE); ADB. 2008. Strategy 2020: The Long-Term Strategic Framework of the Asian Development Bank, 2008–2020. Manila.

[16] ADB. 2013. Project Preparatory Technical Assistance for the Second Greater Mekong Subregion Corridor Towns Development Project. Manila (TA 8425-REG).

[17] With knowledge solutions identified as a "driver of change" in ADB's Strategy 2020, strengthened knowledge management aims to offer "finance ++" by combining ADB's finance with resources from partners, as well as knowledge toward improved development effectiveness. (ADB. 2008. *Strategy 2020: The Long-Term Strategic Framework of the Asian Development Bank, 2008–2020.* Manila; ADB. 2013. *Knowledge Management Directions and Action Plan (2013–2015): Supporting "Finance ++" at the Asian Development Bank.* Manila.) ADB. 2010. Technical Assistance for Public–Private Partnership Development in the Brunei Darussalam–Indonesia–Malaysia–Philippines East ASEAN Growth Area and Indonesia–Malaysia–Thailand Growth Triangle. Manila (TA 7627-REG).

endorsed by the IMT-GT Summit in Nay Pyi Taw, Myanmar, in May 2014 and was adopted by the State of Melaka as the overarching document to operationalize its blueprint to guide integrated urban development as a road map for green growth in Malaysia to be piloted through the implementation of the GCAP in Melaka city.[18] This informed the reimbursable TA with ADB for small-scale capacity development for Sustainable Urban Management (Green Cities) Support for Follow-Up Activities in Melaka.[19] This TA will support Malaysia in developing a benchmarking index to monitor and deliver services efficiently to achieve the set targets for green infrastructure and services.

- **Thailand:** Under the IMT-GT, GCAPs were prepared as scoping studies for Songkhla and Hat Yai, and these are now guiding further engagement in the urban sector focusing on climate change resilience and environmental infrastructure for flood management, heritage conservation, and building competitiveness of cities.[20]

- **Indonesia:** The GrEEEn Cities Initiative guided the development of the TA for the Sustainable Infrastructure Assistance Program – Green Cities: A Sustainable Urban Future in Indonesia (Subproject 4).[21] The TA supports the following outputs for Batam, Kendari, Malang, and Medan: (i) development of a green city action plan, (ii) identification of innovative mechanisms for the financing of urban infrastructure, (iii) development of Urban Management Partnerships, and (iv) implementation of a small-scale pilot project in each city.

- **Myanmar:** The scoping study "Toward a Green Mandalay" acted as input for the investment loan for the Mandalay Urban Services Improvement Project.[22]

Audience

GrEEEn Solutions for Livable Cities reflects on the application of the GCOF. It aims to provide sustainable urban development solutions for local and national government leaders and technical staff, project officers, other international donors and nongovernment organizations, and development practitioners.

---

[18] ADB. 2014. *Green City Action Plan Melaka, Malaysia.* Final report of the Master Plan on ASEAN Connectivity Implementation (2011, TA 8040-REG). Manila.

[19] ADB. 2014. Technical Assistance for Sustainable Urban Management (Green Cities) Support for Follow-Up Activities in Melaka, Malaysia. Manila (S-CDTA 8781-MAL).

[20] ADB. 2015. *GrEEEn City Action Plan for Songkhla and Hat Yai Municipalities.* Manila.

[21] ADB. 2013. Technical Assistance to Indonesia for Green Cities: A Sustainable Urban Future in Indonesia. Manila (TA 8518-INO).

[22] ADB. 2014. *Toward a Green Mandalay: Scoping Study of a Strategic Development Plan for Mandalay.* Final report of Capacity Building Support for Project Identification (2012, TA 8251-MYA). Manila; ADB. 2015. Project Preparatory Technical Assistance for Mandalay Urban Services Improvement Project, Myanmar. Manila (TA 8472-MYA).

Structure

This book is structured in three parts as shown in the figure. Chapters 1 and 2 provide the background to this book by giving an overview of the emergence of green growth approaches in urban development in recent years and introducing the GCOF. The second part of the book presents the building blocks for grEEEn solutions by deepening understanding of the visioning and action planning for integrated urban development (Chapter 3), unbundling the 3Es as applied in concrete projects (Chapter 4), elaborating on Urban Management Partnerships (Chapter 5), and discussing key enablers in the various stages of project planning and implementation (Chapter 6). The final part of this book looks at the key takeaway lessons for improving the quality of life for all citizens (Chapter 7).

Structure of the Publication

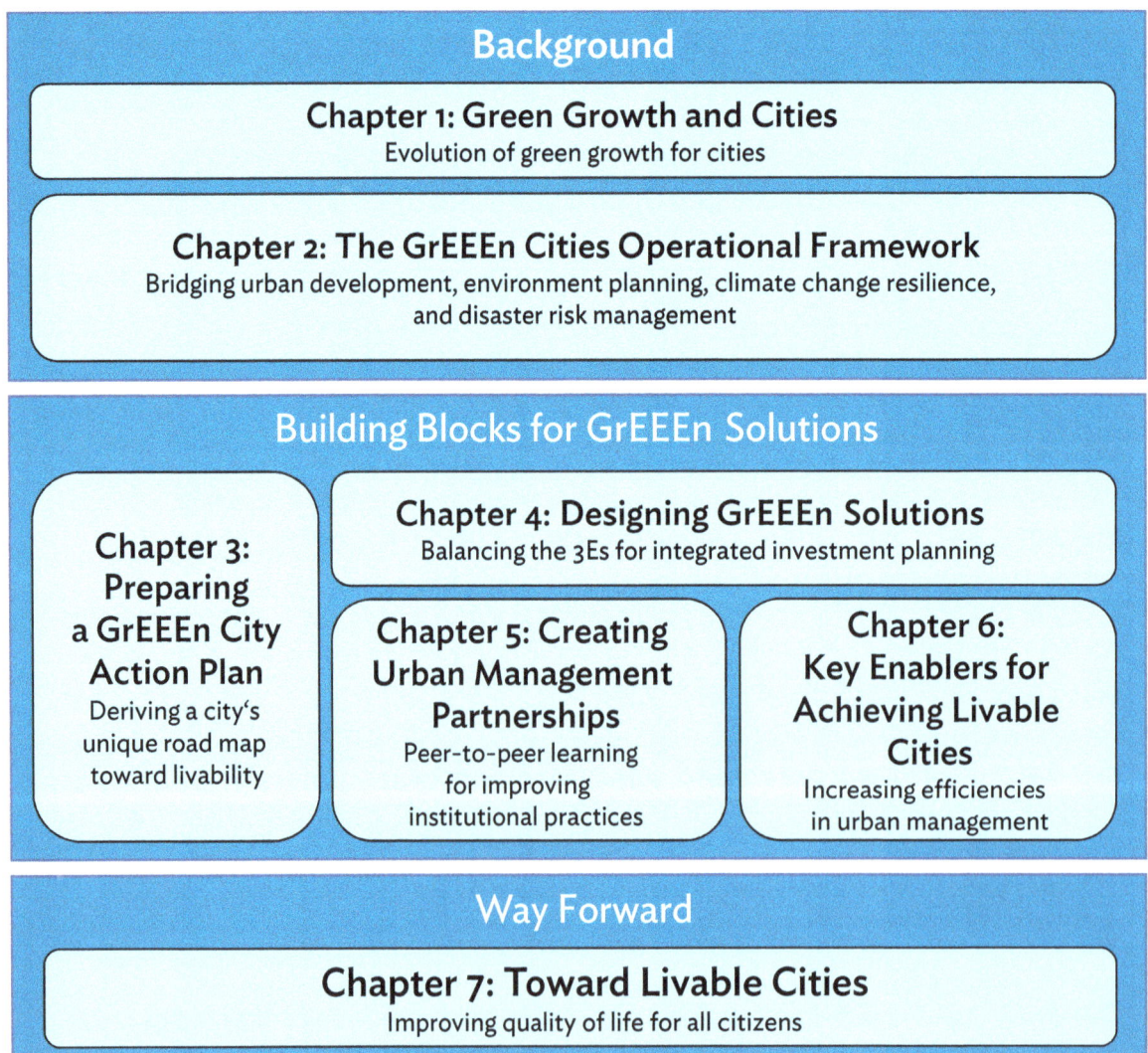

Background

Chapter 1: Green Growth and Cities
Evolution of green growth for cities

Chapter 2: The GrEEEn Cities Operational Framework
Bridging urban development, environment planning, climate change resilience, and disaster risk management

Building Blocks for GrEEEn Solutions

Chapter 3: Preparing a GrEEEn City Action Plan
Deriving a city's unique road map toward livability

Chapter 4: Designing GrEEEn Solutions
Balancing the 3Es for integrated investment planning

Chapter 5: Creating Urban Management Partnerships
Peer-to-peer learning for improving institutional practices

Chapter 6: Key Enablers for Achieving Livable Cities
Increasing efficiencies in urban management

Way Forward

Chapter 7: Toward Livable Cities
Improving quality of life for all citizens

3Es = economy, environmental, and equity.
Source: Authors.

Authors

This publication was prepared by a team led by Sonia Chand Sandhu, senior advisor to the Vice-President for Knowledge Management and Sustainable Development, ADB (team leader) and Ramola Naik Singru, urban development specialist, Urban Development and Water Division, Central and West Asia Department, ADB, with John Bachmann, technical director at the AECOM Asia Sustainability Center; Vaideeswaran Sankaran, environment engineer and climate resilience specialist (consultant); and Pierre Arnoux, social development specialist (consultant). Sameer A. Kamal, urban development specialist, ADB, contributed significantly in restructuring the publication and through his specific contribution on the technical application on urban water systems. Renard Teipelke, urban development specialist (consultant), coordinated the preparation of the publication and contributed significantly to the research and writing. Phuong Nguyen, research analyst and national coordinator (consultant), supported the team in Viet Nam with research inputs and coordination with the participating cities of the GrEEEn Cities Initiative. Tadeo Culla, associate social development officer, SEUW-SERD, administered the project. Mary France Creus and Le Huong Loan assisted on administrative matters. The multidisciplinary team brought together many years of experience from the field in their respective subjects covering environmental engineering, climate change, urban and regional planning, urban design, architecture, social development, economics, and finance to respond to urbanization challenges by proposing a progressive approach toward improving livability in cities. The team greatly benefited from the contributions, comments, discussions, and support of various professionals mentioned in the Acknowledgments.

Photo Credit: Edsel Roman

Philippines: Members of the GrEEEn Cities team at the first Enabling GrEEEn Cities Regional Conference held at ADB headquarters in Manila on 13–14 May 2014

Acknowledgments

This publication was prepared under the technical assistance for Green Cities: A Sustainable Urban Future in Southeast Asia, also known as the GrEEEn Cities Initiative.

We appreciate the guidance and advice of Stephen P. Groff, vice-president for the East Asia, Southeast Asia, and the Pacific departments, Asian Development Bank (ADB), as well as Bindu N. Lohani, vice-president for Knowledge Management and Sustainable Development (retired), ADB, during the first Enabling GrEEEn Cities Regional Conference. We appreciate the guidance and advice of Bambang Susantono, vice-president for Knowledge Management and Sustainable Development during the preparation of this book. We are grateful to James Nugent, director general, Southeast Asia Department (SERD) and Noriko Ogawa, deputy director general, SERD, for their advice and support in the preparation of this publication. We gratefully acknowledge the discussions and input of our colleagues. The authors would like to thank Ramesh Subramaniam, director general, Operations Services and Financial Management Department and Amy S.P. Leung, deputy director general, East Asia Department, for their guidance. We thank Satinder Bindra, principal director of the Department of

Philippines: Participants at the first Enabling GrEEEn Cities Regional Conference held at ADB headquarters in Manila on 13–14 May 2014

External Relations for facilitating the completion of this publication; and Vinod Thomas, director general, Independent Evaluation Department, for his advice. We also thank Tatiana Gallego-Lizon, director, Urban Development and Water Division (SEUW), SERD, for her support to the initiative and comprehensive review of the book. We thank the reviewers of this publication for their critical comments in improving this publication, especially Philipp Rode, executive director, LSE Cities and Urban Age, London School of Economics and Political Science. Thanks go out to Tomoyuki Kimura, deputy director, Strategy and Policy Department and Eric Sidgwick, country director, Viet Nam Resident Mission, as well as staff of the Viet Nam Resident Mission for their support to the project. We appreciate the support from Vijay Padmanabhan, technical advisor, Urban and Water Sector Advisory Group and from colleagues of the Urban Sector Group and SERD.

The authors thank the contributors: Pierre Beauchamp, municipal, civil, and environment engineer (consultant); Royston R.C. Brockman, urban and regional planner (consultant); Niels Van Dijk, Water Operators Partnerships Program team leader (consultant); Mike Sharrocks, urban designer (consultant); Pedro García de Mendoza, specialist in hydrology, flood protection, and decision support systems (consultant); Sushma Kotagiri, social development specialist, EATC-SERD; Rajivan Krishnaswamy, consultant and former managing director and chief executive officer, Tamil Nadu Urban Development Fund; Michael R. Lindfield, institutional specialist (consultant); and Joji I. Reyes, economist (consultant). Thanks go to Savita Mullapudi Narasimhan (consultant, Strategy and Policy Department, ADB) for her inputs on the linkages of the Sustainable Development Goals and financing for development; Gagan Sandhu (infrastructure and operations manager, Town of Georgina, Ontario, Canada) for sharing Canadian good practices on asset management; Lainie Thomas, social development specialist, Human and Social Development Division, SERD, for her contribution on the GMS Youth Caravan; and Jason Rush, principal communications specialist, SERD,

Photo Credit: Edsel Roman

for his advice on the structure of the book. The team especially thanks Balamurugan Ratha Krishnan, deputy director, Center for Indonesia–Malaysia–Thailand Growth Triangle (IMT-GT) Subregional Cooperation, for championing the GrEEEn Cities Initiative in Malaysia and contributing to the publication.

This publication incorporates findings from the ADB regional technical assistance for Public–Private Partnership Development in Brunei Darussalam–Indonesia–Malaysia–Philippines East ASEAN Growth Area and Indonesia–Malaysia–Thailand Growth Triangle and the capacity development technical assistance for Capacity Development Support for Project Identification: Support to the Ministry of Construction of the Union of Myanmar.

The authors are grateful to the leaders and officials from the governments of Malaysia, Myanmar, Thailand, and Viet Nam for their commitment and active engagement throughout the course of the project. We would like to thank Datuk Seri Ir. Hj. Idris bin Hj. Haron, Right honorable chief minister of Melaka in Malaysia; U Tun Kyi, committee member, Mandalay City Development Committee, Mandalay in Myanmar; Songkhla Governor's Office, Mueang Songkhla, and Hat Yai municipality in Thailand; and Nguyen Van Cao and other leaders of Thua Thien Hue province, Phung Quang Hung and other leaders of Vinh Phuc province, and Dam Van Bong and other leaders of Ha Giang province in Viet Nam. We would like to thank Nguyen Thi Thanh Phuong, deputy director general and Nguyen Hoang Phuong from the Foreign Economic Relations, Department of the Ministry of Planning and Investment. We thank the officials from the Office of the National Economic and Social Development Board, and the Centre for IMT-GT Subregional Cooperation; and Aye Aye Myint, director, Planning Department, Department of Human Settlements and Housing Development, Ministry of Construction, Myanmar. The authors thank the IMT-GT team consisting of Alfredo Perdiguero, principal regional cooperation specialist, Regional Cooperation and Operations Coordination Division (SERC), SERD; Gary Krishnan, country specialist, SERC-SERD; and Amit Prothi, urban development specialist (consultant), for their inputs and support for the preparation of the Melaka Green City Action Plan.

We thank all the officials and staff from the different government agencies and organizations in the countries' states and/or provinces and cities, as well as private sector and civil society representatives for their valuable contribution and participation in the project activities including the first Enabling GrEEEn Cities Regional Conference held at ADB in Manila on 13–14 May 2014. We are grateful to councillor Raymond Louie, acting mayor of Vancouver and first vice-president of the Federation of Canadian Municipalities, for his contributions to the regional conference.

Special thanks to the ADB Department of External Relations Publishing Team: Anna K. Sherwood, senior communications specialist; Cynthia A. Hidalgo, associate communications officer; Anthony H. Victoria, associate communications coordinator, for graphics and design; Rommel Marilla for layout; Kae Sugawara and Ma. Theresa Arago for editing; and April Gallega, senior communications assistant, and Leo Magno, senior communications officer, for overall coordination of the publication. The authors also thank Karen Lane, senior external relations specialist and John Larkin, external relations specialist, for expert advice on communications; and Andrew Perrin, communications specialist, and Angeli Mendoza, communications officer, for marketing and dissemination. The authors are grateful to Tadeo Culla, associate social development officer, SEUW-SERD, for his able administration of the project; and Mary France Creus and Le Huong Loan for all their help in administrative matters.

Abbreviations

3Es	economy, environment, and equity
ACCCRN	Asian Cities Climate Change Resilience Network
ADB	Asian Development Bank
ASEAN	Association of Southeast Asian Nations
BAU	business as usual
CBD	community-based development
CBO	community-based organization
CBSWM	community-based solid waste management
CDC	community development council
CDIA	Cities Development Initiative for Asia
CDS	City Development Strategy
CIIPP	City Infrastructure Investment Programming and Prioritization (CDIA)
CIMS	Capital Investment Management System (South Africa)
CIMT	Center for IMT-GT Subregional Cooperation
DMC	developing member country
DSS	decision support systems
GCAP	GrEEEn City Action Plan
GCF	Green Climate Fund
GCIF	Global City Indicators Facility
GCOF	GrEEEn Cities Operational Framework
GHG	greenhouse gas
GIS	geographic information system
ICLEI	Local Governments for Sustainability (formerly: International Council for Local Environmental Initiatives)
ICT	information and communication technology
IMT-GT	Indonesia–Malaysia–Thailand Growth Triangle
ISO	International Organization for Standardization
IWAG	Integrity Watch for Water Anti-Corruption Group
KPI	key performance indicator
LED	light-emitting diode
LSE	London School of Economics and Political Science

MDG	Millennium Development Goal
MPI	management process indicator
MUDF	Municipal Urban Development Fund
NGO	nongovernment organization
ODA	official development assistance
OECD	Organisation for Economic Co-operation and Development
OPI	operational process indicator
PPP	public–private partnership
PPWSA	Phnom Penh Water Supply Authority (Cambodia)
PSAB	Public Sector Accounting Board (Canada)
SDG	Sustainable Development Goal
SMEs	small and medium-sized enterprises
SSIM	Sustainable Systems Integration Model
SWOT	strengths, weaknesses, opportunities, and threats
TA	technical assistance
TNUDF	Tamil Nadu Urban Development Fund (India)
TRAM	Tool for the Rapid Assessment of Urban Mobility
UCLG	United Cities and Local Governments
UK	United Kingdom
UMP	Urban Management Partnership
UNEP	United Nations Environment Programme
UNESCAP	United Nations Economic and Social Commission for Asia and the Pacific
UN-Habitat	United Nations Human Settlements Programme
UPEN	Unit Perancangan Ekonomi Negeri (Melaka Economic Planning Unit) (Malaysia)
US	United States
USP	unique selling point
WOPs	Water Operators Partnerships
WSPF	Water and Sanitation Pooled Fund (India)

Executive Summary

The scale of urbanization in Asia today is unprecedented in urban history. Asia stands apart from other regions in terms of the absolute growth of the urban population as well as the number of densely populated megacities. Between 2010 and 2050, Asia's urban population is anticipated to double in size to 3.2 billion—equivalent to an additional 100,000 urban residents each day. By 2050, two-thirds of Asia's population will be urban.

Asia's urban challenges are characterized by (i) increasing household consumption, (ii) rising demand for urban services, (iii) depletion of natural resources, (iv) increasing levels of pollution and greenhouse gas emissions, and (v) increasing vulnerability to natural hazards and risks from climate change. Asian cities have to cope with pressure on physical infrastructure, rapid environmental degradation, and increased risks to health and real property. As a result, the quality of life for many residents in Asian cities is declining. The livability of many cities is decreasing because of air pollution, traffic congestion, poor transport choices, shortage of public open spaces, and inadequate urban and social services.

The livability challenge in Asia has driven urban policy makers to seek solutions in integrated, holistic urban planning. The consensus is that sector-specific approaches cannot sufficiently address the complexities of urban in-migration and increasing pressure on the natural environment. Many local governments, international organizations, and planning professionals have endorsed an integrated approach, in which (i) aspects such as land use, mobility, water use, and energy consumption are all managed in a coordinated manner across municipal departments; and (ii) stakeholders in government, the private sector, and civil society work together to achieve the socioeconomic goals of their city.

Building on the global research and advocacy around sustainability and green growth in cities, and on Asian Development Bank (ADB) initiatives including its Urban Operational Plan 2012–2020 and Strategy 2020, the GrEEEn Cities Operational Framework (GCOF) was developed to ensure a balance of economic competitiveness, environmental sustainability, and social equity in development. As a flexible and scalable approach to address urban Asia's livability challenge, the GCOF embraces the concept of "doing things differently" through integrated urban development and environmental planning.

To test the GCOF, seven cities in Malaysia, Myanmar, Thailand, and Viet Nam have drawn up GrEEEn City Action Plans (GCAPs) with varying technical scopes and levels of institutional engagement. The GCAPs consist of a shared development vision, and prioritized and time-based investment programs and initiatives with short-, medium-, and long-term actions for improving environmental quality and achieving competitive, inclusive, and resilient growth in cities.

Focus of the Book

By way of background, the first part of the book provides an overview of the emergence of green growth approaches in urban development in recent years (Chapter 1) and introduces the GCOF (Chapter 2). The second part of the book presents the building blocks for grEEEn solutions by deepening understanding of visioning and action planning for integrated urban development (Chapter 3); unbundling the 3Es of economy, environment, and equity as applied in concrete projects (Chapter 4); elaborating on Urban Management Partnerships (UMPs) (Chapter 5); and discussing key enablers in the various stages of project planning and implementation (Chapter 6). The final part of this book looks at the key takeaway lessons for improving quality of life for all citizens (Chapter 7).

GrEEEn Cities Operational Framework

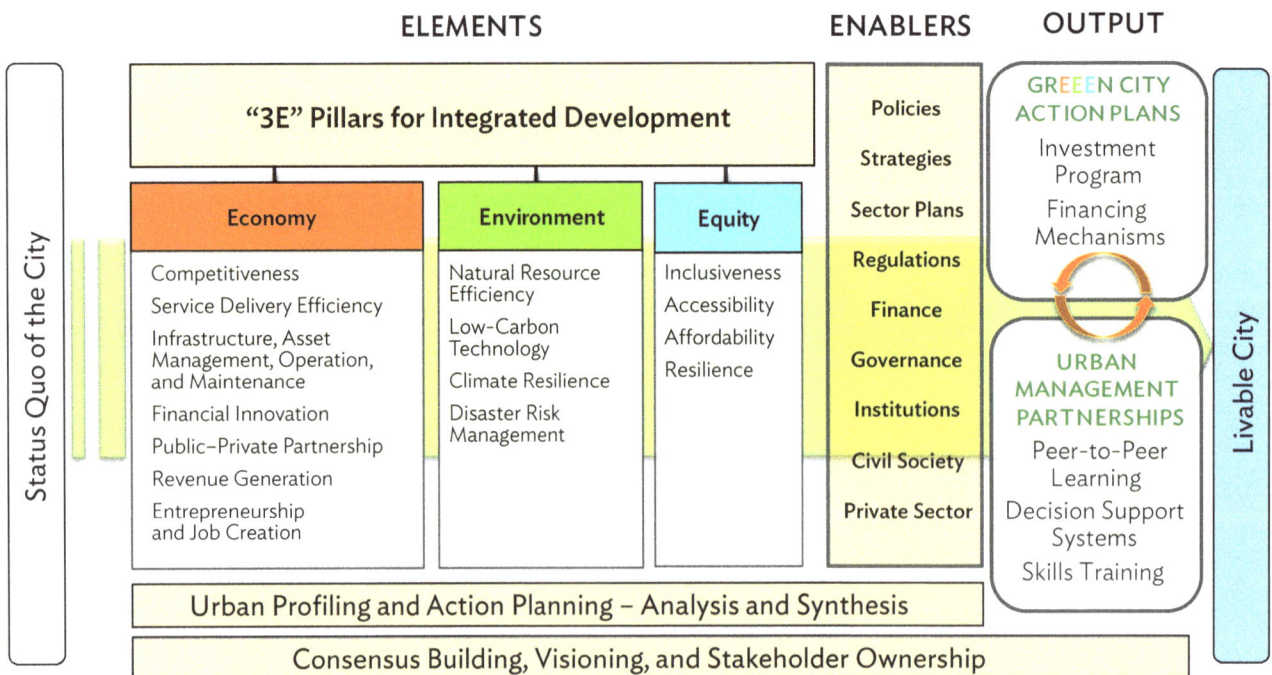

	ELEMENTS			ENABLERS	OUTPUT

Status Quo of the City

"3E" Pillars for Integrated Development

Economy	Environment	Equity
Competitiveness	Natural Resource Efficiency	Inclusiveness
Service Delivery Efficiency	Low-Carbon Technology	Accessibility
Infrastructure, Asset Management, Operation, and Maintenance	Climate Resilience	Affordability
Financial Innovation	Disaster Risk Management	Resilience
Public–Private Partnership		
Revenue Generation		
Entrepreneurship and Job Creation		

Enablers: Policies, Strategies, Sector Plans, Regulations, Finance, Governance, Institutions, Civil Society, Private Sector

GREEEN CITY ACTION PLANS — Investment Program, Financing Mechanisms

URBAN MANAGEMENT PARTNERSHIPS — Peer-to-Peer Learning, Decision Support Systems, Skills Training

Livable City

Urban Profiling and Action Planning – Analysis and Synthesis

Consensus Building, Visioning, and Stakeholder Ownership

3Es = economy, environment, and equity.

Source: S. Sandhu and R. Naik Singru. 2014. Enabling GrEEEn Cities: An Operational Framework for Integrated Urban Development in Southeast Asia. *SERD Working Paper Series*. No. 9. Manila: Asian Development Bank.

GrEEEn Cities Operational Framework

As shown in the figure, the GCOF guides the transformation of a city from the status quo toward becoming a livable city by

- creating a platform for stakeholder engagement for a shared vision and incentives;
- integrating individual investment projects into a coherent whole to generate higher levels of benefits through a strategic combination of investment initiatives and programs;
- striking a balance among the 3Es—economy, environment, and equity—that define livability in the city;
- using a place-based development approach to add value to a city's existing built, cultural, human resource, and natural assets;
- optimizing value-for-money by improving the effectiveness of investments through the use of "enablers" such as incentives, policies, or regulations; and
- facilitating UMPs to ensure stakeholder support, improve coordination, and build local government capacity.

The GCOF has two outputs: the road map (GCAPs) and the operational platform (UMPs) for achieving livability. The key elements of a GCAP are

- a collective vision that enhances and preserves the city's main economic, cultural, and environmental assets;
- an urban profile that assesses the physical, regulatory, institutional, economic, environmental, and social aspects, gaps, and investment and capacity needs, as well as business-as-usual practices in the city;
- a time-bound action plan with initiatives consisting of short-, medium-, and long-term actions for investments and enabling measures (such as policy reform and institutional capacity building) including cost and performance indicators; and
- implementation arrangements including decision support systems (DSS), asset management plans, and monitoring and evaluation mechanisms (such as citizen scorecards to enable feedback and improve responses of the local government in meeting citizens' needs).

The GCOF has the potential to make a substantial contribution to the achievement of the United Nations-sponsored Sustainable Development Goals, which offer a triple bottom-line approach to human well-being through social inclusiveness, environmental protection, and economic competitiveness.

Visioning and Action Planning

The GCOF applies visioning as the starting point in a consultative process of developing the GCAP. The local government leads all major stakeholders in a visioning process that establishes development goals, objectives, and benchmarks. Along with an analysis of a city's strengths, weaknesses, opportunities, and threats (SWOT), the vision helps establish development priorities for investment projects.

Based on the vision and the urban profile (assessment of the city's status quo), the GCAP defines the initiatives and actions required to achieve goals and targets for a livable city. The GCAP establishes a road map that deviates from traditional urban, environmental, and resilience standards. Instead, the road map leads a city toward the standards of GrEEEn Cities, where urban planning is risk-sensitive and outputs are optimized through cross-sector coordination. GCAPs help cities to become more competitive through smart investments in infrastructure, human resource development, natural capital conservation, and technological innovation.

Designing GrEEEn Solutions

Cities in Asia and around the world offer excellent examples of how to design projects that achieve cobenefits related to the economy, environment, and equity—the 3Es of GrEEEn Cities.

GrEEEn Cities identify ways to achieve competitive and resilient economic growth by enhancing a city's unique selling point. Broadly, this can be achieved with a focus on demand-driven urban development (i.e., by developing and maintaining infrastructure assets) and through placemaking for economic success (i.e., by ensuring that a city is attractive for businesses, workers, entrepreneurs, residents, and visitors). Mixed land uses, human-scale development, low levels of pollution, high-quality public open spaces, and multimodal transportation are essential components that make up economically successful places.

Key elements in unbundling the E for "environment" include natural resources management and low-carbon technologies for increased efficiency, protected biodiversity, climate resilience of infrastructure, and disaster risk management for improved protection of communities and assets. Greening infrastructure, resource "looping" and "cascading," compact urban forms, urban design, and mixed land uses can help reduce carbon footprint. Green technologies such as air pollution abatement, water supply conservation, wastewater treatment, land and soil remediation, solid waste treatment and management, recycling and/ or recovery, and energy conservation also contribute to the 3Es. The congruence between urban development patterns and urban infrastructure poses huge opportunity for reducing carbon emissions and conserving natural resources.

GrEEEn Cities put people first. Embracing a holistic view of prosperity, GrEEEn Cities create urban environments for all citizens to flourish and thrive. Making such people-centric cities work requires the engagement and involvement of a full cross section of society. Tools for accountability in urban service delivery include participatory planning and budgeting, citizen's charters, citizen monitoring tools and committees, citizen report cards, and community report cards. GrEEEn Cities also look at the distributional efforts of basic urban development processes. Fundamentally, cities grow by urbanizing peripheral lands and constructing buildings and infrastructure on them. But what is the distribution of these "products" of urbanization? Inclusive approaches to urban development emphasize the assessment of the needs of vulnerable groups, willingness-to-pay studies, appropriate standards, redistribution instruments such as subsidies (where required), and other features of socially sound urban development to ensure equal opportunities to access affordable and efficient services and infrastructure.

GrEEEn Cities are concerned with making great urban places. It is not enough to build networks of urban roads. The aspirations of GrEEEn Cities go further: to make being in the city more rewarding. GrEEEn Cities explicitly seek to create a high-quality public realm that all residents can enjoy. This approach improves access to urban open spaces in low-income communities, enhances connections to employment areas, and improves the quality of life.

Urban Management Partnerships

UMPs are a formal vehicle for engaging local stakeholders and creating social, economic, and environmental value. The complexity of the urban realm and the large number of interconnected partners make the use of a partnership vehicle particularly critical to success. A forum for cooperation allows for the negotiations to unfold, trade-offs to be made, and packages of risks and rewards to be tailored to suit the needs of each participant. The bonds that develop during this process form the foundation for implementing joint activities, for which the partners provide financial and nonfinancial resources. The UMP is not a one-shot initiative, but rather a process of building a cooperative forum for tackling a city's challenges and jointly realizing its potentials. UMPs provide clear benefits for implementing projects in terms of consultation and coordination. More importantly for agencies implementing urban development projects, however, UMPs

- create win–win projects that have multiple positive outputs for related sectors and agencies;
- avoid negative impacts on the goals of other related sectors and/or agencies and avoid repetition or duplication across sectors and/or agencies;
- increase political and community acceptance and approval by leveraging combined influence;
- provide access to finance by pooling government budgets and/or partnering with external agencies (including international finance institutions), the private sector, and local community groups;
- provide enhanced knowledge sharing and lasting skills and capacity development through a mentor–mentee relationship; and
- meet broader global objectives such as conservation of natural resources.

Enablers

Enablers are mechanisms and systems that can help make grEEEn solutions possible. Enablers include policies, strategies, sector plans, regulations, financial incentives, technologies, governance institutions, civil society, and private sector interventions. Asset management tools, financing mechanisms, performance monitoring and indicators, DSS, and information and communication technology in Smart Cities are key enablers for achieving livable cities.

Asset management involves balancing costs, opportunities, and risks against the desired performance of assets. Different analytical approaches can be used to manage an asset throughout its life cycle—from the initial demand for the asset, through its use, to its disposal. In the context of GrEEEn Cities, asset management is an established platform that can be used as an enabling tool to ensure the resilience of urban infrastructure. A preventive management approach based on risk and condition assessments can be a conduit for ensuring continued operation and maintenance and compliance with planning, design, and construction standards as well as regulatory requirements for long-term asset performance and continued service delivery.

First, cities can take charge of their revenues by maximizing conventional finances such as increasing efficiency in the collection of user charges; introducing new "green" charges such as emission or effluent charges for maintaining the environment and, in addition to user charges, for the public service provided by government or industry; and assessing the revenue potential of tradable development rights and marketable permits. Second, cities can leverage private sector finance by identifying and unbundling potentially profitable investments and funding these from the capital markets. Finally, cities can seek specialist green financing such as the Clean Development Mechanism, Global Environment Facility, Climate Investment Funds, and the Association of Southeast Asian Nations (ASEAN) Infrastructure Fund, among others. In terms of total value, however, these funds tend to be small when compared to investment needs. There is a need for city governments to position and market their green initiatives in such a way that they become an attractive investment target.

GrEEEn Cities use DSS to integrate urban development with environmental planning for achieving livability. DSS are tools and mechanisms to structure, improve, and integrate the planning, design, construction, and operation and maintenance of urban projects and places. Enabled by technological change including increased computing capacity, DSS are being more widely utilized in the urban development field. DSS applications such as computer modeling of infrastructure performance, integrated planning systems, and information and communication technology-enabled Smart Cities are further discussed in Chapter 6.

Toward Livable Cities

Over time, citizens' demands for urban infrastructure and services have exponentially increased. These have exceeded the carrying capacity of cities due to the overconsumption of natural resources. Reconciling the demands and needs of people that make up the urban ecosystem, within defined resource limits, and confronting environmental and climate externalities are a major challenge faced by city managers, urban practitioners, and the academe. Decision makers recognize the potential of green growth and the need to move toward livable cities, but only a few cities have moved forward with green growth strategies and implementation is varied. This book suggests a way forward to improving the quality of life for all and shares key insights and learning for "doing things differently":

1. Learn from current conditions and approaches
2. Unbundle the 3Es at the city-region level to internalize risks and capture opportunities
3. Recognize the fourth E: enablers—harnessing the power of partnerships
4. Use DSS for informed decisions
5. Promote asset management as a platform for sustainability and resilience
6. Partner for better ways of green infrastructure financing

Building on lessons learned from previous conceptual approaches and practical experiences from across the world, the GCOF demonstrates a new paradigm in decision making for urban transformation. This places livability at the core of an air, water, and land pyramid, enabling city managers to identify critical natural parameters that impact the quality of life. A platform for synergistic planning is created for stakeholders to formulate and achieve a vision for their city on the 3E principles—economic competitiveness, environment, and equity—defining an exclusive triple bottom line. This innovative approach enables cities to commence smart and optimal planning from any point in their development journey to a sustainable path that will progressively deliver livable cities using GCAPs as road maps.

The value added of the GCOF is the mainstreaming of such integrated approaches for sustainable investments. Moving beyond the adoption of the Sustainable Development Goals in September 2015, it is now of great importance to customize the goals for sustainable development to regional, national, and local contexts. It is here that the GCOF is a conduit to help translate global development commitments into urban-level actions.

1 Green Growth and Cities

Background

The scale of urbanization in Asia today is unprecedented in urban history. Asia's urbanization is unique compared with that of other regions in terms of the absolute growth of the urban population as well as the number of densely populated megacities (ADB 2012a, Dahiya 2012). Between 2010 and 2050, Asia's urban population is anticipated to double in size to 3.2 billion, which is equivalent to an additional 100,000 urban residents each day. By 2050, two-thirds of Asia's population will be urban (ADB 2012a).

Asia's urban challenges are characterized by (i) increasing household consumption, (ii) rising demand for urban services, (iii) depletion of natural resources, (iv) increasing levels of pollution and greenhouse gases, and (v) increasing vulnerability to natural hazards and risks from climate change variations. Asian cities have to cope with pressure on physical infrastructure, rapid environmental degradation, and increased risks to health and real property. As a result, the quality of life for many residents of Asian cities is declining. The "livability" of many cities is decreasing because of air pollution, traffic congestion, lack of choice in transport options, shortage of public open spaces, and inadequate urban and social services.

The livability challenge in Asia has in recent years driven urban policy makers to seek solutions in integrated, holistic urban planning. Sector-specific initiatives alone are insufficient for accommodating urban in-migration and protecting the natural environment. Many local governments, international organizations, and planning professionals have endorsed an integrated approach, in which (i) land use, mobility, water, and energy are all managed in a coordinated fashion across municipal departments; and (ii) stakeholders in government, the private sector, and civil society work together to achieve the socioeconomic goals of the city.

Solutions integrating the 3Es—economy, environment, and equity—are key to addressing livability challenges in Asian Cities.

Recent Evolution of Green Growth Approaches

The concept of sustainability in the urban arena has evolved rapidly in recent decades (UN-Habitat 2009b). In the 1990s, the emphasis was on minimizing the negative impacts associated with urban development through protection of ecological assets and better management of wastewater, stormwater, and solid waste through unilateral investments. Given the wide range of urban activities that put pressure on the natural environment, a multidisciplinary approach to urban management was therefore favored. The challenge was to find a way to get urban professionals out of their traditional technical "silos" and into a collaborative mode where land use, resource consumption, infrastructure services, and economic growth could be managed in a coordinated fashion. Such horizontal collaboration has over time been encouraged by multilateral and bilateral donors.

Since 2000, the objective of environmental sustainability has become more closely linked in urban policy circles to that of economic growth (Figure 1.1). In the mid-2000s, many development agencies and research organizations began to advocate for "green growth," which holds that appropriate levels of environmental protection will contribute to the renewability of natural resources, which in turn facilitates economic production and the satisfaction of basic needs over the longer term. In a more ambitious iteration, the growth of both green technology and services enables environmental protection and drives economic growth (UNEP 2011). Before gaining heightened global attention during the Rio+20 Summit in 2012, the concept of the "green economy" was already well established in the regional policy dialogue in Asia and the Pacific. At the Association of Southeast Asian Nations (ASEAN) Fifth Ministerial Conference on Environment and Development in 2005, green growth was proposed as a regional strategy to enable environmentally sustainable economic growth (Box 1.1).

Photo Credits: Renard Teipelke (top left to bottom right); ADB/Lester Ledesma (lower left)

Traffic-choked streets, uncontrolled dumpsites, clogged rivers, and informal housing in high-risk areas are symptoms of unsustainable patterns of urban development.

Figure 1.1: Timeline of Selected Green Growth Programs and Publications

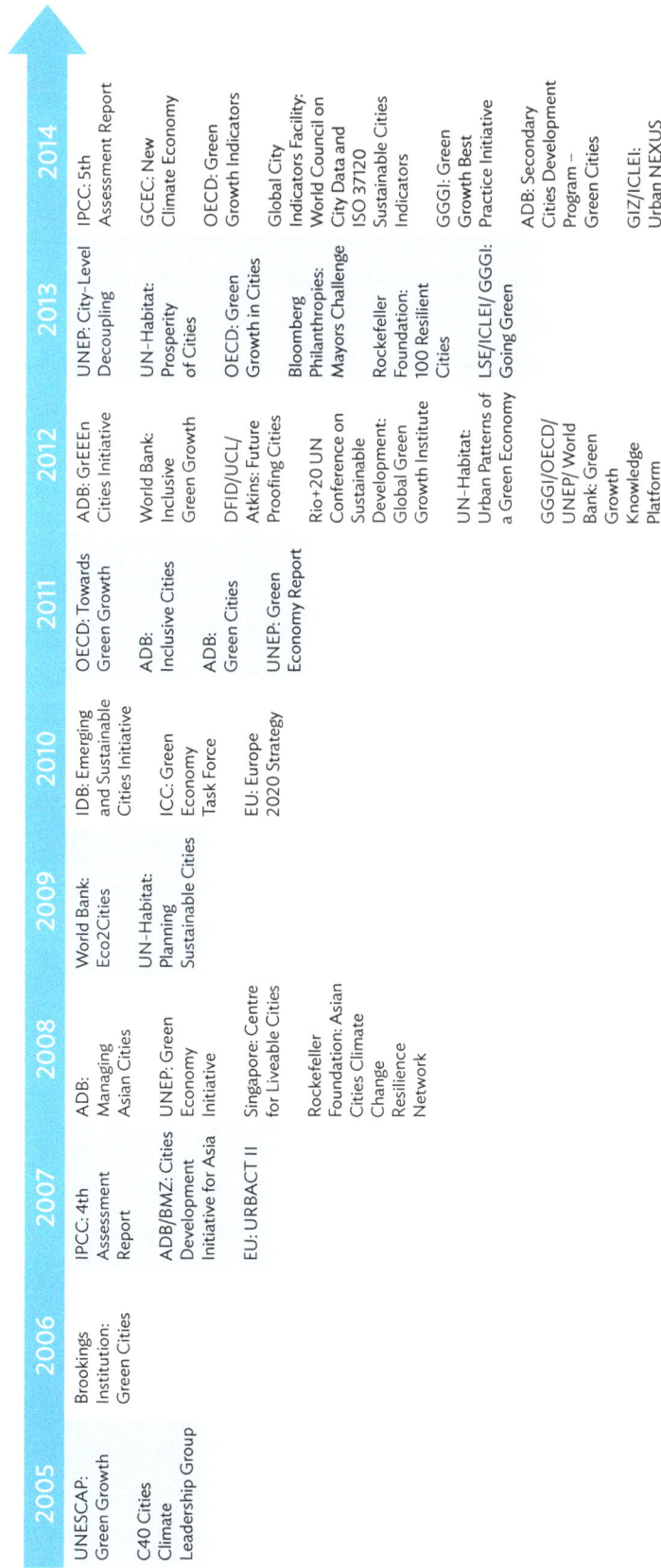

2005	2006	2007	2008	2009	2010	2011	2012	2013	2014
UNESCAP: Green Growth	Brookings Institution: Green Cities	IPCC: 4th Assessment Report	ADB: Managing Asian Cities	World Bank: Eco2Cities	IDB: Emerging and Sustainable Cities Initiative	OECD: Towards Green Growth	ADB: GrEEEn Cities Initiative	UNEP: City-Level Decoupling	IPCC: 5th Assessment Report
C40 Cities Climate Leadership Group		ADB/BMZ: Cities Development Initiative for Asia	UNEP: Green Economy Initiative	UN-Habitat: Planning Sustainable Cities	ICC: Green Economy Task Force	ADB: Inclusive Cities	World Bank: Inclusive Green Growth	UN-Habitat: Prosperity of Cities	GCEC: New Climate Economy
		EU: URBACT II	Singapore: Centre for Liveable Cities		EU: Europe 2020 Strategy	ADB: Green Cities	DFID/UCL/Atkins: Future Proofing Cities	OECD: Green Growth in Cities	OECD: Green Growth Indicators
			Rockefeller Foundation: Asian Cities Climate Change Resilience Network			UNEP: Green Economy Report	Rio+20 UN Conference on Sustainable Development: Global Green Growth Institute	Bloomberg Philanthropies: Mayors Challenge	Global City Indicators Facility: World Council on City Data and ISO 37120
							UN-Habitat: Urban Patterns of a Green Economy	Rockefeller Foundation: 100 Resilient Cities	Sustainable Cities Indicators
							GGGI/OECD/UNEP/World Bank: Green Growth Knowledge Platform	LSE/ICLEI/GGGI: Going Green	GGGI: Green Growth Best Practice Initiative
									ADB: Secondary Cities Development Program – Green Cities
									GIZ/ICLEI: Urban NEXUS

ADB = Asian Development Bank, BMZ = German Federal Ministry for Economic Cooperation and Development, DFID = Department for International Development of the United Kingdom, EU = European Union, GGGI = Global Green Growth Institute, GIZ = German Development Corporation, IDB = Inter-American Development Bank, ICC = International Chamber of Commerce, ICLEI = Local Governments for Sustainability (formerly: International Council for Local Environmental Initiatives), IPCC = Intergovernmental Panel on Climate Change, ISO = International Organization for Standardization, LSE = London School of Economics and Political Science, OECD = Organisation for Economic Co-operation and Development, UCL = University College London, UNEP = United Nations Environment Programme, UNESCAP = United Nations Economic and Social Commission for Asia and the Pacific, UN-Habitat = United Nations Human Settlements Programme.

Source: Authors.

Box 1.1: UNESCAP Green Growth Strategy

A series of energy, water, food, and financial crises in Asia since the 1990s highlighted the dangers of resource-driven development based on "growth first, clean-up later." In response, the United Nations Economic and Social Commission for Asia and the Pacific (UNESCAP) formulated six pillars for achieving less resource-dependent, more climate-friendly, and more socially inclusive development:

- **Sustainable consumption and production:** more efficient use of resources; life-cycle approach; and triple bottom line of environmental, economic, and equity aspects in the production process
- **Greening business and markets:** companies as agents of change toward a sustainable development path, right incentives and support measures, and corporate social responsibility
- **Sustainable infrastructure:** more efficient flow of things, people, information, natural resources, and money; and fewer negative social and environmental impacts
- **Green tax and budget reform:** price reflection of negative externalities associated with increasing consumption, environmentally based taxing, and elimination of subsidies that have perverse effects
- **Eco-efficiency indicators:** impact monitoring, improved decision making, and adjusted policies for enhanced green growth
- **Investment in natural capital:** ecosystem services, local livelihoods and resource cycles, and climate-friendly investments in natural assets

Practical experience in recent years has underscored how the green growth concept must be adjusted to the local context. At the same time, the overarching regional concept has been enriched by local experiences, knowledge, and expertise.

Sources: Green Growth Best Practice Initiative (GGBP). 2014. *Green Growth in Practice: Lessons from Country Experiences.* Seoul: GGBP/Global Green Growth Institute. http://www.greengrowth.org/?q=publication/full-report-green-growth-practice-lessons-country-experiences; UNESCAP. 2015. Green Growth. http://www.greengrowth.org/

The Organisation for Economic Co-operation and Development (OECD) defines green growth as "fostering economic growth and development while ensuring that natural assets continue to provide the resources and environmental services on which our well-being relies" (OECD 2013, p. 3). The OECD also identified recommendations on how green growth can happen in the urban context (Box 1.2). Thus, green growth raised the potential of putting natural assets to use in fostering a low-carbon economy, thereby opening up new markets, creating jobs, and spurring innovation (UNESCAP 2015a).

ECO2Cities, a World Bank initiative, emphasized the "interdependence of ecological and economic sustainability, and their fundamental ability to reinforce each other in the urban context" (World Bank 2010b). Strategic use of a smaller, renewable resource base, it was argued, could generate the same value for the economy while reducing harmful pollution and unnecessary waste. This linkage was made in the context of a "one system" approach, in which the city is viewed as an organic whole composed of various subsystems (land, water, energy, and transport) to be developed and operated in harmony with each other.

Box 1.2: OECD – Enabling Green Growth in Cities

As part of its Green Growth Studies, the Organisation for Economic Co-operation and Development (OECD) has identified recommendations on how green growth can happen in the urban context. Retrofitting buildings for increased energy efficiency is favorable for creating jobs. An intelligent transport system can help attract skilled labor and investors. If green products and services are to be promoted, a closer look at locational potentials and support for innovation, research, and development are recommended. For an increase in urban land values, various urban redevelopment options can help, including eco-districts and infill development. These actions can be enhanced through various governance mechanisms, for instance, incentives and clear enforcement of rules as well as cooperation and through data collection and monitoring across administrative boundaries, cross-sector collaboration, and local capacity building. On the financial side, public–private partnerships, carbon finance, loans, bonds, value capture taxes, and development fees and charges are the broad categories of options. The OECD report underscores that no city action can become fully successful and sustainable without some national action; national governments can support cities through financing, technical assistance, monitoring mechanisms, the right price signals, adjusted standards, reassessment of incentive schemes, and programs to support green infrastructure investment.

Source: OECD. 2013. *Green Growth in Cities*. Paris. http://www.oecd.org/regional/green-growth-in-cities.htm

The 2000s also witnessed the broadening of the concept of sustainable urban development to include the third pillar: social equity (UN-Habitat 2014). The concept of cobenefits—interventions that produced both social and economic benefits—was popularized. This shift reflected the increasing emphasis on the livability of urban communities, promoted by smart growth and other planning movements that valued walkable, human-scale environments with high-quality open spaces and recreational areas.[1] Social equity was combined with environmental sustainability and economic competitiveness in the concept of the "triple bottom line."

The introduction of the City Development Strategy (CDS) by Cities Alliance (2014) also contributed to the emphasis on the social impacts of urban development. The goal of the high-level strategic planning process espoused by the CDS is to maximize the economic impact of urbanization and ensure some of the benefits reach the low-income population. It emphasized interagency coordination and a strategic prioritization of investment projects, which facilitated the preparation of loan projects by international donor agencies. Many CDS interventions have directly impacted the poor by concentrating attention and resources on urban upgrading projects.

As part of its flagship *State of the World's Cities* report series, the United Nations Human Settlements Programme (UN-Habitat) reintroduced the concept of "prosperity" to address stark inequalities around the world (UN-Habitat 2013b). While citywide economic growth rates were high, many socioeconomic segments of the population were not benefiting from the rising tide. UN-Habitat therefore proposed the City Prosperity Index, which broadens the

---

[1]   For an overview, see Birch (2009).

Malaysia: The KLCC Park in Kuala Lumpur provides quality green space accessible to the public

definition of success to include not only economic growth, but also access to infrastructure, environmental sustainability, generational justice and equity, and quality of life (Table 1.1). UN-Habitat argues in the report that cities are in a position to contribute solutions to some of the multiple crises (financial, economic, political, environmental, etc.) that countries are experiencing in the 21st century.

120,000
people move into cities per day

Asia's cities will become home to another 1.1 billion people in the next two decades as the poor continue to be drawn to better opportunities. Many of these people go into slums.

520 million
people live in urban squalor

Currently, about 520 million people in the region live in urban squalor and by 2015 that is expected to rise to 700 million.

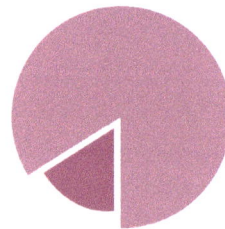

80%
of most Asian countries' GDP

According to the March 2011 report, McKinsey Global Institute's Urban World, half of the 600 cities that account for 60% of global gross domestic product are in Asia. In most countries in Asia, cities generate more than 80% of gross domestic product.

70%
of all new jobs in India by 2030

By 2030, cities will provide 70% of all new jobs in India. By that time, the economy of the city of Delhi will be bigger than Malaysia's economy is today, according to McKinsey.

The role of cities to a country's prosperity cannot be overestimated

Source: ADB Green Cities Multimedia Feature. Green Cities: A Sustainable Urban Future in Southeast Asia. http://www.adb.org/green-cities/index.html

Table 1.1: Defining a Prosperous City

A prosperous city is one that provides ...	
Productivity	Contributes to economic growth and development, generates income, and provides decent jobs and equal opportunities for all through effective economic policies and reforms
Infrastructure development	Provides adequate infrastructure—water, sanitation, roads, and information and communication technology—to improve living standards and enhance productivity, mobility, and connectivity
Quality of life	Enhances the use of public spaces for the sake of community cohesion and civic identity, and guarantees individual and material safety and security
Equity and social inclusion	Ensures equitable (re)distribution of the benefits of prosperity; reduces poverty and the incidence of slums; protects the rights of minority and vulnerable groups; enhances gender equality; and ensures civic participation in the social, political, and cultural spheres
Environmental sustainability	Values the protection of the urban environment and natural assets while ensuring growth, pursues energy efficiency, reduces pressure on surrounding land and natural resources, and reduces environmental losses through creative environment-enhancing solutions

Source: UN-Habitat. 2013. *State of the World's Cities 2012/2013: Prosperity of Cities*. New York: Routledge. pp. 11–12. http://unhabitat.org/books/prosperity-of-cities-state-of-the-worlds-cities-20122013/

Since 2010, urban sustainability has advanced to focus on climate change resilience. The ability of cities to expand and redevelop in a way that minimizes the impact of natural hazards and climate change risks has dominated sustainability initiatives and projects in Asia and around the world. ICLEI's GreenClimateCities Program, for example, offers decision-making tools and a planning process for preparing broad-based climate change mitigation programs at the city or regional level (ICLEI 2015). The Rockefeller Foundation has also committed substantial resources to achieve its objective of "making people, communities and systems better prepared to withstand catastrophic events—both natural and manmade—and able to bounce back more quickly and emerge stronger from these shocks and stresses" (Rockefeller Foundation 2015b).

In 2013, LSE Cities at the London School of Economics and Political Science, supported by ICLEI and the Global Green Growth Institute, published *Going Green: How Cities Are Leading the Next Economy* (Box 1.3). The project concluded that "going green" has reached the mainstream of urban management internationally, as witnessed by the substantial progress in areas such as solid waste, water supply, wastewater, and green open spaces. However, other areas such as energy security and resource efficiency still lag. While green policies have been initiated in many cities, integrated cross-sector approaches for green growth are still

Box 1.3: Going Green: How Cities Are Leading the Next Economy

In the first part of this report, the London School of Economics and Political Science (LSE) concludes, following a survey of city governments, that many cities worldwide have instituted green growth policies. The nonbinding nature of these policies has undermined their impact, however. Another observation is that while coordination among environment, transport, and planning departments in city governments has improved, timely inputs from economics, technology, and/or finance departments are often still lacking.

The second part of the report presents findings from eight case studies of cities on their path toward green growth. The main findings confirm the important role of local leadership in promoting and implementing green growth strategies. It was observed that cities strongly dedicated to going green establish a leadership position that attracts investment and leads to accumulation of expertise over the medium and long term. Whereas the direct and indirect downstream benefits of investment in green growth are known, quantitative evidence of green growth's high benefit–cost ratio is still scarce, mostly for lack of study. Funding shortages and lack of capacity in the public sector can be overcome through partnerships with private firms. In the case of lower-income countries, international funds for low-carbon development can also help make green projects financially viable. The report notes that green growth can be enhanced through an integrated spatial planning approach, regulatory frameworks that support research and development in niche markets, and the formulation of higher standards, which in turn trigger innovation in businesses and industries.

Source: LSE Cities, ICLEI, and Global Green Growth Institute. 2013. *Going Green: How Cities Are Leading the Next Economy*. London: LSE.

rare (GIZ and ICLEI 2014). The study also noted that funding shortages and unsupportive national policy frameworks continue to impede the progress of local governments toward their green development goals.

An integrated, multisector approach was and still is the key to achieving sustainable urban development (Centre for Liveable Cities 2014). A snapshot of city examples from the past decade (Figure 1.2) illustrates that there have been numerous efforts across the globe to achieve urban development that is integrated, with a view to creating sustainable and livable cities. Each of these city examples is embedded in a specific national and local context of economic, political, social, cultural, and environmental conditions.[2] Of course, each of these examples requires an individual evaluation of which aspects of a particular approach have (or have not) been successful.

The GrEEEn Cities Operational Framework

Building on the global research and advocacy around sustainability and green growth in cities, and ADB's own initiatives to ensure an integrated, sustainable approach to urban development as part of its operations, the GrEEEn Cities Operational Framework (GCOF) was developed as a flexible, scalable approach to address urban Asia's livability challenge (Sandhu and Naik Singru 2014).

---

[2]   See, for instance, video of Portland Development Commission (2011).

Figure 1.2: A Decade of Green City Examples for Integrated Urban Development

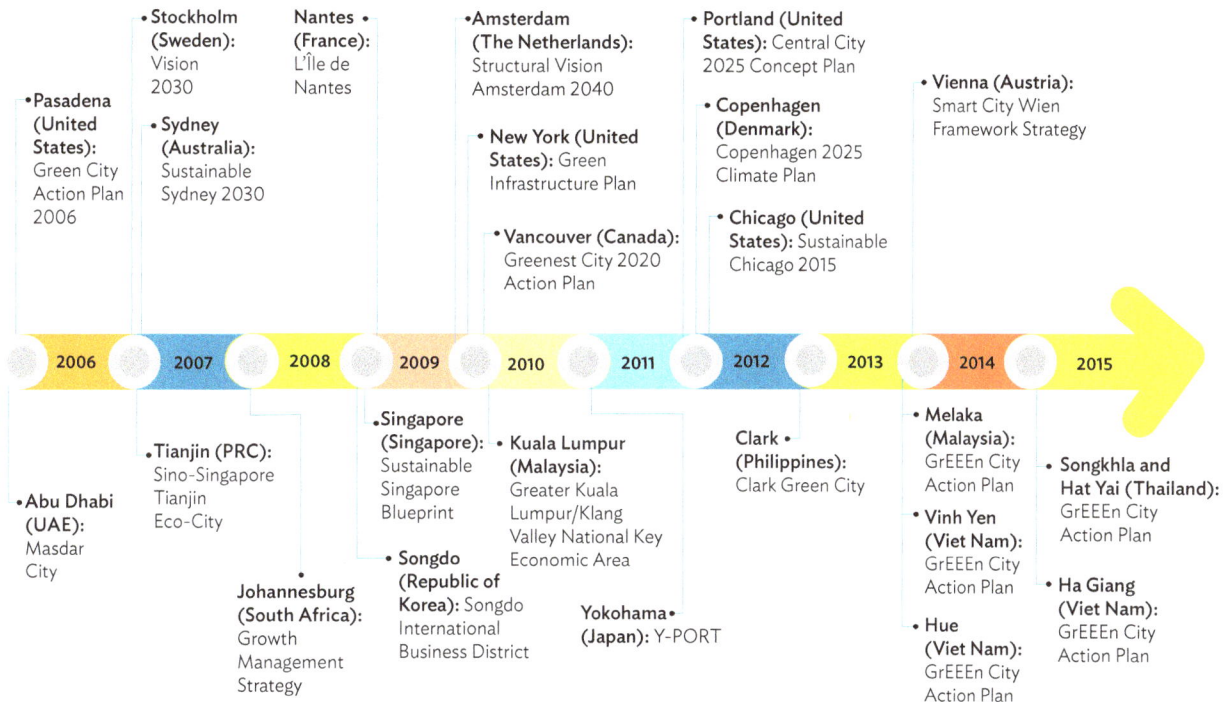

- **Pasadena (United States):** Green City Action Plan 2006

- **Stockholm (Sweden):** Vision 2030
- **Sydney (Australia):** Sustainable Sydney 2030

- **Nantes (France):** L'Île de Nantes

- **Amsterdam (The Netherlands):** Structural Vision Amsterdam 2040
- **New York (United States):** Green Infrastructure Plan
- **Vancouver (Canada):** Greenest City 2020 Action Plan

- **Portland (United States):** Central City 2025 Concept Plan
- **Copenhagen (Denmark):** Copenhagen 2025 Climate Plan
- **Chicago (United States):** Sustainable Chicago 2015

- **Vienna (Austria):** Smart City Wien Framework Strategy

| 2006 | 2007 | 2008 | 2009 | 2010 | 2011 | 2012 | 2013 | 2014 | 2015 |

- **Abu Dhabi (UAE):** Masdar City

- **Tianjin (PRC):** Sino-Singapore Tianjin Eco-City
- **Johannesburg (South Africa):** Growth Management Strategy

- **Singapore (Singapore):** Sustainable Singapore Blueprint
- **Songdo (Republic of Korea):** Songdo International Business District

- **Kuala Lumpur (Malaysia):** Greater Kuala Lumpur/Klang Valley National Key Economic Area
- **Yokohama (Japan):** Y-PORT

- **Clark (Philippines):** Clark Green City

- **Melaka (Malaysia):** GrEEEn City Action Plan
- **Vinh Yen (Viet Nam):** GrEEEn City Action Plan
- **Hue (Viet Nam):** GrEEEn City Action Plan

- **Songkhla and Hat Yai (Thailand):** GrEEEn City Action Plan
- **Ha Giang (Viet Nam):** GrEEEn City Action Plan

PRC = People's Republic of China, UAE = United Arab Emirates.
Source: Authors.

ADB addresses the urbanization challenge through Strategy 2020, its long-term strategic framework for 2008–2020. Together with its recently concluded midterm review, Strategy 2020 identifies environmentally sustainable growth, including infrastructure and climate change, as a priority for development and operations (ADB 2014i). The framework has been articulated in different sectors through specific operational plans, such as the Water Operational Plan 2011–2020, the Environment Operational Directions 2013–2020, and the Sustainable Transport Initiative (ADB 2011e, 2013c, 2010a).

In the urban sector, Strategy 2020 has been articulated through ADB's Urban Operational Plan 2012–2020, which calls for an integrated, sustainable approach to urban development anchored on addressing the environmental (green), equity (inclusiveness), and economic (competitiveness) issues facing cities today (ADB 2013i). The plan was discussed extensively both within ADB and with clients, utilizing a set of background documents prepared describing the 3E (economy, environment, and equity) basics—green, inclusive, and competitive cities (ADB 2011a, b, c). This 3E approach was seen as a significant departure from business as usual for ADB, its developing member countries, the urban sector, and the international community (ADB 2013i). The Urban Operational Plan also stated that ADB's regional departments first run pilot tests with the 3E approach to then gradually mainstream it in their urban operations (ADB 2013i). In parallel, there was a demand from countries in

Southeast Asia, in particular the Indonesia–Malaysia–Thailand Growth Triangle (IMT-GT) and Viet Nam, to apply their national green growth strategies toward developing green cities.

Eleven cities in Indonesia, Malaysia, Myanmar, Thailand, and Viet Nam have tested the GCOF and have prepared GrEEEn City Action Plans (GCAPs) with varying technical scopes and levels of institutional engagement. The GCAPs, which represent the key output from the GCOF process, consist of prioritized, time-based investment programs with goals and short-, medium-, and long-term actions for improving the environmental quality and achieving competitive, resilient growth in cities.

The comprehensive GCAPs prepared by Vinh Yen and Hue in Viet Nam respond to the urbanization challenges facing both these cities (ADB 2012d, 2015b, 2015c). A limited scoping study based on the 3Es was carried out in Mandalay (Myanmar) (ADB 2014n). GCAPs were prepared for the cities of Melaka (Malaysia) and Songkhla and Hat Yai (Thailand) under a regional cooperation initiative of the IMT-GT (ADB 2010b, 2015d). A high degree of consensus was achieved in Melaka (Malaysia) among city government departments, local residents, the business community, national ministries, and development agencies about the way forward for enhanced sustainability; the Melaka GCAP is under implementation

Singapore: The efforts in sustainable urban development in Singapore are one example of the different pathways toward urban livability

(ADB 2010b). A GCAP has been prepared in Ha Giang (Viet Nam), building upon the initial learning in Vinh Yen and Hue (ADB 2014l). In Indonesia, GCAPs are under preparation in four cities under an ADB-financed technical assistance project (ADB 2013g).

The experience of applying the GCOF in the context of ADB's sector work and operations on the ground have demonstrated the added value of this approach and its ability to complement and augment traditional (and often top-down) master planning processes. The result of these test applications is that the seven cities are on a clear path toward environmentally, economically, and socially sustainable development. Having used this results-oriented approach, the pilot cities are more likely to achieve their development vision.

Each of these experiences has provided unique insights and perspectives on how an approach like the GCOF can offer local governments and stakeholders, including development finance institutions such as ADB, an operational platform for integrated urban development and environmental planning. The chapters that follow represent an effort to capture, document, and reflect on these experiences, and to provide replicable examples of good practices from cities in different regions and at different stages of development.

Photo Credit: Renard Teipelke

Solutions emerge
When bridges are built
People crossing
....exploring
.......tranquility
...............livability

---Authors

2 The GrEEEn Cities Operational Framework

Building on previous concepts and experiences from around the world, the GrEEEn Cities Operational Framework (GCOF) enables the systematic and thorough integration of urban development and environmental planning for improved livability and balanced growth in cities (ADB 2014d, Sandhu and Naik Singru 2014). This requires breaking down institutional compartmentalization; deploying effective decision support systems; investing in urban profiles and assessments; and recognizing that environmental, economic, and social systems complement technical soundness.

As shown in Figure 2.1, the GCOF is a framework that guides the transformation of a city from its existing status quo toward becoming a livable city, depicted by the underlying green arrow. It is a combination of processes, activities, and actions leading to the preparation of a GrEEEn City Action Plan (GCAP) and identifying options for Urban Management Partnerships (UMPs). The vertical bars represent elements that will be assessed and analyzed. The horizontal bars represent reiterative processes required to develop the outputs. The entire process is driven through consensus building to develop stakeholder ownership in the transformation of the city.

The GCOF is sequenced to begin with the urban profile, a diagnostic review of the status quo of the city with a business-as-usual assessment for understanding the baseline. Assessments are conducted along the elements identified under the 3E pillars of economy, environment, and equity based on available secondary data and other existing reports including master plans for the city.[3] The elements listed in the boxes under each of the 3E pillars need to be analyzed and tailored to the individual city context with a relative emphasis on those that align with the city's vision and key assets identified through stakeholder consultations. The analysis and synthesis is reiteratively conducted and confirmed through visioning and SWOT (strengths, weaknesses, opportunities, and threats) analysis to arrive at a shared vision. The urban profile ensures that the assessments take into consideration existing urban realities and the future needs of the growing urban population (cf. gap analysis). It identifies the city's key assets and drivers of urban growth, outlines existing urban conditions, and evaluates future patterns of urbanization. It takes into consideration the "enablers," such as the political and legislative dimensions of urban development that are critical in the creation of an enabling environment, the governance and management platforms, and the institutional structures that are the mechanisms for implementation. The analysis of the enabling

The GrEEEn Cities Operational Framework is a platform that enables the unfolding of various institutional and technical "compartments" to respond to citizens' vision of livability for their cities.

---

[3]   The urban profile process has been explained in the manual by Naik Singru and Lindfield (forthcoming) with the appropriate tools identified for conducting it. The three phases of the national urban assessments are urban profiling, urban strategy and prioritization, and urban actions. The GCOF is aligned with these phases.

Figure 2.1: GrEEEn Cities Operational Framework

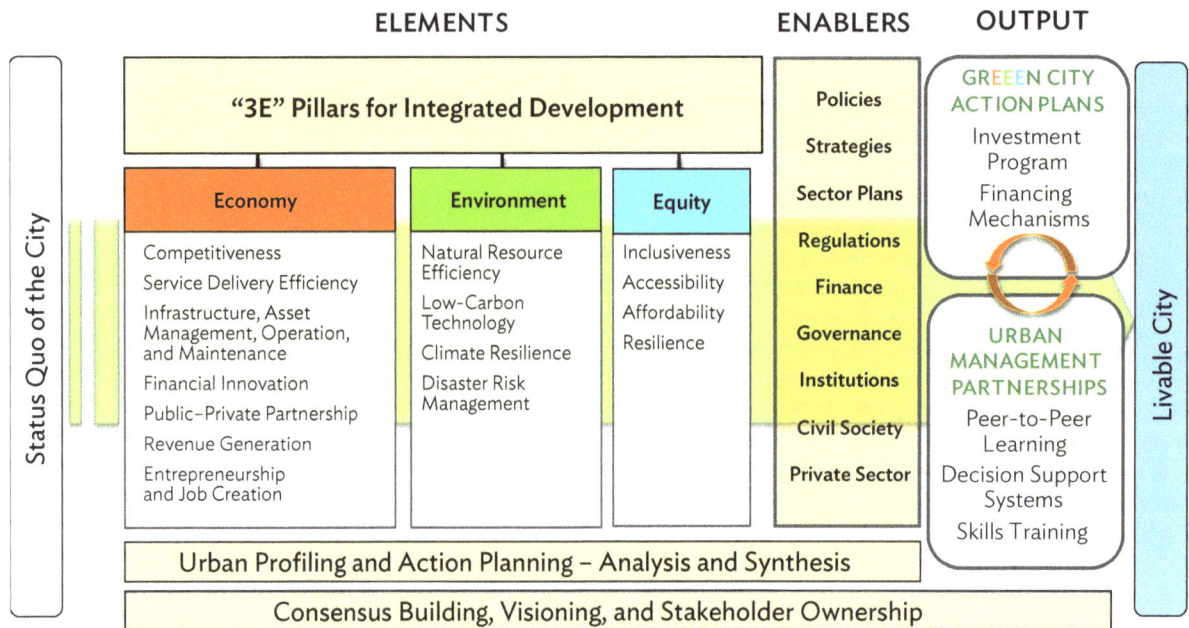

Note: The 3E pillars of economy, environment, and equity were derived from ADB. 2013. *Urban Operational Plan 2012–2020*. Manila.

Source: S. Sandhu and R. Naik Singru. 2014. Enabling GrEEEn Cities: An Operational Framework for Integrated Urban Development in Southeast Asia. *SERD Working Paper Series*. No. 9. Manila: Asian Development Bank.

environment comprises the regulatory, institutional, capacity, and resource frameworks. Socioeconomic factors and the environment, natural resource consumption, resilience to climate and disaster risks, technologies for low-carbon growth, and financial resource flows of a city are assessed and its natural and revenue-generating assets are identified, along with other enablers, such as national strategic priorities, policies, institutional mechanisms, and partnerships with civil society and the private sector, with which the city is able to maximize its asset advantage. The 3E criteria are established for prioritizing investments and actions to improve the efficiency of urban services and the sustainability of urban infrastructure.

The city's comprehensive urban profile thus serves as the basis for identifying the actions that are required to bring about the transformation of the city. The action planning process considers iteratively the connections between the 3E elements to improve the correlation between these for integrated city planning to develop the actions required to implement the vision for the city. These actions consist of investments (including financing mechanisms), "enablers" (policies and strategies), and institutional mechanisms that could be developed through UMPs to support the implementation of the actions. The entire process and outputs are captured in the GCAP, which is meant to be a dynamic and evolving document that presents an investment program aimed to augment livability for the balanced growth of a city.

The GCOF guides the preparation of GCAPs as well as the creation of UMPs (Figure 2.1). Led by the local government, the preparation of the GCAP integrates local stakeholders, national ministries, implementing agencies, and investors into the planning and implementation

Photo Credit: ADB/Lester Ledesma

Malaysia: The Kuala Lumpur skyline as seen from Lake Titiwangsa

process with the right incentives for achieving the city's short-, medium-, and long-term development goals. At a glance, the GCOF encompasses the following:

- Creates a platform for stakeholder engagement for a shared vision and incentives
- Integrates individual investment projects into a coherent whole to generate higher levels of benefits through a strategic combination of investment initiatives and programs
- Unbundles the economic competitiveness, environmental, and equity dimensions of all interventions in the context of the city
- Identifies and adds value to a city's existing social, cultural, and natural assets by using a place-based approach
- Optimizes value-for-money by improving the effectiveness of investments through the use of "enablers" such as incentives, policies, or regulations
- Facilitates UMPs to ensure stakeholder support, improve coordination, and build local government capacity
- Results in enhanced livability and quality of life.

The key elements of a GCAP include

- a collective **vision** that enhances and preserves the city's main economic, cultural, and environmental assets;
- an **urban profile** that assesses the regulatory, institutional, economic, environmental, and social aspects and business-as-usual practices in the city and identifies corresponding gaps to be addressed in the city's urban development;
- a time-bound **action plan** consisting of short-, medium-, and long-term initiatives for investments and enabling measures (such as policy reform and institutional capacity building) including costs and performance indicators; and

- **implementation arrangements**, including decision support systems, asset management plans, and monitoring and evaluation mechanisms (such as citizen scorecards to enable citizens feedback and to improve the local government response in meeting citizens' needs).

UMPs through city-to-city peer learning and knowledge sharing are designed to improve skills and competence in integrated urban development, environmental planning, and project management at various levels of government as well as in civil society and the private sector. UMPs facilitate collaboration among city administration, local stakeholders, and successful external organizations, including the private sector, to enable learning and building capacity.

An Integrating Platform

The platform created by the GCOF enables deeper analytical understanding for bridging the 3Es through urban profiling and synthesis. In order to achieve multiple benefits across the 3Es, it is possible to carry out an analysis of how one single intervention can generate a series of direct and indirect benefits that impact the livability in a city. Often, the planning and management of cities is out of alignment with their natural resource flows, resulting in overextraction and inefficiency (GIZ and ICLEI 2014). The GCOF seeks to enhance that alignment by siting development (i) in areas with excess capacity in infrastructure systems, (ii) near or downstream from potable water sources, and (iii) along existing transport corridors. Such a multi-criteria analysis informs the design of strategic investments to provide cumulative positive impacts. For example, this approach has been used in recent years to integrate climate change mitigation programs with other more traditional socioeconomic development efforts, enabling cities to advance simultaneously on all fronts of sustainable development (Hammer et al. 2011, p. 16).

Building GrEEEn Cities is by nature an incremental process, building on and connecting to existing initiatives. The GCOF adds value to the status quo (i) by establishing a programmatic approach for the city's urban development by situating ongoing initiatives within based on value enhancement of the 3Es and (ii) by creating the opportunity to retool existing projects. A clean slate may not be necessary to initiate green growth. Existing physical development plans can be used as is or optimized to generate better results in the 3Es. The GCAPs mentioned in Chapter 1 incorporated and updated existing plans and development initiatives into an operational framework with specific benchmarks for implementation. The GCAPs demonstrated their application as a flexible and scalable approach at different times in a city's growth trajectory and at different stages of socioeconomic development (ADB 2014b). Success across the board in the short term is not a requirement. The iterative process should trace an upward spiral, in which a number of small victories can over time add up to a more livable city (EuroFoundationCentre 2013).

Drawing an analogy with a beehive, which is a complete, interlinked ecosystem where each cell is productive and contributes to the entire system in a coordinated manner under strong leadership, a city is made up of several spatial components that add up to a whole. Each neighborhood can be viewed as a complete ecosystem that contributes to the larger spatial scale in a GrEEEn Cities system (Figure 2.2). One or more initiatives can be implemented within each cell of the city. While the initiatives may be implemented by different agencies of

Figure 2.2: GrEEEn Cities System

Public transport

Community participation

Local prosperity

Inclusive housing

Green spaces

Nonmotorized mobility

Green economy

Renewable energy

Water for All

Note: All elements conjunctively form a mixed GrEEEn Cities system in a flexible and scalable manner from the neighborhood to the city scale.

Source: Authors.

the city, the core of the system is to integrate planning and build complementarities across the different sectors and services such as water, energy, transport, and social services to scale up to a livable GrEEEn City. The GrEEEn Cities system thus is scalable and flexible in its application.

A livable city, similar to a living organism, has a unique DNA structure—a genetic code, which is made up from its built assets, as well as cultural, natural, and human resource assets (Crowhurst Lennard and Lennard 1995). Building on established concepts for increasing competition and place branding, the GCOF carefully analyzes a city's assets to enhance its unique selling point (USP).[4] The GCOF is a relevant framework for city branding and provides the building blocks for addressing economic and resource competition as well as the challenges of social equity in an integrated manner (Kavaratzis 2004). The GCOF being a place-based approach identifies a city's key assets (e.g., a surface water body, vibrant commercial district, or emerging industrial cluster) and supports their emergence through capital improvements, investment incentives, and/or regulatory reforms. In each case, the combination of investments that leverages the USP to deliver a city's vision will vary.

Most often, typical urban projects group together disparate infrastructure investments that, though worthwhile on their own, do not achieve synergies and therefore fail to maximize the value they add to a city. For example, a package of roads improvements, water pumping stations, and stormwater drainage channels in different neighborhoods across the city may not achieve the city's vision for urban transformation. The returns are greater when investments are clustered in one or more districts.

---

[4]   Building on place branding concepts versus generic city marketing approaches, see, for example, Kavaratzis, Warnaby, and Ashworth (2015).

Figure 2.3: Exemplary Urban Management Partnership for the Development of the Citadel in Hue, Viet Nam

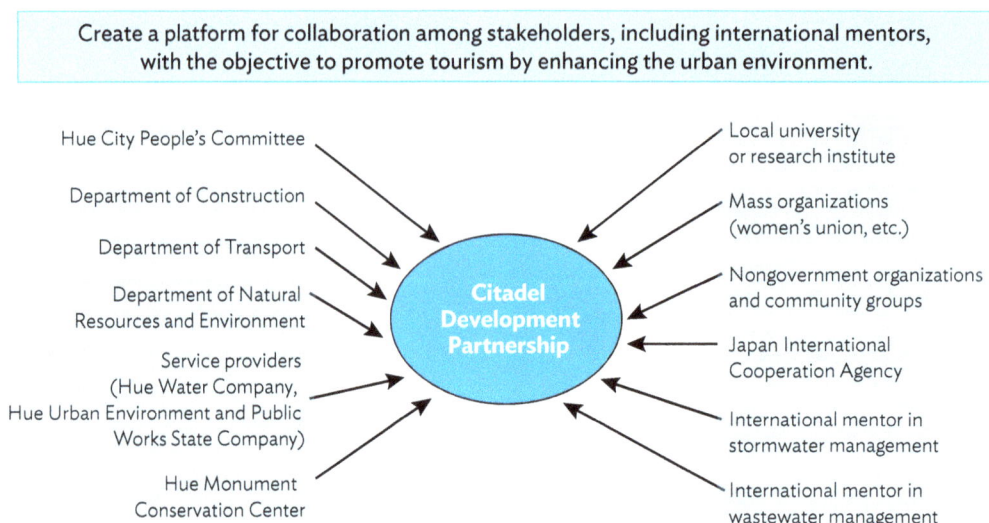

Create a platform for collaboration among stakeholders, including international mentors, with the objective to promote tourism by enhancing the urban environment.

Hue City People's Committee

Department of Construction

Department of Transport

Department of Natural Resources and Environment

Service providers (Hue Water Company, Hue Urban Environment and Public Works State Company)

Hue Monument Conservation Center

Citadel Development Partnership

Local university or research institute

Mass organizations (women's union, etc.)

Nongovernment organizations and community groups

Japan International Cooperation Agency

International mentor in stormwater management

International mentor in wastewater management

Source: ADB. 2015. *Enabling GrEEEn Cities: Hue GrEEEn City Action Plan.* Manila.

The GCOF enables a platform for engagement of stakeholders and integration of development efforts at all spatial and governance levels. This provides a chance for local leaders to align their urban development initiatives with the mandates and resources that flow down from higher levels of government.

UMPs can be structured to create this platform for coordination and collaboration among all stakeholders and investors. The UMP brings together all the major players with a stake in the socioeconomic and physical development of a city (see example in Figure 2.3). Under the leadership of the local government, the UMP usually includes business associations, large employers, civil society organizations, and community groups. The UMP is a mechanism for "horizontal" coordination of the various projects and programs into one overarching investment program, and for strengthening "vertical" connections among local governments, central agencies, and national policy and regulatory frameworks. In doing so, it creates the chance to "connect some dots," achieve synergies, and maximize long-term value creation for the city.

Meeting the Sustainable Development Goals

The year 2015 has been a milestone year for the future of development. The international dialogue on the sustainable development agenda has widened. In alignment with the post-2015 development agenda, the Millennium Development Goals (MDGs) have been replaced by the Sustainable Development Goals (SDGs) (UNDESA 2015b). Adopted in September 2015, they embrace a triple bottom-line approach to human well-being, covering environmental, social, and economic challenges, and their ambition is to be global and inclusive. Negotiations among 193 member countries of the United Nations have concluded to finalize 17 goals and 169 targets for countries to meet in the next 15 years (UNDESA 2015a).

SDG Goal 11 is to "make cities and human settlements inclusive, safe, resilient and sustainable" and the inclusion of this "urban goal" among the 17 SDGs underscores the broadly recognized transformative role of cities for sustainable development (Cardama 2015).[5] A number of other goals also relate to livability of urban areas: Goal 6 on water and sanitation, Goal 9 on resilient infrastructure, Goal 13 on climate change, Goal 15 on sustainable ecosystems, and Goal 16 on accountable and inclusive institutions.

Scaling down these global goals and targets to the city level is critical to their achievement. Convergence of the top–down international goals with the bottom–up city-level urban transformations can only be achieved through integration of specific indicators into the design of investments at the city level (Figure 2.4). The GCAP provides a mechanism for coordinating institutional partnerships, finance, and implementation linked to the integration of indicators mapped across the initiatives for urban transformation in a city. Thus in a loop-back, the development and implementation of the GCAP can contribute to the incremental achievement of global targets such as the SDGs. Linking investments with the indicators, targets, and goals is a prerequisite to achieving the goals.

Financing for Development is the new paradigm for making money work more effectively.[6] The SDGs will require much larger sums than before to back. Under the MDGs, the predecessor to the SDGs, the focus was on addressing deprivations.

A recent ADB (2015f) publication, *Making Money Work: Financing a Sustainable Future in Asia and the Pacific,* highlights not just the need to inject more money into investments that contribute to sustainable development, but also the need to attract funds toward them. Development finance was seen mainly as public money, partly domestic and official development assistance (ODA)—money that is programmable for development.

The SDGs are far more ambitious in scope and will require the best and innovative use of all sources of funding. According to some estimates, it could require as much as $1 trillion per year to meet the SDGs in Asia and the Pacific (ADB 2015f). With ODA in the region at only $27 billion (2012), a dramatic change in the landscape of finance requires moving beyond an aid-centric approach on development finance to much wider financing for development. The recently concluded Third International Conference on Financing for Development reiterated that every dollar should count for meeting the SDGs and the international finance institutions' model of "a dollar in" resulting in "more than a dollar out" for development seems the best model among development partners.

Putting Asia and the Pacific on track to achieve sustainable development will not be an easy process. Traditionally, developing countries in the region looked to ODA as a primary source

---

[5]   Also see video of United Cities and Local Governments (UCLG 2014).

[6]   The Third International Conference on Financing for Development adopted the Outcome Document of the Conference, the Addis Ababa Action Agenda, endorsed by the General Assembly of the United Nations in July 2015. See http://www.un.org/esa/ffd/ffd3/wp-content/uploads/sites/2/2015/07/Addis-Ababa-Action-Agenda-Draft-Outcome-Document-7-July-2015.pdf (accessed 5 August 2015).

Figure 2.4: Convergence of International Goals and Financing with City Development

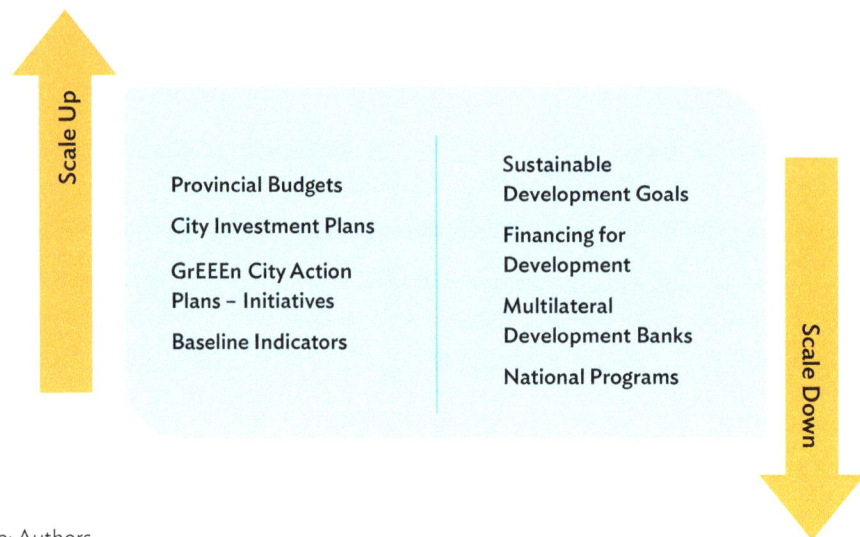

Scale Up

Provincial Budgets

City Investment Plans

GrEEEn City Action
Plans – Initiatives

Baseline Indicators

Sustainable
Development Goals

Financing for
Development

Multilateral
Development Banks

National Programs

Scale Down

Source: Authors.

of development finance. But in many, ODA is now dwarfed by domestic fiscal space, which has grown significantly on the back of dynamic economic growth. Greater still are private sources, yet so far they have been only partially responsive and accountable for sustainable development priorities. In Asia, sources of private finance, beyond remittances and foreign direct investment, are far larger than ODA and domestic public finance combined. The region currently has $6.2 trillion in private savings, $3.5 trillion in sovereign wealth and pension funds, and $1.3 trillion in insurance premiums (ADB 2015f). The challenge is to align these funds toward meeting sustainable development.

Moving more money into development will require some new perspectives. The first relates to going beyond the past emphasis on mainly supplying funds, aggregating and leveraging them to pump money toward development. More money does need to flow; but equally important is the increased attractiveness of development investments so they become not just destinations for pumping funds to, but also magnets pulling in money from all possible sources. A second issue involves diverse motivations, which vary considerably across the public and private realms. Incentives for public and private actors are not mutually exclusive, but they do require new capacities to bring them together. The public sector might pursue projects with more well-defined measurable outcomes that inspire private interest, for example. Private actors can begin to see the pitfalls of a purely short-term profit orientation, such as the irreversible loss of natural resources required for production or consumer disaffection with practices seen as violating human rights standards or harming the planet.

In both of the above cases, urbanization presents new options for local funds and finance. With urbanization accelerating at a historic rate, responsibilities for both finance and decision making shall increasingly fall on subnational governments. Cities and municipalities shall begin to operate as both—sources of funds and also destinations for pulling in money from all possible sources. Increasing own source revenues will contribute to pumping funds. These can include effective collection of a balanced variety of fees, fines, levies for services rendered, and taxes on immovable property. In Asia, own source revenues cover a broad range. On the one hand, the Philippines has more than 33 different types of local user fees and charges, ranging from animal registration to garbage collection. The Republic of Korea, on the other hand, has its Local Tax Act that dictates the basic framework and allows local governments to determine the rates of 11 local taxes within certain limits (Brosio 2014). Where options such as bonds and local taxes are not available, in cities in the People's Republic of China, for example, negative fallouts can occur. According to the Ministry of Finance, the gross income share from land transference fees at 9% of local finance revenues rose to 44% in 2009 (UNDP 2013). From a sustainability viewpoint, different sources should be assessed and perverse incentives that lead to unsustainable use of land or other resources should be avoided.

Nurturing market options for municipal financing will make them attractive destinations for all sources of money. In addition to developing mechanisms to access financial markets, municipalities should build the right capacities for risk assessment, planning, and management. For selected municipalities, borrowing through bonds can be explored, including options for cofinancing. In case of public–private partnerships (PPPs), building project management capacities is imperative. With the right capacities, tailoring PPP frameworks and contracts based on local needs that apply appropriate safeguards that deliver verifiable sustainable development returns can widen options in identified cases.

Sustainable development requires linking different economic, environmental, and social issues. Making links across sectors early in project design can not only improve the quality and impact of local projects but also go a long way in assisting a country to meet its targets and contribute to transforming the world. One such way could be to design national-level programs that address crosscutting issues such as environmental quality, which impacts quality of life through, for instance, national air quality programs, given that environmental pollution and climate variations are by their very nature not localized issues.

Photo Credit: ADB/Rakesh Sahai

India: Integrated urban programs, such as the Karnataka Urban Development and Coastal Environmental Management Project, can address a variety of development goals by bundling different sectoral actions together

Preparing a GrEEEn City Action Plan

Formulation Process

The preparation and the implementation of the GrEEEn City Action Plan (GCAP) are led by a city government in coordination with key stakeholders. In this role, the city government faces two main challenges: (i) getting its staff out of their technical silos and (ii) ensuring the participation of private sector and civil society stakeholders. The obstacles and work-arounds related to interdepartmental collaboration are set out in Chapter 2.

The GCAP requires a long-term commitment for sustainable results and lasting benefits. Leadership and political commitment is necessary from the beginning of the GCAP formulation process through to implementation, and during the operations and maintenance phase. Strong leadership and political commitment is needed in high-level committees to overcome institutional barriers and enablers for the development of GrEEEn Cities. For instance in Viet Nam, in the dialogue and engagement with the national government on moving the strategic vision of green growth forward, the city selection criteria included evidence of strong leadership and commitment on the part of the provincial and local governments.

The process of how the GCAP is formulated is shown in Figure 3.1.

Visioning

A vision for a city is the aspirational description of the future of the city to guide its development in consensus with citizens. The vision has descriptive elements that capture the aspirations of the citizens on how the city should feel, function, and respond to their needs. It sets the direction for the city's development and helps in improving the adaptive capacity of a city to meet its future urban development needs. The challenge is to articulate a vision statement that encompasses the needs of the diverse stakeholders, while synergizing their priorities to create an image of a livable city that is competitive, green, and inclusive. A well-conceptualized vision statement provides a long-term perspective that enables informed decision making. The vision statement is the outcome of a stakeholder visioning exercise. "As much as a successful visioning process is a potential

The GrEEEn City Action Plan is a result of a citizens and stakeholder participatory process starting with a Vision for livability to be achieved over time through strategic investments in plans, programs, and projects.

Figure 3.1: GrEEEn City Action Plan Formulation Process

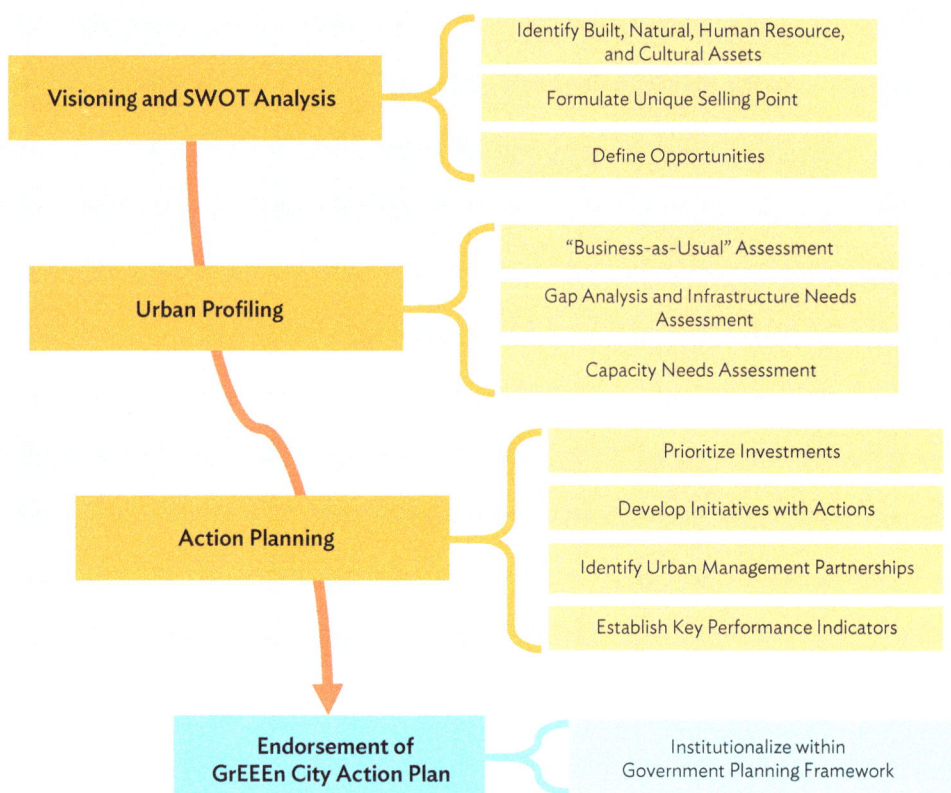

Visioning and SWOT Analysis	Identify Built, Natural, Human Resource, and Cultural Assets
	Formulate Unique Selling Point
	Define Opportunities
Urban Profiling	"Business-as-Usual" Assessment
	Gap Analysis and Infrastructure Needs Assessment
	Capacity Needs Assessment
Action Planning	Prioritize Investments
	Develop Initiatives with Actions
	Identify Urban Management Partnerships
	Establish Key Performance Indicators
Endorsement of GrEEEn City Action Plan	Institutionalize within Government Planning Framework

SWOT = strengths, weaknesses, opportunities, and threats.
Source: Authors.

and powerful leverage for changing the culture of participation, so can a vision generate a powerful momentum for changing and improving the quality of life in a certain territory" (UN-Habitat 2012, pp. 19–20).

Stakeholder Visioning Exercise

Visioning is an effective tool that can be used to develop a strategic urban vision at the city level and the national level. From its origins in the 1970s, collaborative and community visioning has become a widely used tool for participatory planning at all stages, from strategy to action (UN-Habitat 2012, ch 3; Robinson 2008). Strategic planning allows planners and stakeholders to define together an overall development perspective, identify priority areas for action, and focus implementation in these areas to refine traditional master plans (UN-Habitat 2012, ch 3).

Qualitative methodologies for rapid assessments were primarily developed through business studies for strategic action planning of business corporations. Urban planning has adopted strategic planning techniques popularized in business management strategies

Photo Credit: Soliman Carina

Georgia: Visioning and strengths, weaknesses, opportunities, and threats (SWOT) analysis with stakeholders in Tbilisi

(Naik Singru and Lindfield, forthcoming). Developed in the 1960s as a strategic planning method for data analysis; strengths, weaknesses, opportunities, and threats (SWOT) analysis evolved as a matrix for organizational analysis of internal (strengths and opportunities) and external factors (weaknesses and threats) (Naik Singru and Lindfield, forthcoming). It has gained popularity as an urban strategic planning tool to prepare Cities Alliance's (2014) City Development Strategy (CDS). The process for the visioning exercise is similar to that followed by other strategic planning methods such as the CDS.

Visioning exercises are scalable and require relatively few resources. However, other visioning methods are possible in order to match the community needs and available resources. They include surveys, online surveys, charettes, focus groups, panel studies, etc.[7] These tools can make relevant contributions to the visioning stage of a GCAP. The visioning exercise itself is, however, indispensable to generate community-based ideas and to capture vision, particularly for GrEEEn Cities.

Visioning can only be achieved through broad public participation and feedback on issues from members of the community. Facilitating a visioning exercise is in itself a challenge, as it requires external planning professionals to help connect the local vision in both vertical and horizontal ways: vertically to ensure the interrelationships with other government layers (national, regional, and local) and horizontally to ensure connectivity with neighboring

---

[7]   Based on its experience in Kosovo, UN-Habitat (2012, ch 3) developed a visioning tool kit, which identifies different ways of visioning in a planning perspective. Some of the methods are more generic and broad in scope, such as community planning events, roundtable workshops, and field workshops, while others are more specific and narrow, such as vision fairs or electronic mapping. Based on the purpose of visioning and the resources available, different methods can be used.

Photo Credits: Ramola Naik Singru (top left and right); Renard Teipelke (bottom left)

The strengths and opportunities of a city can be characterized by its history, cultural endowments, public spaces, local entrepreneurs, and many other valuable assets, which can often be revealed through a proper stakeholder consultation

communities and to provide a regional perspective (UN-Habitat 2012, ch 3). If done correctly, this can ensure continued stakeholder ownership and engagement during further planning and implementation to initiate in business-as-usual (BAU) practices.

While key decision makers often know the diverse range of stakeholders in their cities very well, it might pose a challenge to them to adjust the style of which, how, and when stakeholders are engaged in the urban planning process. It is important to underline that the experience-based knowledge of local stakeholders offers critical insights into the current situation and provides out-of-the-box options to address urban development challenges.

Stakeholders refer to persons or groups who are directly or indirectly affected by any activity in the city. Stakeholders are usually categorized into three major groups: (i) government, including at the national, regional, provincial, city, and neighborhood levels; (ii) civil society, including citizens, civil society organizations, community-based organizations (CBOs), nongovernment organizations (NGOs), and academe; and (iii) the private sector, including small and medium-sized enterprises (SMEs) and professional associations. For many stakeholders, the visioning exercise may be the first and only time they are involved in such an intensive collaborative planning. Multiple stakeholders will bring multiple visions to the table, which are articulated into a coherent vision statement through consensus building.

Photo Credit: Renard Teipelke

Viet Nam: GrEEEn City Action Plan workshops with different stakeholder groups in Hue and Vinh Yen

This process inherently involves trade-offs. No one vision can capture all preferences of all stakeholders. Depending on the degree of overlap among the preferences and priorities of the different participating groups, however, it is sometimes possible to find a core vision that will satisfy most parties to a large extent. Politics and power relations among the stakeholders always play a role in determining the trade-offs and forging the final outcome, even when the levers of influence are not exercised publicly during the consultation exercises. Sometimes it is useful for facilitators to meet with the major stakeholder representatives individually prior to the public meetings in order to understand in advance the position of the weaker groups.

The GrEEEn Cities Operational Framework (GCOF) applies visioning as the starting point in a consultative process of developing the GCAP. Visioning is used in conjunction with an analysis and synthesis of a city's SWOT, to support the development of an urban profile. This aims to establish sector priorities and ranking criteria for prioritizing investments. The visioning is designed to identify cities' assets, unique selling points (USPs), and priority development needs. Visioning and SWOT analysis have been applied at the city level in Vinh Yen, Hue, and Ha Giang in Viet Nam; Songkhla and Hat Yai in Thailand; and Mandalay in Myanmar. This was also applied at the national level for ADB's national urban assessment for Georgia (Naik Singru et al., forthcoming). This enabled the articulation and translation of national strategies into city-level actions, combining top–down and bottom–up approaches. The example of the visioning and SWOT analysis in Hue is shown in Figures 3.2 and 3.3.

Figure 3.2: GrEEEn City Vision for Hue, Viet Nam

What do you want your city to be in 10 years?

"A city with excellent physical conditions is not enough if the people who live there are not happy."

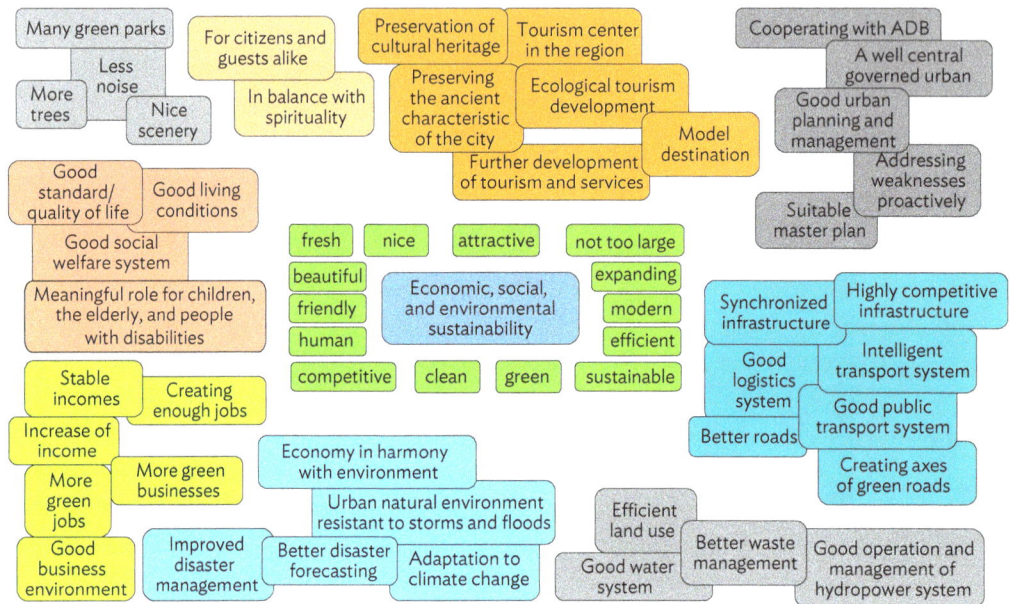

Many green parks	For citizens and guests alike	Preservation of cultural heritage	Tourism center in the region	Cooperating with ADB
Less noise		Preserving the ancient characteristic of the city	Ecological tourism development	A well central governed urban
More trees	Nice scenery	In balance with spirituality		Good urban planning and management
			Model destination	Addressing weaknesses proactively
Good standard/ quality of life	Good living conditions	Further development of tourism and services		Suitable master plan

fresh, nice, attractive, not too large

beautiful, friendly, human — Economic, social, and environmental sustainability — expanding, modern, efficient

competitive, clean, green, sustainable

Good standard/ quality of life · Good living conditions · Good social welfare system · Meaningful role for children, the elderly, and people with disabilities

Stable incomes · Creating enough jobs · Increase of income · More green jobs · More green businesses · Good business environment · Improved disaster management · Better disaster forecasting · Adaptation to climate change

Economy in harmony with environment · Urban natural environment resistant to storms and floods

Synchronized infrastructure · Highly competitive infrastructure · Good logistics system · Intelligent transport system · Better roads · Good public transport system · Creating axes of green roads

Efficient land use · Good water system · Better waste management · Good operation and management of hydropower system

ADB = Asian Development Bank.

Source: ADB. 2015. *Enabling GrEEEn Cities: Hue GrEEEn City Action Plan*. Manila.

Constraints and Barriers to Achieving Consensus

The visioning exercise differs from a simple stakeholder meeting because building consensus on a shared GrEEEn City vision among the various stakeholders is a reiterative process to ensure representation, ownership, and equity. Therefore, real participation of a diverse range of stakeholders, especially the disadvantaged, is needed to build inclusiveness through a people-first approach. Some authors also argue that contrary to long-held assumptions about the relationship between democratization and social equality, this expansion of political equality has been accompanied by a corresponding decline in social and economic equality (Lee, McQuarrie, and Walker 2015). However, in emerging countries, where public participation is relatively new, democratization and public participation are a key enabler of broader social equality.

Involvement of the civil society in many countries is often difficult. For example in Viet Nam, mass organizations, such as the Women's Union, Farmers' Union, Youth Union, or Fatherland Front, continue to dominate the space for civil society with the increasing number of nongovernment actors. New civil society organizations are emerging and are engaged in a wide range of issues, from environmental protection to gender equality and disaster relief. It is essential that nongovernment actors join such visioning exercises and get the chance to voice ideas for their city's vision next to the established, traditional CBOs and unions.

Figure 3.3: Strengths, Weaknesses, Opportunities, and Threats (SWOT) Analysis for Hue, Viet Nam

Strengths

- Geographical location (hub function)
- Diversity (land, water)
- Naturally preserved areas
- Natural scenery maintained, low pollution
- Ecological assets
- Strong historical and cultural heritage
- Human capital
- Education center
- International cooperation and partnerships
- Medical provision and facilities
- Established brand "Hue"

- Economic growth in province (10%)
- Well-developed infrastructure (education, water supply, medical)
- Tolerance
- Political commitment
- International airport
- Transport connectivity (also rail)
- Security system
- Developed industries (tourism, textiles, construction materials, [sea]food processing, high tech, beverage)

Weaknesses

- Slow urbanization
- Lack of raw natural and financial resources
- Lack of infrastructure and outdated technologies (drainage, waste treatment, transportation)
- Encroachment into heritage site
- Low climate resilience
- Low capacity in environmental protection
- Lack of planning and preservation of open spaces/natural environment
- Low community awareness for environment
- Rate of deforestation

- "Laid-back" attitude inhibits thrive for development/ innovation
- Unemployment
- Complexity of government system and management
- Limited number of investors vis-à-vis potential
- Water bodies not well maintained, with negative impacts on citizens
- Lighting and signage system insufficient
- Dependence on external tourist operators
- Connectivity between tourist destinations

Opportunities

- Support from central government and external donors/investors
- Tourism center (and development in other locations)
- Vocational training and jobs in tourism, health care, and handicrafts

- (New) tourism niches (spiritual, etc.)
- Health center development
- Building on the brand
- Heritage preservation strategy

Threats

- Effects of climate change (sea-level rise, etc.)
- Disaster-prone geographical features
- High construction/ development
- Degradation of heritage sites and shortening of tourist season due to climate change

- Geographical separation of coastline
- Integration leading to intensified (inter-)national competition
- Growth of (facilities in) Da Nang
- Balance between economic growth and heritage preservation

SWOT = strengths, weaknesses, opportunities, and threats.

Source: ADB. 2013. Technical Assistance for Green Cities – A Sustainable Urban Future in Southeast Asia (TA 8314-REG). GCAP Visioning and SWOT Analysis Workshop, 22 November, Hue, Viet Nam.

Barriers to such participation arising from formal arrangements or traditional practices may need to be overcome or navigated to reach equal participation of women, and to involve vulnerable and disadvantaged groups, in particular people living in poverty and other low-income groups or their representatives, as well as ethnic minorities and indigenous peoples. To reach consensus, each stakeholder must have the opportunity and needs to be encouraged to individually express themselves and participate fully in the discussion. Different viewpoints and aspirations need to be explored until every issue is placed on the table and an acceptable solution can be reached. There is always a risk that the vision will be only that of key government staff solely due to their position and influence.

Viet Nam: The UNESCO-recognized Citadel is Hue's key cultural asset and unique selling point, attracting more than 2 million visitors

Another hurdle is the restricted vision that most of the stakeholders have regarding GrEEEn Cities. Stakeholders' understanding of the "green vision" is often limited to trees, parks, and a clean environment. The two Es of economy and equity do not immediately come to mind to key stakeholders when talking about GrEEEn Cities. Visioning exercises need to establish the concept of GrEEEn Cities and enlarge the understanding of participants, particularly for such an integrated interpretation.

A City's Unique Selling Point and Competitive Advantage

Culture, heritage, industry, and nature are all assets that are often neglected in cities. Identifying the city's assets requires an understanding of the city's evolution. The USP of a city is derived from an analysis of the assets and can be the basis for developing policies and strategies toward improving the city's competitive advantage and economic development, while also being a platform for city residents to develop a stronger sense of belonging and ownership of the city's future (Kavaratzis 2004, pp. 58-73).

Photo Credit: Ramola Naik Singru

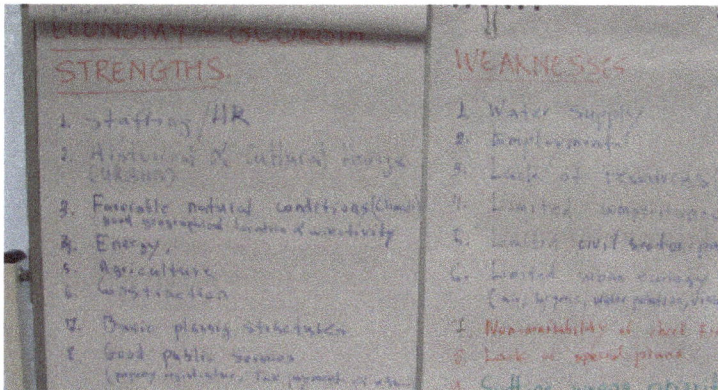

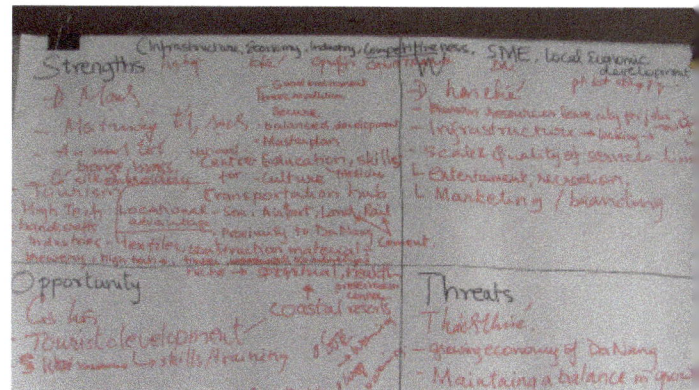

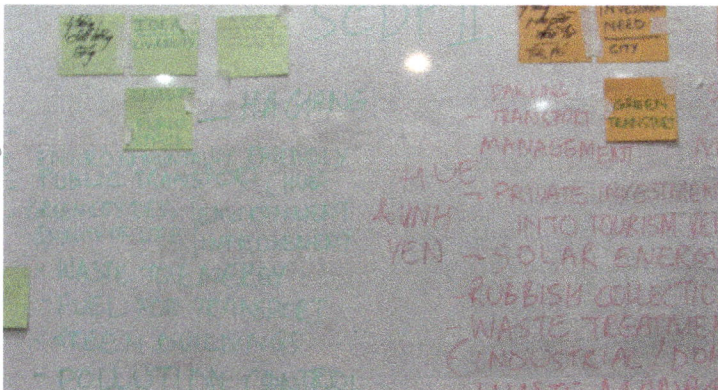

Problem tree analysis and strengths, weaknesses, opportunities, and threats analysis of Ha Giang, Hue, and Vinh Yen, Viet Nam; visioning exercise of Tbilisi, Georgia

The GCOF aims to protect and enhance a city's assets. Natural assets are important due to their biodiversity and the long-term sustainability of the city and for its recreation and education role for citizens and tourists. For instance, Vinh Yen in Viet Nam has the Dam Vac Lake in the heart of the city as its natural asset. In Melaka, it is the Melaka River that concentrates both the city's main challenges (water pollution, lack of green spaces, flood risks, and deteriorating urban infrastructure) and its key potentials (river rehabilitation, dense low-carbon development, local businesses, heritage and tourism, enhanced mobility, and joint stakeholder engagement). New York City has a 100-hectare botanical garden and the 341-hectare Central Park that serve as the city's lungs, and it also has beaches that maintain the city's connection with nature.

With culture and tourism playing an important role in a city, joining forces around a shared image of how to develop a city can be enhanced. In tourism-oriented cities, technical aspects such as infrastructure improvements can be combined with the preservation and support of cultural traditions, thereby planning and managing a city's different challenges in an integrated manner. For example, revenue generators such as traditional handicraft and old architecture are cultural and heritage assets that provide authenticity to the tourism industry. For example, Hue in Viet Nam has the river waterfront as its natural asset and the Citadel as its cultural heritage asset. The Citadel, a 19th-century walled district surrounding the Imperial Palace of the former Nguyen Dynasty, is the USP of the city and the anchor of its growing tourism industry.

Viet Nam: Mother Temple Festival in Ha Giang

Thailand: Songkran (New Year's Day) Festival in Chiang Mai

Myanmar: Festival of Lights in Mandalay

Photo Credits: Renard Teipelke (*top left*); Takeaway (*bottom left*); Ramola Naik Singru (*right*)

Festival time is an incentive to boost local tourism and showcase the city to a larger crowd of national and international visitors.

These assets need to be supported through investments in heritage conservation, urban upgrading, SME development, and capacity training to preserve local skills. Traditional skills are often practiced by minority ethnic groups and particularly by women. Economic support policies can be specifically tailored and targeted to be inclusive (Naik Singru 2015).

Each city has an economic driver. This has its roots in the evolution of the city's economy. Generally, the main sector of the local economy will reflect the city's competitive advantage. For instance, financial markets are London's competitive advantage in a similar way that Bangalore's information technology cluster is the city's key economic sector. In another city, the USP may be an informal industrial area that manufactures textiles, a bustling riverfront, or a thriving art district.

In new planned cities, where a new competitive advantage is to be developed, stakeholder consensus about its suitability is essential. For instance, the periphery of the Indian city of Chennai was developed as an automobile hub in the region. Over 2 decades, the city of Chennai grew to overtake Detroit in terms of automobile production. The availability of a strong skilled and disciplined labor force was identified through stakeholder consensus as the key factor. Once determined, the various stakeholder organizations came together to actively

Figure 3.4: From Visioning to Action Planning

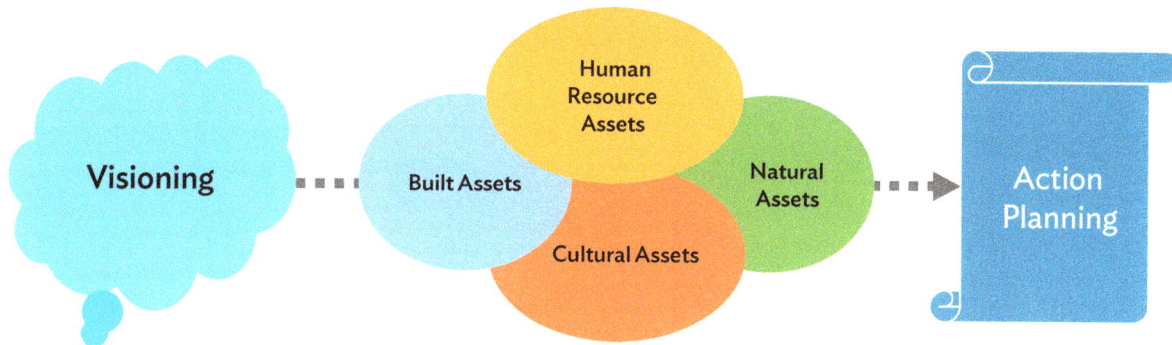

Source: Authors.

and aggressively pursue policies, programs, and plans to put Chennai on the automobile map of the world. This example shows how a city's competitive advantage has to be viewed from a regional perspective. The GCAP does not only account for the internal factors of a city, but also identifies the city's external relations, for instance, with export markets (as in the case of Chennai's automobile industry) or regional tourism (as in the case of Hat Yai as an entertainment and shopping destination).

In summary, a visioning exercise helps to

- build consensus on a shared vision for the city's future among all stakeholders;
- develop ownership for the GCAP among its stakeholders;
- confirm high-level political commitment;
- identify the city's USP from its built, natural, human resource, and cultural assets (Figure 3.4); and
- define opportunities to be taken up through action planning.

Urban Profiling

The GCAP is based on an understanding of business as usual (BAU) arrived at through comprehensive urban profiling, including an assessment of the regulatory, institutional, environmental, social, and economic aspects of urban development. The institutional assessment looks into any current trends toward decentralization and the role of local governments in the delivery of essential urban services, amid the stresses due to the exponential physical and economic growth in cities. Existing capacity and resource constraints on core urban services—water supply, sanitation, solid waste management, mobility, education, health, and trade support—are key considerations discussed with stakeholders during visioning. Institutional, operational, and financial recommendations for reducing the impact on natural resources, improving service delivery to end users, and sharing risks with the private sector are determined through the GCAP process.

The BAU analysis elucidates current conditions and trends with respect to economic competitiveness, the environment, and equity (3Es). Particular emphasis is placed on any *unsustainable* aspects of the current development path, which strengthen the case for

The GrEEEn City Action Plan is based on a clear understanding of "business as usual" and the institutional development paths and technology solutions that need to be altered to achieve livability goals.

adopting a different approach that can make the city more livable in the future. Typically, these should also come out from a SWOT analysis, which is conducted as part of a visioning workshop. In Vinh Yen, for example, the province's rapid industrial estate expansion plans were not consistent with the push to develop a livable urban environment conducive to tourism and education sector development. In Melaka, traffic congestion was understood to increasingly constrain tourism development, the mainstay of the local economy. Poor wastewater and stormwater management in Hue and associated surface water pollution were having a similar negative impact on tourism in that city.

Going along the 3Es of economic competitiveness, the environment, and equity (not necessarily in that order), an understanding is developed of the factors that are impacting each aspect of the "triple bottom line." A combination of environmental, economic, and social benefits enhance livability. The BAU generally builds on existing assessments. The idea is to integrate the findings and conclusions with a view to creating synergies and highlighting any contradictions or incompatibilities. In case of data gaps, a number of existing rapid assessment tools can be applied. For instance, a strategic environmental assessment, which provides "a range of analytical and participatory approaches that aim to integrate environmental considerations into policies, plans and programmes and evaluate the inter linkages with economic and social considerations"(OECD 2006, p. 17).

ADB has developed several tool kits that outline tools to be used for green, competitive, and inclusive cities, while the *Manual for National Urban Assessments* provides guidance on tools applicable at the national level (ADB 2015e; Naik Singru and Lindfield, forthcoming; Roberts 2015).

To facilitate a 3E analysis, a combination of tools could be considered, such as the ones outlined in the following:

Economy
- Enterprise surveys (sample surveys of business owners or operators)
- Business-operating environment surveys and indexes
- Focus groups with businesspeople, chambers of commerce, property owners associations, etc.

Malaysia: Melaka Ekocalendar showing zero waste enterprise

Environment

- Strategic environmental assessment to integrate environmental and social considerations
- Time-series analysis of satellite images to identify physical development trends
- Hydraulic and hydrological analysis and flood mapping
- Climate change and natural hazard risk mapping

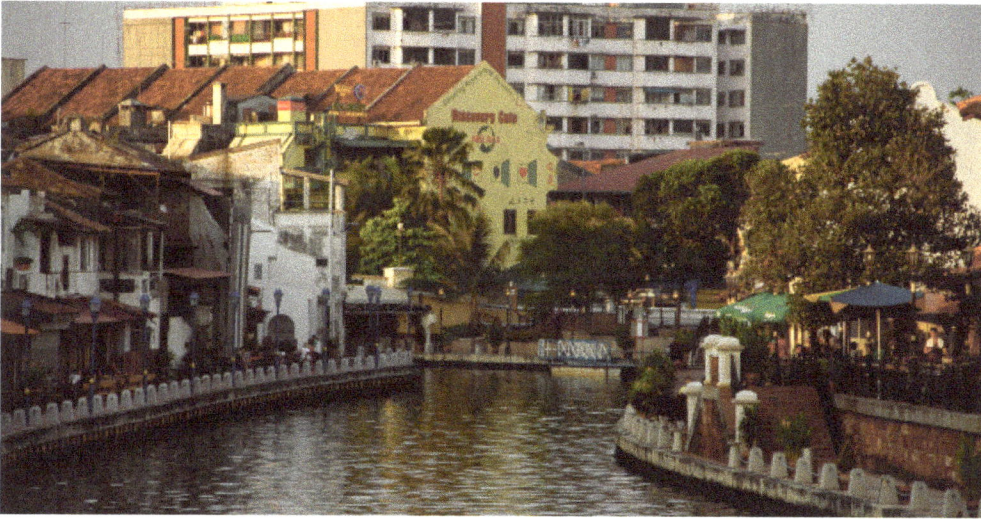

Photo Credit: ADB/Lester Ledesma

Malaysia: The Melaka River as the city's most important natural landmark

Equity

- Legal review
- Sample household surveys
- Focus groups with representatives of local communities
- Housing needs assessment model

Photo Credit: Ramola Naik Singru

Myanmar: Women gathering at a meeting in Mandalay

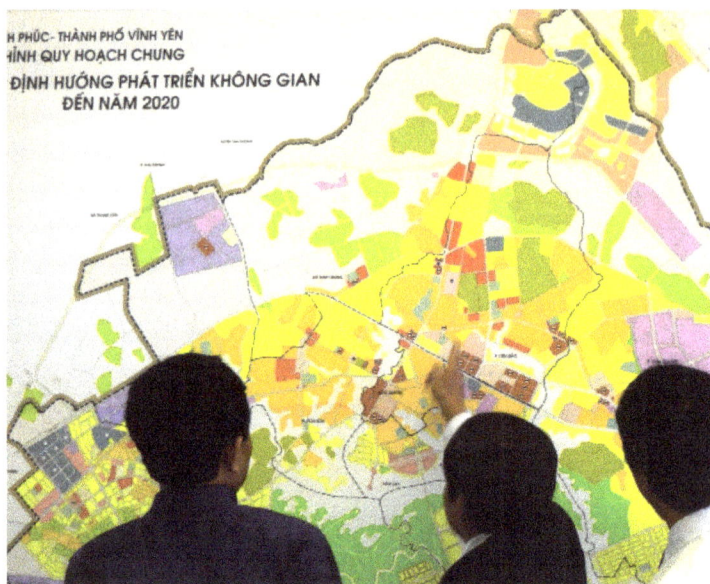

Viet Nam: Site inspection and action planning in Hue and Vinh Yen for their GrEEEn City Action Plans

Satellite imagery can be used to understand how development trends are impacting specific locations that are related to a city's USP. Where data have a spatial dimension, overlays can be used to see where environmental, economic, and social factors intersect in the fabric of the city. For example, an energy and water use assessment or audit provides an understanding of natural resource consumption, correlated with urban service provision and efficiency of service delivery. An urban mobility analysis helps in the assessment of connectivity between inner-city neighborhoods and regional growth centers, and between critical infrastructure assets. Unique environmental and ecological aspects of the city and its surroundings are regarded as core assets in the existing urban development plan. Enabling institutional, governance, and civil society participation mechanisms for increased competitiveness and revenue generation are also identified. Investment projects are prioritized in this context and designed such that these are resource and energy efficient, and supported with improved technologies to the extent possible.

The conclusions of the BAU are presented during postvisioning consultations, and feedback is sought from stakeholders to identify practices and trends that can be changed to initiate urban transformation.

Action Planning

The GCAP is envisioned as a business plan for the city, outlining initiatives and actions required to achieve the goals and targets for a livable city. As in a typical corporate business plan, the GCAP reviews a city's status quo, evaluates demand, formulates livability goals, analyzes its competitive advantages, and proposes solutions. The GCAP builds on city development strategies and master plans to form a city's blueprint for urban transformation.[8] Green city

---

[8]   See, for example, Greater London Authority (2015) and City Council of Kansas City, Missouri (2014).

Figure 3.5: From Master Plan to Action Planning

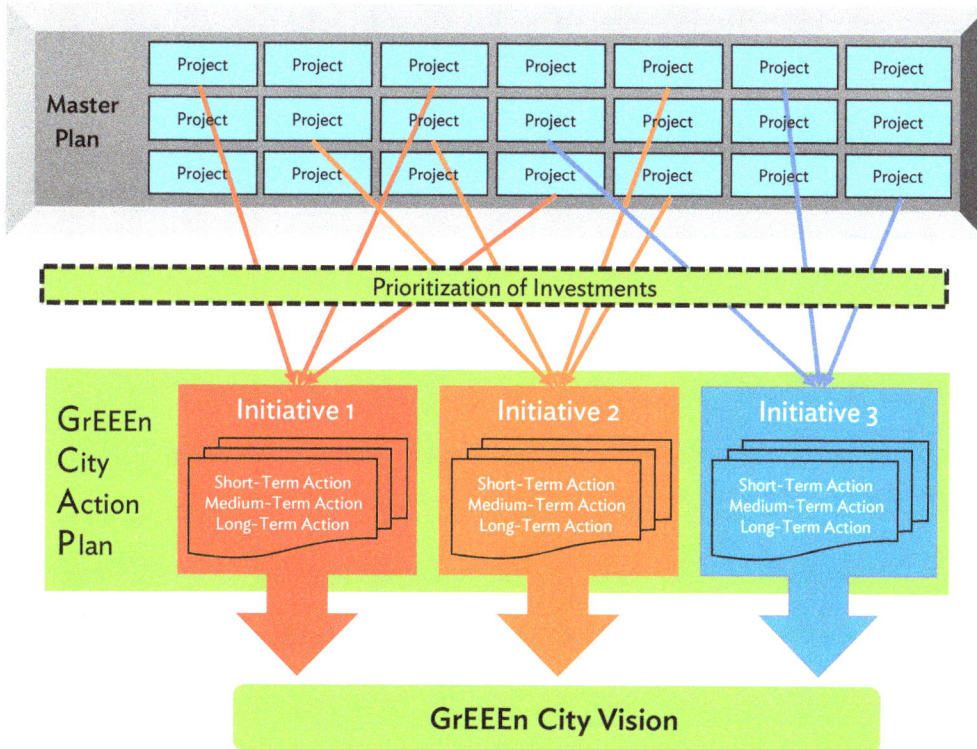

Source: Authors.

action plans have been initiated in cities such as Pasadena in the United States and Vancouver in Canada, with focused environmental initiatives and as road maps for sustainable urban development (Box 3.1).[9] Such green city action plans are environmentally driven, while the city development strategies are driven from an urban services and infrastructure perspective. The GCAP bridges the two for initiating integrated approaches in a city's development.

Urban master plans have a detailed, spatial planning perspective with a long time frame and a long list of projects identified for the city; the GCAP comprises a short list of a matrix of investments. Moving beyond the master plan, the GCAP organizes a smaller number of projects into high-priority development initiatives (Figure 3.5). Prioritization tools can help in refining the investments. For instance, for the cities of Ha Giang, Hue, and Vinh Yen in Viet Nam, the Cities Development Initiative for Asia (CDIA) tool kit for City Infrastructure Investment Programming and Prioritization (CIIPP) was applied to undertake structured planning, prioritization, and programming of the cities' intended investments (CDIA 2014). The resulting prioritized list informed the GCAP.

The GCAP integrates urban planning, environmental management, decision making, financial innovation, and consensus building. It establishes a pathway leading the city away from its current urban, environment, and resilience standards and toward the standards of GrEEEn Cities, where urban planning is risk sensitive and environmentally responsive, and

---

[9] See, for example, Cities of Melbourne, Port Phillip, Stonnington, Yarra and Maribyrnong (2009); City Council of Pasadena (2006); City of Vancouver (2011a, b); and City of Vienna (2011).

Box 3.1: Vancouver's Greenest City 2020 Action Plan

The Greenest City 2020 Action Plan for Vancouver was developed as an ambitious, necessary, and feasible road map for the city to become the greenest city in the world by 2020. The plan sets the course toward realizing a healthy, prosperous, and resilient future for Vancouver and calls on all citizens to transform the community to create a better life for future generations. The action plan sets out a clear vision, with concrete targets and steps required to achieve each one of them. The city considers four key ingredients as requirements for their success:

- **Vision:** to create opportunities today while building a strong local economy, vibrant and inclusive neighborhoods, and an internationally recognized city that meets the needs of generations to come
- **Leadership:** required from all stakeholders including staff and officials, government, and sector organizations and all residents
- **Action:** identified highest priority actions for the first 3 years as well as strategies and actions for the longer term (with baseline indicators and clear targets to work toward)
- **Partnerships:** considered as key to achieving the plan given the limited sphere of influence and resources of the city

The Greenest City 2020 Action Plan of Vancouver is divided into 10 smaller plans, each with a long-term goal (up to 2050) and medium-term targets (up to 2020): green economy, climate leadership, green buildings, green transport, zero waste, access to nature, lighter footprint, clean water, clean air, and local food. Together these 10 plans address three overarching areas of focus: carbon, waste, and ecosystems. While the smaller plans are organized separately in the Greenest City 2020 Action Plan, the actions from each plan work together to form one integrated plan. For example, increasing composting and gardening helps achieve the green economy, zero waste, access to nature, and local food targets; and improving transit services supports the climate leadership, green transport, and clean air targets.

Raymond Louie, Councillor of the City of Vancouver, said in his speech at the first Enabling GrEEEn Cities Regional Conference in 2014 sharing lessons from the Vancouver experience, "One important lesson from the Greenest City 2020 Action Plan of Vancouver is that through a proper public engagement process, it was advocated and agreed that the city needs to set an example in its own operations." As a result, four high-priority actions in the city's operations have been identified:

- Plan and implement a comprehensive corporate waste reduction and diversion program for all city facilities.
- Develop a procurement policy and practice that supports local food in city-run facilities.
- Look for opportunities for greening community events of the city.
- Plan and implement a program to reduce greenhouse gas emissions and fossil fuel use in city-run buildings and vehicles, and achieve carbon-neutral operations.

During the past years, the implementation progress has been tremendous: greenhouse gases have been reduced by 6% since 2007; 23,400 new trees planted since 2010; 3,200 new local food and green jobs created since 2010; 93 charging stations set up for electric vehicles; solid waste to landfill or incinerator decreased by 12% since 2008; water consumption fell by 18% since 2006; and trip share by transit, walking, and biking raised to 44%, with a bike network capacity of 265 kilometers in Vancouver. Not surprisingly, these efforts have received numerous national and international awards.

Sharing the learning is, according to Councillor Louie, "an important part of the 'give' from a city's standpoint… to share the wealth, share the understanding and a common goal to make our world more sustainable and without that type of 'give' back into the local, national, and global community, the world will suffer."

Sources: ADB. 2014. Diverse Views on the Green Cities Initiative. Enabling GrEEEn Cities Regional Conference, Manila, 14 May. https://www.youtube.com/watch?v=lea8kaaRiOE
City of Vancouver. 2011. Greenest City 2020 Action Plan. http://vancouver.ca/files/cov/Greenest-city-action-plan.pdf
City of Vancouver. 2014. Greenest City 2020 Action Plan: 2013–2014 Implementation Update. http://vancouver.ca/files/cov/greenest-city-2020-action-plan-2013-2014-implementation-update.pdf

Figure 3.6: Initiatives and Actions toward Ha Giang's GrEEEn City Vision, Viet Nam

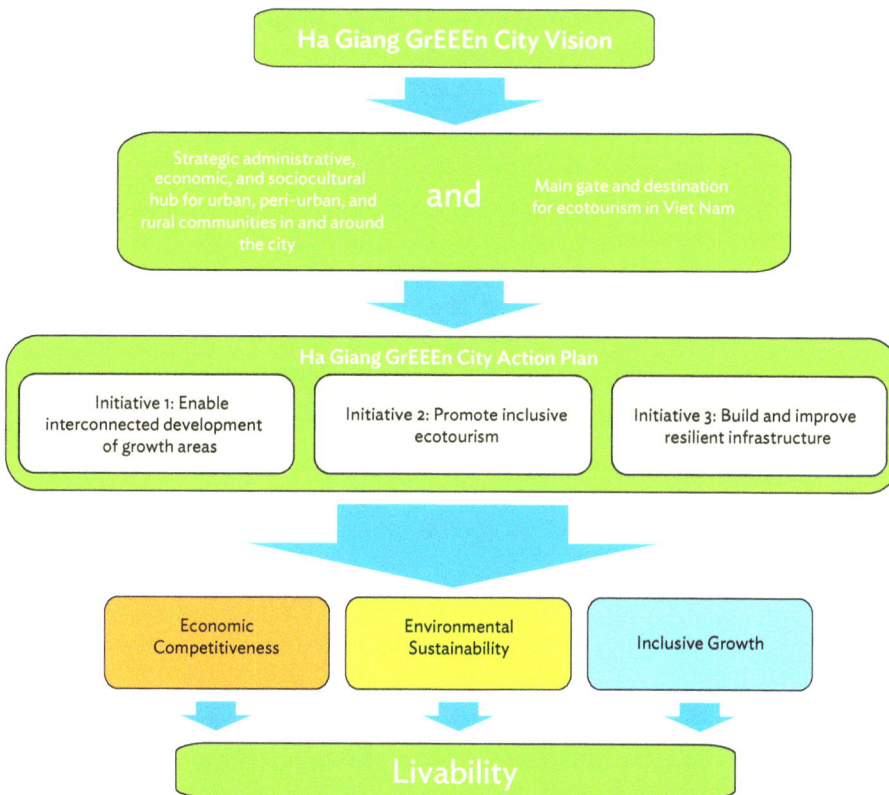

Ha Giang GrEEEn City Vision

Strategic administrative, economic, and sociocultural hub for urban, peri-urban, and rural communities in and around the city **and** Main gate and destination for ecotourism in Viet Nam

Ha Giang GrEEEn City Action Plan

Initiative 1: Enable interconnected development of growth areas

Initiative 2: Promote inclusive ecotourism

Initiative 3: Build and improve resilient infrastructure

Economic Competitiveness

Environmental Sustainability

Inclusive Growth

Livability

Source: ADB. Forthcoming. Ha Giang GrEEEn City Action Plan. Manila.

cross-sector optimization is achieved. Through smart investments in infrastructure, human resource development, natural capital conservation, and technological innovation, the city can become more competitive.

Most cities in the world already have sustainability initiatives. One department is installing low-energy streetlights; another is designing flood protection works. One nongovernment organization is engaging small informal businesses into the mainstream economy; a multilateral donor is financing part of a public transit system; a private firm plans to build a new factory. How do these individual actions add up to an overall sustainability impact? What missing pieces are needed to reach higher? How are the dozens of actors being held accountable to a process of achieving the city's goals?

The GCAP can fulfill the functions of connecting the dots and maximizing sustainability impacts by clearly outlining the content and structure of implementing GCAP initiatives and actions (Figure 3.6).

The initiatives of a GCAP are generally place-based and are designed to preserve and enhance a city's USP. A GCAP emphasizes the cumulative economic benefits that result from the coordinated implementation of multiple measures (actions) in a spatial context.

Taken together, the outputs of the GCAP constitute a platform for "connecting the dots": bringing together actors and integrating programs into one strategic, coherent, and effective implementation framework.

The GCAP comprises the following:

(i)   GrEEEn City vision with goals and targets;
(ii)   urban profile with assessments of economic, environmental, and social baselines, climate change and disaster risks, and infrastructure needs;
(iii) initiatives with short-, medium-, and long-term actions, with associated cost estimates, cumulative benefits, and identified roles and responsibilities;
(iv)   institutional arrangements for implementing the GCAP;
(v)   budgetary resources and innovative financial mechanisms;
(vi)   monitoring and evaluation framework with key performance indicators and citizen feedback mechanisms;
(vii) management information systems for data collection and management;
(viii) decision support systems, such as geographic information system-based thematic maps, hydraulic and hydrological simulation models, and early warning systems;
(ix)   enablers for GCAP implementation: policies, regulations, strategies, sector plans, financial incentives, institutions, private sector initiatives, community participation;
(x)   capacity and skills improvement plans, including vocational training; and
(xi)   proposals for Urban Management Partnerships (UMPs) to develop partnerships between government, the private sector, and civil society for implementation of specific actions.

The GCAP encompasses recommendations derived from the urban profiling and assessment for translation into initiatives, plans, programs, and investments, which, individually or in combination, are expected to achieve the targets and goals agreed on during the visioning and consensus building. Some of the identified interventions could include construction of wetlands as part of a stormwater management strategy or a decentralized wastewater treatment system, composting or waste-to-energy systems like biogas or incinerator-based systems, or on-grid solar systems. Greener urban development strategies aimed at improving a city's environmental quality and lowering its carbon footprint could involve adopting green building and development standards, greening existing urban development through adaptive design and retrofits, introducing urban forestry, or recycling nutrients in community kitchen gardens or urban farms. It identifies initiatives such as wastewater and waste management, energy efficiency improvements, renewable energy, low-carbon transport options, and the need to strengthen community resilience by integrating climate adaptation into disaster risk reduction and expanding green cover. The three examples in Boxes 3.2–3.4 provide insight into the adaptation of the GCAP process in different country contexts and development stages.

Implementation Arrangements

GrEEEn City Action Plan Institutional Mechanisms

Effective institutional arrangements are critical to the achievement of the long-term vision of achieving a livable city. The GCAP needs first and foremost high-level political commitment and strong leadership to overcome barriers. Parallel to the process of bringing together all stakeholders, local governments are faced with the critical challenge of breaking down the "silos" that separate city departments. This requires formalizing new organizational arrangements to ensure that the actors responsible for land use, environment, energy, transport, the economy, etc. work together. Some cities have removed the policy and planning functions from each of the relevant departments and merged them into a new cross-sector policy and planning department. More commonly, cities create supradepartmental policy and planning committees in which the relevant departments and agencies are represented.

For example, the Vinh Yen GCAP catalyzed an "out-of-the-box" thinking within the Vinh Phuc People's Committee in Viet Nam to establish an executive committee for implementation of its GCAP as illustrated in Figure 3.7. The committee will have the following functions:

- Facilitate inputs of all major stakeholders in GCAP implementation
- Ensure coordination among the different municipal and provincial departments involved in implementing all of the actions under the GCAP
- Make sure that decision making for individual investment projects is consistent with the approach and the objectives of the GCAP
- Monitor and evaluate progress on the implementation of the GCAP
- Report to stakeholders on the status of the implementation of the GCAP

According to Figure 3.7, the GCAP implementation committee could be the steering committee of the UMP. Stewardship of that committee by the UMP gives the local government the appropriate leading role in the development process.

The national government can take steps toward institutionalizing the preparation of a GCAP for each city or for cities that want to access national-level green funding for improved urban infrastructure. In that sense, a GCAP does not replace existing plans, nor does it go into the level of detail of, for instance, master plans. Instead, the GCAP enables and guides city managers to implement the most crucial projects, which can realize the most cross-sector benefits under a 3E paradigm of economic competitiveness, environmental sustainability, and social equity. For example, in Viet Nam, the GCAPs are being endorsed by the Provincial People's Committee and will form the basis for the forthcoming Secondary Cities Development Program (ADB 2014l). Another approach to institutionalizing GCAPs has been through endorsement under a regional cooperation platform (e.g., IMT-GT for the Melaka GCAP).

Capacity-building needs will be addressed according to the gaps identified. Awareness, training, and competence building will be done to address the gaps pertaining to human resources. In building this capacity, particular attention will be given to all 3E dimensions. Whereas social

Box 3.2: GrEEEn City Action Planning in Myanmar

Under an Asian Development Bank (ADB) capacity development technical assistance, a scoping study for a Strategic Development Plan for a GrEEEn Mandalay was developed. The study used elements of the GrEEEn Cities Operational Framework to conduct a rapid assessment and recommend actions for the plan. The idea was to develop a model in one city that could serve as a model for the management of urban development throughout Myanmar. Mandalay was the chosen city for developing this model, and the recommendations of the plan are presently being used to develop a full-fledged investment project.

Mandalay is the second-largest city in Myanmar with an estimated population of over 1.3 million and a historic growth rate of just over 2% per year. With the opening up of the country to foreign investment, and with its critical location on the crossroads between India and Bangladesh to the west, the Lao People's Democratic Republic and Thailand to the east and south, as well as the People's Republic of China to the north, it is expected to grow at a far faster rate of nearly 3% over the next 25 years. Developing a plan using the GrEEEn Cities Operational Framework was timely and relevant for the city.

The scoping study focused on the principles contained in the ADB Urban Operational Plan that emphasizes looking at the three complementary components—the environment, economy, and equity. Using secondary information sources, the study developed an urban profile for the city and identified the key issues and challenges. Using a socioeconomic survey that was administered by the municipality officials, feedback from the citizens about the key issues and challenges was obtained. Stakeholder workshops—one focused on the issues and challenges and another on solutions and actions—were conducted to confirm the findings of the scoping study.

One of the most critical problems identified was the lack of any planning law, regulations, or the capacity to prepare and monitor the implementation of such plans, in particular the use of privately owned land. This has had a great impact on the increased risk of flooding and on the lack of open space, both of which were also identified as high priorities. Groundwater sources were recognized to be at risk, primarily due to the industrial wastewater that drains untreated toward the Dottarwaddy. Likewise, without a sewage treatment plant, domestic wastewater is not treated and runs in open drains, predominantly to larger water bodies such as the Kandawgyi and Taung Tha Man. Solid waste is widely collected, but still only covers about 74% of domestic waste. Much of the waste still finds its way into waterways and causes clogging of the drainage channels. Their clogging is one of the contributory causes of flooding. There are inadequate preventative measures to stop water draining into the lower land to the northwest of the city Aung Myay Thar Zan. While the city is protected from floods from the Ayeyarwaddy by an embankment and pumps are used to get water out from the lower ground behind these embankments, more pumps are needed. Furthermore, flooding occurs in Pyi Gyi Dagon to the east and south of the city as the agricultural land has become urbanized.

The scoping study's recommended actions for the development plan is to realize the city's mission "… to keep the city clean, to make the city beautiful, and to enable the city dwellers to enjoy a pleasant life." (ADB 2014, p. 4). The vision for the year 2040 envisages Mandalay City to become a "green cultural city, with clean air, a center of tourism, a trade and logistics hub, and an IT center for upper Myanmar" (ADB 2014, p. 4). To achieve the status of a GrEEEn City which is at the same time sustainable, inclusive, and competitive, a number of actions are proposed covering investment proposals as well as legal and institutional development for each sector. These include, among others, the following:

- Strengthening the spatial planning and building regulations to facilitate the city's development, alongside establishing the institutional capacity to undertake, approve, and monitor spatial planning aspects.
- Minimizing the carbon and water footprint of human settlements as well as addressing the carbon footprint of transport using appropriate technologies and methods.
- Lessening the risk of flooding by improving the solid waste collection and controlling development on natural floodplains, while improving the drainage system and the means of flood mitigation.

- Improving the access of the poor to basic services, including housing, through government-subsidized housing, upgrading of settlement areas, and the creation of new low-cost housing areas where the infrastructure is in place but the houses are built by the beneficiaries.
- Strengthening financial management through better monitoring of fund flows and the computerization of accounts and budget preparation. In addition, it suggests the review of the tariff system and how it might be altered to cover at a minimum operations and maintenance costs through a restructuring of the tariffs and savings in the nonrevenue services provided.

The scoping study subsequently formed the base input during the preparation of ADB's Urban Services Improvement Project in Mandalay.

Myanmar: Mandalay's city landscape features busy streets and cultural assets

Myanmar: Hot spots for urgent infrastructure and service improvements in Mandalay were identified through site inspections

Myanmar: It was the first time for many stakeholder representatives in Mandalay to participate in an open consultation workshop

Source: ADB. 2014. *Toward a Green Mandalay: Scoping Study of a Strategic Development Plan for Mandalay.* Final report of Capacity Building Support for Project Identification (2012, TA 8251-MYA). Manila.

Box 3.3: GrEEEn City Action Planning in Thailand

For the two southern cities Mueang Songkhla and Hat Yai in Thailand's Songkhla Province, a GrEEEn City Action Plan (GCAP) scoping study was carried out as an initial step toward putting the two cities on a path to becoming GrEEEn Cities. It was supported by the Asian Development Bank (ADB) under the Indonesia–Malaysia–Thailand Growth Triangle (IMT-GT), a subregional economic cooperation program aimed at spurring economic development in participating provinces and states in the three countries and also at prioritizing sustainable urban development. The National Economic and Social Development Board, with its aim to promote Thailand's national agenda toward developing ecocities and as a participant in the IMT-GT, is also supporting the two cities to become pioneer GrEEEn Cities in the region. Mueang Songkhla is a port city that is looking to enhance its livability by promoting economic development related to cultural and natural tourism. Hat Yai is already a popular tourist destination for entertainment and shopping, as well as a center for commerce and education, that is keen to enhance its livability by increasing its resilience to urban flooding and continuing its economic dominance in the region.

The scoping study is guided by ADB's operational framework for GrEEEn Cities that places emphasis on "doing things differently," to respond to environmental degradation, inefficient resource consumption, inequitable growth, and increased risks of climate change and natural disasters related to rapid urbanization. The scoping study (i) provides a snapshot of the existing conditions and key issues related to livability in each city, which are based on a review of existing documents and interviews with public officials and key stakeholders; (ii) through a stakeholder and visioning workshop organized in each city, a general consensus among government leaders, residents, and business community members toward sustainable urban development was established; and (iii) broad potential actions were scoped out, including implementation mechanisms, which could help Mueang Songkhla and Hat Yai initiate activities toward becoming GrEEEn Cities. Concluding the scoping study, initiatives and actions, which are summarized in the following, were proposed to address these challenges. In the city of Mueang Songkhla, four major initiatives—with several actions under each—are being proposed. Under the initiative to promote tourism, pursuing world heritage city designation and working with the private sector to improve historic preservation are proposed. In the initiative on enhancing land management, conducting a land availability assessment and redeveloping low-income housing are suggested. Under enhancing environmental quality, establishing a linkage between fishery productivity and human

Photo Credit: Amit Prothi

settlements on the deteriorating water quality of Songkhla Lake is of the highest priority. And lastly, pursuing innovative financing mechanisms to raise resources from the oil and gas sector, other private sector segments, and the central government require further exploration.

In the city of Hat Yai, the major initiatives have both commonalities and differences with Songkhla. In terms of strengthening land management, enhancing environmental quality, and pursuing innovative financing mechanisms, the actions are more or less similar. Addressing the issues pertaining to climate change and its induced impacts are also major initiatives in Hat Yai. More than 80% of the city suffers from the seasonal floods. Studying alternatives for flood avoidance, cleaning and dredging the canal prior to the rains, and continuing the Living with Floods Initiative are vitally important. As for tourism, the present focus on entertainment and shopping needs to be diversified into a more regional approach toward tourism.

Photo Credit: Amit Prothi

Thailand: The GrEEEn City Action Plans for Mueang Songkhla and Hat Yai aim at balancing the economic, environmental, and social aspirations under a joint vision

Source: ADB. 2015. *GrEEEn City Action Plan for Songkhla and Hat Yai Municipalities*. Manila.

Box 3.4: GrEEEn City Action Planning in Malaysia

The Indonesia–Malaysia–Thailand Growth Triangle (IMT-GT) is a subregional economic cooperation program aimed at spurring economic development in participating provinces and states in the three countries. The IMT-GT focuses on enhancing trade and investment opportunities, tourism, infrastructure links and institutional arrangements, among others, to achieve a vision of "a seamless, progressive, prosperous and peaceful subregion with improved quality of life" (IMT-GT 2011). The Ninth IMT-GT Chief Ministers and Governors Forum, held in early September 2012, proposed to pursue a new initiative for Green Cities in IMT-GT. The proposal was deliberated and supported by IMT-GT Ministers during the 18th IMT-GT Ministerial Meeting held at Port Dickson, Malaysia, on 27 September 2012. The IMT-GT requested the Asian Development Bank (ADB) to further elaborate on the proposed concept of sustainable urban development, which could be applied in the subregion and potentially to other member states of the Association of Southeast Asian Nations (ASEAN), linking with ASEAN's larger effort in developing sustainable cities. ADB agreed to assist the cities of Melaka (in Malaysia), Songkhla (in Thailand), and Medan (in Indonesia) to develop a comprehensive GrEEEn City Action Plan (GCAP). The action plan takes into account existing GrEEEn City examples, frameworks, development master plans, and planned anchor projects to identify potential actions and projects that will support these communities to become models of urban sustainability. Melaka has prepared the first GCAP as part of this initiative and will set an example that will be emulated by other cities within the subregion. Capacity building will also be a significant part of the IMT-GT Green Cities Initiative, which was formally endorsed by the Seventh IMT-GT Summit on 25 April 2013 in Brunei Darussalam.

In 2010, Melaka established a vision to become a Green Technology State by 2020. Melaka was driven by the Malaysian Prime Minister's pledge during the Conference of the Parties (COP15) meeting in Copenhagen in 2009 to reduce Malaysia's carbon intensity relative to its gross domestic product by 40% by 2020. Melaka became the first state in Malaysia to adopt the United Nations Urban Environmental Accords (UEA) green city rating system. Melaka adopted the Melaka Green Technology Blueprint and prepared a list of indicators as recommended by the UEA to pursue green development. Melaka also established the Green Technology Council to oversee the efforts to achieve Melaka's green city vision.

Melaka has started its renewable energy program to reduce carbon emissions from the energy sector as well as inaugurated a 5-megawatt solar farm in 2013. Melaka has also established an area called the Melaka World Solar Valley to promote the development of green technology industries specializing in solar energy. For its efforts, Melaka received the Green Apple Award from an environmental organization based in the United Kingdom for the ongoing transformation of the Melaka River waterfront. Through an integrated approach and over nearly a decade, Melaka

Photo Credit: Adiput

has been able to start transforming the Melaka River from a polluted backyard drainage canal to a popular cultural amenity, tourist attraction, and enjoyable green space for city residents. Melaka has also started several other efforts, including a pilot energy efficiency project to upgrade streetlights and selected public buildings, introducing electric vehicle charging stations, developing the Hang Tuah Jaya Green City, converting diesel buses into electric buses, and developing the Melaka Green Seal—a green rating tool for residential and nonresidential buildings from the stage of building permissions to certification of completion and compliance, enabling green knowledge to be transferred down to the developers and contractors.

Even though Melaka has initiated numerous green initiatives and has already done award-winning work, a lot still needs to be done. The GCAP reflects Melaka's long-term commitment to pursue low-carbon growth, improve environmental quality, and strengthen economic competitiveness. The GCAP provides a set of recommendations that are aimed at maintaining Melaka's competitiveness as a popular tourist and investment destination, keeping environmental challenges to a minimum, and establishing the state as a role model for livability in the region. The action plan provides Melaka a clear path toward becoming a sustainable community, and it reflects a comprehensive approach that brings together individual actions that have already started. It also provides clear direction on what Melaka needs to do in the coming years. The Green Cities Initiative proposes for Melaka to improve its understanding of the underlying causes that affect livability in urban areas, enhance planning so that resources are invested in the right place and at the right scale; collect data so that investment decisions are based on good information and can support monitoring of implemented actions, try out pilot projects so that it can learn what works and what does not work before committing to large amounts of resources, prepare better project designs so that the quality of the projects is better, and improve the institutions so that decisions are made in a coordinated manner and with buy-in from key stakeholders. This may require enacting new laws, engaging directly with important constituents, prioritizing investments, seeking innovative avenues of funds, and sharing knowledge to learn from the experience of others. Also important will be engaging with the private sector to bring in financing, technical knowledge, and innovation to this process. The GCAP will transform Melaka into a livable city and establish itself as one of the leading green states in the region.

Photo Credit: Government of Melaka

Malaysia: Chief Minister of Melaka presenting Melaka GrEEEn City Action Plan to ADB. In addition to already initiated actions, Melaka wants to further strengthen its economic basis, decrease environmental impacts from growth, and become a role model for GrEEEn City development

Sources: Balamurugan Ratha Krishnan. 2015. IMT-GT's Green Cities Initiative. Background write-up; IMT-GT. 2011. Director's Message. http://www.imtgt.org/director_msg_feb2011.htm

Figure 3.7: Institutional Arrangements for GrEEEn City Action Plan Implementation in Vinh Yen, Viet Nam

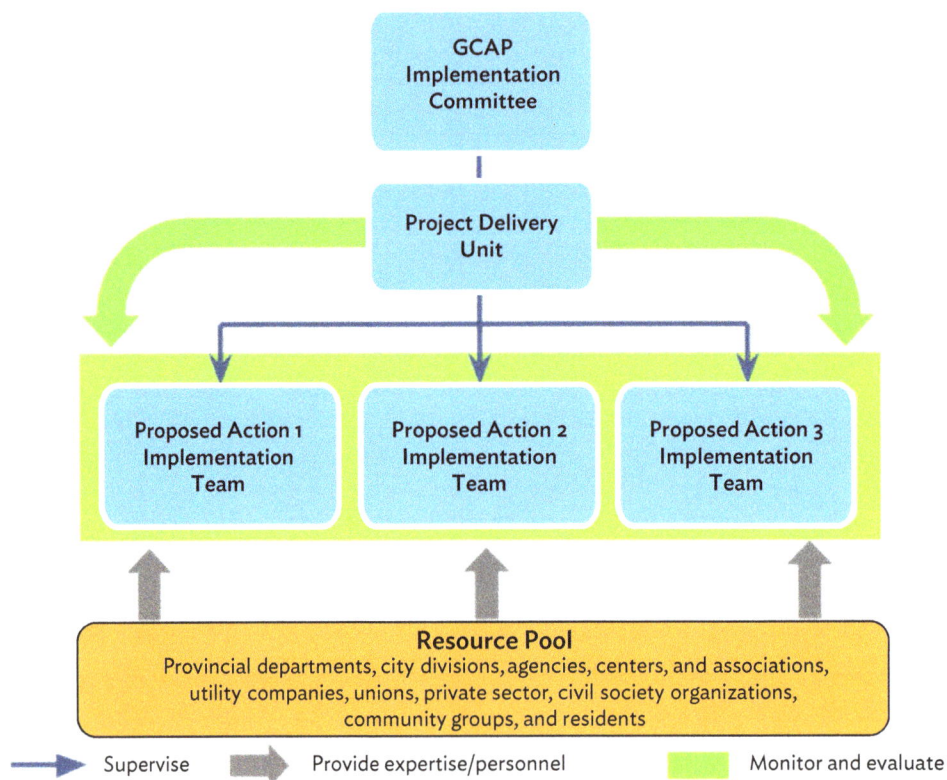

GCAP = GrEEEn City Action Plan.
Source: ADB. 2015. *Enabling GrEEEn Cities: Vinh Yen GrEEEn City Action Plan*. Manila.

scientists may have the knowledge and skills pertaining to equity considerations, the need to build their capacity to better understand economic competitiveness and environmental issues will be the focus. Through such an approach, a new capacity to consider and address situations taking into account the three dimensions will be realized.

The institutional structure of local governments can create a "silo mentality" among the staff of individual departments that can obstruct GCAP development and implementation. Lack of exchange of information and coordination between departments is not a good basis for GCAP development. Creating bridges between departments within the same (city or province) institution, having multidisciplinary teams in the institutional structure for addressing different perspectives, and having strong leadership from higher levels of government are some of the options to overcome barriers.

Public participation in the implementation and monitoring of the GCAP is also a key enabler. Involvement of citizens in the monitoring of the GCAP implementation will raise ownership of the GCAP and empower communities. For the Vinh Yen GCAP, a community scorecard was introduced. The aim is to monitor the improvement of the Dam Vac Lake environment (i.e., water quality, public access, timeliness of development of infrastructures, etc.) and gather feedback from local residents about the results and effectiveness of the protection activities. This will lead to the community mind-set shift that is required for the sustainable management of the lake.

Financing Mechanisms

As will be further discussed in Chapter 6, bringing national actors into the development planning and implementation process also opens up additional financing options for the city. Local governments can use the GCAP to align their interventions with national sustainability and climate change policies, thereby taking advantage of any subsidies or financial incentives that national governments are offering.

Cities can also tap into international funding sources that target particular types of sustainability programs, such as the Rockefeller Foundation's (2015a) 100 Resilient Cities. Successful applicants to the program receive funding support for a resilience staff, development of a resilience strategy, as well as access to an international network of resilience partners and experts. In general, the way to mobilize financing for GCAP implementation is the same as any other urban development plan. Rather than financing the whole plan, the challenge is to finance each action (or occasionally each initiative) within it. The financing of a wastewater treatment plant is very different from that of a bus rapid transit system. Some projects generate a cash flow stream, and some do not. Some urban projects can be financed by private companies, while many will require some public sector funding to be successful. Downstream from the GCAP preparation is the feasibility analysis of the different actions. The capital improvement projects will require individual scrutiny. In some cases, however, they can be packaged together to achieve economies of scale or attract outside investors for project packages that balance the different risks of single investments bundled together.

Sometimes, all that is needed to get the sustainability ball rolling is some working capital. Many cities have had success with revolving funds that are targeted to sustainability projects. Eligibility criteria are defined in advance. City government and/or outside funding sources can be used to capitalize the fund initially. Projects that can pay for themselves over time, thereby allowing the borrower to pay back the fund, should be prioritized. Revolving funds are particularly well adapted to energy-saving projects, projects that generate land value increases for owner-borrowers, urban services network extension projects in which hookup fees are unaffordable to low-income households, and other projects.

With the GCAP, the city can leverage catalytic funding from multilateral or bilateral agencies, from green funds such as the Global Environment Fund or the Climate Investment Funds, from public–private partnerships, or even from the business sector's corporate social responsibility initiatives. In exploring various financial mechanisms with financial stakeholders, the city can clearly explain the intended use of the funds.

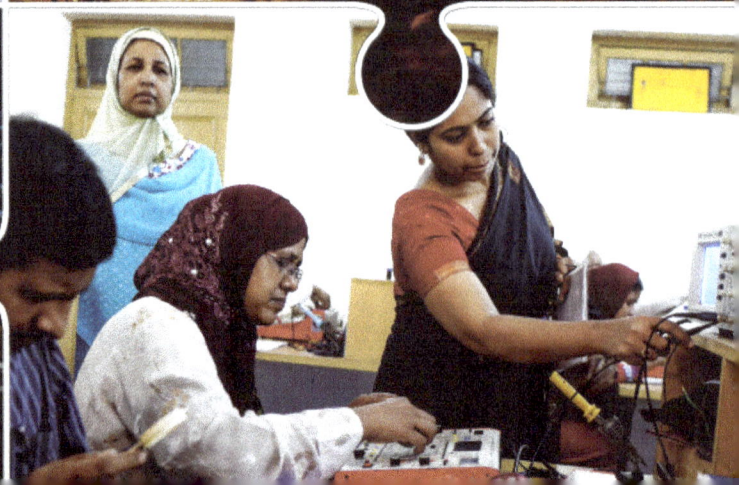

4   Designing GrEEEn Solutions

Unbundling the 3Es

Designing grEEEn solutions begins with translating theory to practice by unbundling the 3Es—economy, environment, and equity—in a city's spatial and temporal context. Precursors to conceptualizing and designing integrated projects are based on a multidisciplinary approach, analytical rigor, optimizing on shared experience, and a focus on results. A multidisciplinary approach plans to achieve positive economic, environmental, and social benefits. It requires a combination of technical and institutional skills.

Analytical rigor is essential to deepen the understanding of interconnectedness of the disciplines and the various factors that drive urban development. For example, addressing water shortage problems by building a desalinization plant poses the question of the impact on energy consumption and associated greenhouse gas (GHG) emission. Life-cycle cost analysis requires engineers and financial experts to focus their joint attention on the development and operating costs of alternative designs for selected assets and services, while taking into account nonmonetary environmental costs to derive a design solution that achieves the highest cost–benefit ratio over the life of the asset. Learning from shared experiences and optimizing existing good practices help to scope out potential solutions.

A focus on results for a long-term development impact can be achieved by setting tangible goals, specific targets, and measurable indicators that contribute to the improvement of the quality of life in the city. The results focus can be strengthened through performance monitoring systems that establish the baseline and periodically track progress over time. A more ambitious approach is to use a rigorous results-based framework in which project performance is measured on the achievement of agreed results. This approach has been initiated under the results-based lending (RBL) modality by the Asian Development Bank (ADB) and the Program for Results (PfR) by the World Bank in the design of investments.[10]

GrEEEn City Action Plans (GCAPs) capture the above elements and inform the design of investments in line with the GrEEEn City vision. All initiatives tap the 3Es—the balance among the three and the extent to which these different dimensions of livability will be emphasized

Analytical rigor to understand the interconnectedness of the 3Es and capitalize on synergies is essential for designing GrEEEn solutions.

---

[10]   See, for example, ADB (forthcoming) and World Bank (2014).

will vary from project to project. Detailed consideration of the 3Es can inform project design. Citywide capital improvement programs and master plans often include projects that were designed earlier, which can benefit from retrofitting through the 3E perspective. Such retrofitting design features come at a cost, which may not always be higher, taking into consideration the operating costs over the life of the asset. The capital and operating costs of such a project should be evaluated in the context of additional benefits accrued from grEEEn design features.

Improving efficiencies begins with understanding processes and disciplines that come together in a city to deliver services to its citizens. Unbundling the 3Es helps to focus attention on key actions to fuse resources more effectively. It provides an understanding of the interconnection of required disciplines that need to be connected in a city. The city can be understood as one system that is made up of a number of subsystems (such as land, water, energy, and mobility) (World Bank 2010b). GrEEEn projects focus on one or more of the subsystems and the interconnections among them. In every city, there are opportunities to improve the performance of subsystems and to realize a cumulative positive impact on the carbon performance of the whole city system. Additionally, one activity in an urban space often impacts other activities. These cause-and-effect relations influence the balance of the 3Es.

For example, consider the construction of a customs processing center next to an industrial park. This convenience may spur more industrial investment, which generates jobs and strengthens the ability of some households to satisfy their own basic needs—two positive socioeconomic outcomes—but the additional industrial production may generate negative environmental impacts. In such a case, adverse environmental impacts will need to be mitigated. Risk management is an essential part of addressing and mitigating risks through specific environmental and social safeguard measures and management plans (ADB 2009b).

The challenge is to balance and prioritize the various dimensions of livability through unbundling the 3Es. For example, everyone resides in a watershed. In an urban watershed, rain runs off hardscapes such as streets, rooftops, sidewalks, and parking areas flowing through catch basins, sewers, and treatment plants before being discharged to the bay or ocean. Infrastructure needs to be planned, taking into consideration urban watershed-based planning to ensure natural resource efficiency and, at the same time, increase the protection of communities from natural disasters such as Typhoon Ondoy (internationally known as Ketsana) in Manila or the floods in Bangkok (ADB 2014o; International Research Initiative on Adaptation to Climate Change 2015). The example "The GrEEEn Cities Operational Framework Applied to Urban Water Systems" (Insert C) showcases the unbundling of the 3Es with respect to urban service delivery. The following sections of this chapter provide a partial menu of effective and innovative solutions for integrated urban development, which can inform future project design to improve how we plan and actually develop urban spaces.

E for Economy

GrEEEn Cities identify ways to achieve competitive and resilient economic growth, by enhancing their unique selling point. Broadly, this can be achieved with a focus on green jobs (i.e., environment-friendly manufacturing, eco-innovation, green skills enhancement), demand-driven urban development (i.e.. by developing and maintaining infrastructure assets), and through placemaking for economic success (i.e., by ensuring that a city is attractive for businesses, workers, entrepreneurs, and residents).

Green Jobs

Increasing opportunities for revenue generation can be achieved through skills development, green jobs and enterprises, and partnerships with the private sector (UNEP 2008). Urban transformation and green growth rely heavily on changing environmental practices. Competitiveness in response to the emerging green growth challenges is reliant on creating new opportunities for shifting to a low-carbon green economy. The GrEEEn Cities Operational Framework (GCOF) is a conduit for identifying avenues for incentivizing such green skills and talent development for future markets (ADB 2012c). Incentivizing entrepreneurs and small and medium-sized enterprises (SMEs) is important for enabling innovation. This requires a favorable policy environment for research and development in emerging technologies to realize the potential of green entrepreneurship (UNEP 2011).

Household-level businesses and SMEs contribute significantly to urban gross domestic product, but often function in unregulated environments requiring a change in production practices. With good environmental practices and regulations, SMEs can be incubators of eco-innovation and green manufacturing across different industries (OECD 2010). Technical and vocational education and training programs provide a very good opportunity to internalize such skills through innovative practice modules (Jagannathan and Geronimo

Photo Credit: Ramola Naik Singru

Thailand: Street food vendors in Koh Samui

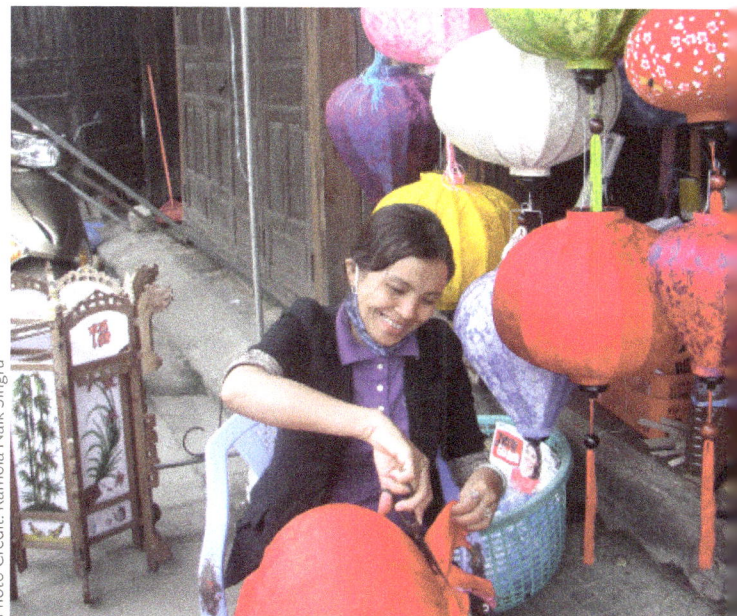

Photo Credit: Ramola Naik Singru

Viet Nam: Traditional art stores in restored heritage center of Hoi An

Thailand: Small store vendor adding to the products diversity in market

Photo Credit: ADB

Viet Nam: Active streets with souvenir shops and restaurants in Ha Noi

Photo Credit: Renard Teipelke

Pakistan: Busy shopping in festival preparation at Liberty Market in Lahore

Photo Credit: ADB/Syed Muhammad Rafiq

Japan: All-weather design ensures for dynamic local economy throughout the year in Tokyo

Photo Credit: Renard Teipelke

Viet Nam: Household bronze manufacturer sustains traditional manufacturing in Hue

Photo Credit: Renard Teipelke

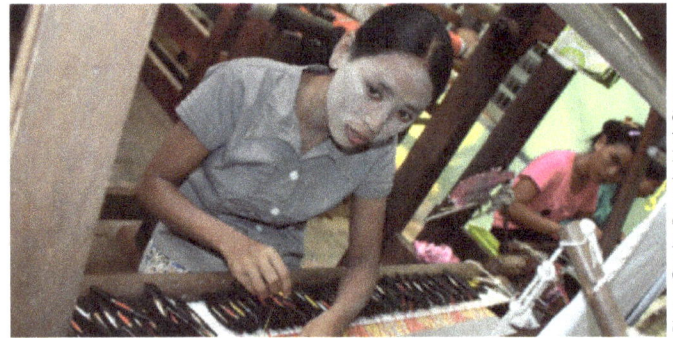

Myanmar: Home-based small-scale handloom weaving in Mandalay

Photo Credit: Ramola Naik Singru

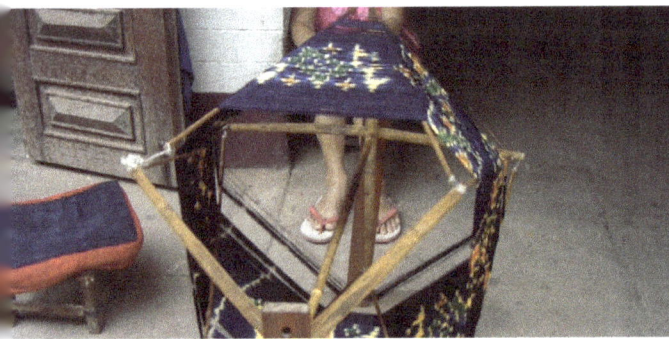

Lao People's Democratic Republic: Household lamp handicraft and weaving in Vientiane

Photo Credit: Ramola Naik Singru

Bangladesh: Vocational training on electronics under a skills development project

Photo Credit: ADB/M R Hasan

2013). Eventually, the skills base of a city, or even of a country, will slowly progress toward the required transformation.

Cities can choose different paths toward a green economy, for instance, by promoting dynamic streets with food vendors and home-based craftspeople, designing public spaces with markets and stores for local entrepreneurs, and supporting the development of training for skills in cultural manufacturing or SMEs.

Demand-Driven Urban Development

The GCOF proposes urban planning and management from an economic development perspective. When assessing urban requirements, cities must think beyond the traditional approach of safeguarding the natural environment and the provision of basic services to local residents. Urban authorities must strive to answer the question: How can urbanization and infrastructure improvements contribute to promoting local economic growth? And a corollary question: What are the needs of businesses to flourish in the city?

For example, manufacturers require stable water and electrical power services for efficient production, as well as waste management services to satisfy local environmental regulations in an affordable manner. Tourism operators require an attractive and clean public realm, which in turn requires stormwater management, pedestrian facilities, solid waste collection, landscaping, and other urban infrastructure and services. As part of citywide and district planning, information on the preferences and priorities of urban services (e.g., through enterprise surveys) must be collected from key stakeholders and enterprises in a city. This information is key to formulating demand-driven urban investment programs.

The types of urban service improvements required will vary depending on the economic sectors being targeted in a city. For example, the tourism sector has high benchmarks for environmental quality, where the management of solid waste, wastewater, and stormwater may be needed to ensure that areas frequented by tourists are clean, safe, and usable. Cities that target education and health care will emphasize environmental and public realm quality. Workers in finance, information and communication technology (ICT), and related

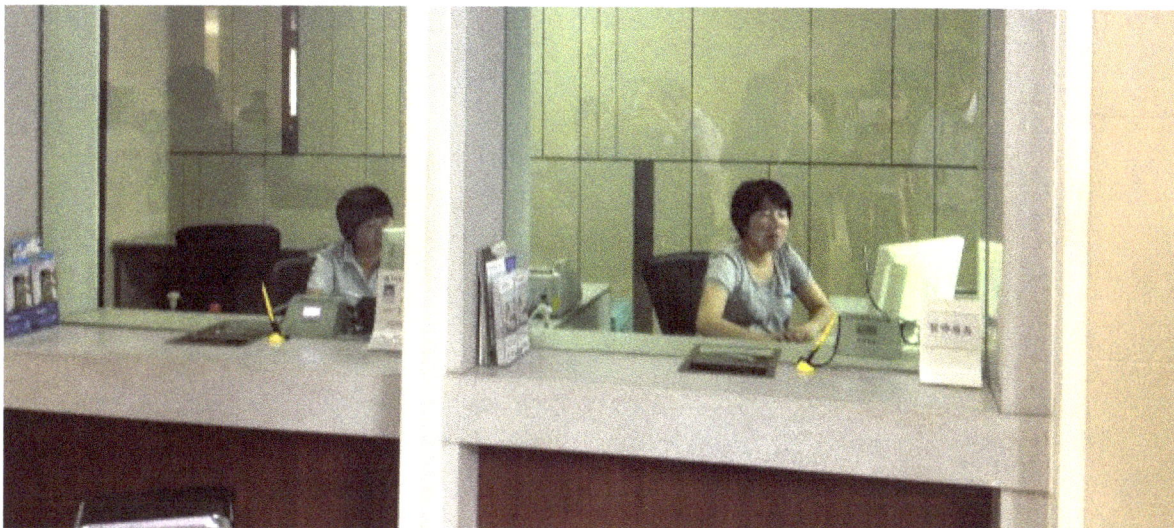

People's Republic of China: One-stop window for integrated government services in Shaoxing, Zhejiang

service industries also value those qualities; in addition, they have high expectations for the dynamism of districts (lively and engaging neighborhoods) and the depth of cultural amenities (Florida 2005).

Cities targeting green industrial development would first and foremost want to ensure the adequacy of water, power, and other key services that industries need for production. Second, the ability of industries to dispose of their waste in a compliant manner at a reasonable cost is an important criterion in industrial investment location decisions. Cities may choose to address wastewater and solid waste management challenges at the district level, with municipal or privately financed infrastructure, so that the marginal costs to industries are affordable. An area-based approach, where industries are clustered in zones where certain key services are provided, could be pursued. Third, road improvements and public transport services make it faster or easier for workers to reach employment areas, as well as to transfer raw materials and products. Once infrastructure assets are identified, a city will need to focus on financing mechanisms and partnerships to build these assets and on revenue generation for the sustainable management of these assets (see Chapter 6).

Local governments can also provide services that promote a pro-business operating environment, such as (i) establishing a "one-stop shop" or other agency to liaise, on behalf of the investors, with all of the government departments that regulate investment and provide public services; (ii) helping investors access the right kind of labor locally, by providing information on the availability of workers and offering training in the relevant skills required by investors in target economic sectors; and (iii) developing and maintaining a level playing field where investors and businesses can compete against each other according to clear and consistent rules and procedures.

Placemaking for Economic Success

Placemaking refers to a people-centered approach to the planning, design, and management of public spaces, with the intention of creating spaces that promote people's health, happiness, and well-being (Duany, Speck, and Lydon 2010). By focusing on placemaking for economic success, a city must answer the question: What are the ingredients of a distinctive urban environment that attracts businesses, entrepreneurs, residents, and visitors alike? And why is it that some cities are successful in creating these kinds of environments, while others fail? Placemaking goes beyond urban infrastructure and services, in the sense that it includes intangible assets that make a city attractive.[11] These intangible assets are unique for every city, and many can be subjective in the sense that they depend on individual preferences.[12] Guidelines that can promote these intangible assets through integrated urban design are presented with illustrative images in Insert A. The following are some of the common elements of placemaking:

- **Mixed land use.** Colocating employment areas with residential and commercial areas allows people to commute, shop, and recreate with greater ease and at lower cost. This can be combined with transit-oriented development, which contributes directly to urban efficiency and therefore economic competitiveness. Moreover, short distances also make it more feasible to use nonmotorized forms of transport (walking or biking), which have a lower carbon footprint than motorized transport.

---

[11] See, for instance, video of the School of Life (2015).

[12] City indexes that attempt to capture some of these dimensions are highlighted in Chapter 6.

Successful placemaking through quality open spaces, high environmental quality, mixed uses, pedestrian-oriented mobility, and human scale in Ho Chi Minh City, Viet Nam, and Little India, Singapore

Photo Credit: Renard Teipelke

Thailand: Open-air duty-free zone at Koh Samui Airport showcasing "out-of-the-box" design solutions

Photo Credit: Ramola Naik Singru

- **Human scale.** Walkable urban environments with a strong sense of place often have low- to mid-rise buildings, with an urban fabric that is composed of many smaller buildings rather than a fewer larger ones. This can be achieved during land subdivision by laying out smaller blocks and smaller plots.
- **Low level of pollution.** Garbage-free streets, clean river and pond water, and clean air all contribute to making urban places more attractive and life-supporting. Such places draw people to actively use and enjoy these spaces and to identify with them, which can result in community-based initiatives for maintenance and upgrading.
- **High-quality public open space.** Streets, plazas, parks, and recreation facilities should be designed and maintained for accessibility, comfort, and ease of use. Many cities these days greatly enrich the public realm by developing a large number of small parks that are dispersed throughout the urban fabric.
- **Urban mobility and multimodal transport.** A wide variety of modes (including pedestrian and bicycle networks, metro and buses, and private vehicles) with easy connections among them should be made available.

The case of Singapore exemplifies how these broad aspects have been translated into principles for a livable city (Box 4.1), merging placemaking for economic success with urban design for inclusive and sustainable development.

These types of elements combine in specific districts or cities to create a distinctive sense of place as well as a high level of livability. They can impact the sense of community, civic engagement, work–life balance, and satisfaction that residents, workers, and entrepreneurs experience in the city. The livability of a city relates to the quality of life it can afford, which relates to the city's economic viability. This is particularly true for cities that are trying to promote the development of a knowledge-based economy, as highly educated workers tend to place a high premium on livability, environmental quality, and urban vibrancy (City of Hamburg 2011).

Box 4.1: Singapore's Lessons for Livable High-Density Cities

The Urban Land Institute and the Centre for Liveable Cities in Singapore have summarized lessons learned from Singapore's path toward strong livability in light of rapid urbanization and a necessity for high-density urban development. Based on a number of case studies and assessments, as well as two stakeholder workshops, the resulting 10 principles for high-density, livable cities address potential repercussions and stresses, which can follow from dense urban development, and they also highlight the abundant opportunities from such places, where people of all different walks of life come together to further social and economic progress.

Principle 1: Plan for Long-Term Growth and Renewal
Takeaway: Long-term concepts and planning for livable cities are useful in guiding urban development. At the same time, these plans need to be revised regularly. They facilitate the most efficient and grEEEn use of land, instead of being rigid and out of touch from the dynamic flows of urban life. In that sense, strategic planning and flexibility go hand in hand.

Principle 2: Embrace Diversity and Foster Inclusiveness
Takeaway: Enabling harmony among diverse people living in dense urban areas can be facilitated through the establishment of public, semipublic, and private places, which are not segregated from each other, in order to enhance a sense of community. This is exemplified by Singapore's public housing plans, policies, and designs.

Principle 3: Draw Nature Closer to People
Takeaway: Rather than seeing nature as a separate element of a city, it is to be integrated into the urban fabric. This can be done by greening of the built environment and by interconnecting natural habits with each other to create a system of urban greenery throughout the city, strongly enhancing placemaking, environmental quality, and access to leisure activities.

Principle 4: Develop Affordable Mixed-Use Neighborhoods
Takeaway: Mixed-use communities combine a diverse set of housing for different groups of residents and they feature multiple functions present in a neighborhood, covering work, life, and play. Once walkability to the key social services and between residential housing and workplaces is ensured, commuting times can be reduced and dynamic neighborhoods can be furthered.

Principle 5: Make Public Spaces Work Harder
Takeaway: Cities cannot afford to have "dormant spaces"—most kinds of spaces can be put to

continued on next page

Box 4.1. *continued*

intelligent and multiple uses. This also refers to underground or rooftop areas. Adjusted building and zoning bylaws can function as enablers to accommodate flexible, multitask spaces.

Principle 6: Prioritize Green Transport and Building Options

Takeaway: Urban density is about efficient resource use. Once noncar transport options are improved and made into enjoyable mobility alternatives, car use can be successfully discouraged. This requires incentives the same way as the greening of buildings or neighborhoods only happens when initially higher costs are offset through various development schemes and longer-term savings from the use of innovative technologies.

Principle 7: Relieve Density with Variety and Add Green Boundaries

Takeaway: Green boundaries can make dense cities appear more like a natural network of livable neighborhoods. In addition to density differentials and height gradation in the urban fabric, so-called "spaces of relief" can provide room to breathe. Variety instead of design repetition can enhance the unique characters and identities of neighborhoods.

Principle 8: Activate Spaces for Greater Safety

Takeaway: Combining the concepts of "eyes on the street" and "visual access," spaces can be made active, lively, and safe. Place management performs an important role here in the activation of spaces during different times of the week. Interlinkages of neighborhoods can help strengthen colocation. This, in turn, depends on a mixed-use setup of spaces in the first place.

Principle 9: Promote Innovative and Nonconventional Solutions

Takeaway: Innovative urban development means trying out new solution sets and going step by step in incrementally changing the urban fabric. It also means to critically assess previous planning decisions and to reinvent places to meet current and future demands. A crucial foundation for this innovation is research and development, undertaken, coordinated, supported, and/or enhanced by the public sector, private enterprises, academe, and civil society.

Principle 10: Forge 3P Partnerships

Takeaway: The 3P principle, as in "people, private, public," acknowledges the problem of possibly conflicting interests and needs by different stakeholder groups, while also seeing the synergies that can emerge from a joint action in addressing urban development challenges. A multitude of perspectives, experiences, and capacities can help in designing solution sets that are carried by multiple actors. However, in contrast to previous government-driven approaches, such a process requires different styles of communication and cooperation.

Source: Centre for Liveable Cities. 2013. 10 Principles for Liveable High-Density Cities: Lessons from Singapore. Singapore: Urban Land Institute and Centre for Liveable Cities. http://uli.org/wp-content/uploads/ULI-Documents/10PrinciplesSingapore.pdf

Photo Credits: Renard Teipelke *(top)*; ADB *(bottom)*

Multiple uses of public spaces during different times of the day and week in Singapore *(top)*; and Ho Chi Minh City, Viet Nam *(bottom)*

The link between placemaking and real estate market economics must be acknowledged, as in many cases, property and business owners will benefit the most from successful placemaking initiatives. Renters, visitors, and workers will also enjoy benefits (such as new jobs, improved environmental quality, and additional economic opportunities), but the largest share of the benefits will accrue to the property owners in the place enjoying the growth. This has important implications for how financing for initiatives targeting both tangible and intangible assets can be raised. Financing for cities is discussed further in Chapter 6.

The following are urban design principles, which would contribute to sustainable urban development, livability, and a sense of place in integrated GrEEEn City planning.

Promote higher densities, mixed uses, and a variety of facilities. The pursuit of high-density mixed-use development, especially in central urban areas, which would help to avoid urban sprawl and maintain city cohesion and the compactness of built form, thereby reducing utility and infrastructure costs. A number of secondary or smaller cities worldwide are experiencing a "hollowing out" of their centers as sprawl undermines the urban core and its functions. Higher-density development would lead to shorter road lengths and more efficient utility servicing for the same number of residents, which in turn would result in lower utility costs per household. Urban infrastructure management and maintenance costs would also be reduced.

Viet Nam: High density, mixed, and fine grain of uses in Hoan Kiem in Ha Noi

Photo Credit: Mike Sharrocks

Singapore: Facade enhancements and refurbishment of heritage properties for mixed uses in Tanjong Pagar

Focus on inner urban areas and urban renewal. Sustainable urban planning and urban design should focus on the development of inner urban *brownfield* sites, infill development and urban renewal, and the reuse of old or heritage buildings. This approach will help reduce the demand for *greenfield* development and avoid urban sprawl.

Photo Credit: Ramola Naik Singru

People's Republic of China: Economically vibrant and well-restored heritage street in Hangzhou, Zheizang province

Incorporate the natural environment into design. The natural environment and ecological systems should be incorporated into design to promote an urban character and enhance recreational and landscape planning. At the very least, development proposals must be sensitive to the natural context. Thus, there should be new planting and reforestation within urban areas, as well as the creation of ecology or wildlife corridors extending from suburban edges and rural environments. As a *general* rule, for example, where parks or gardens are proposed, the following design principles should be applied:

- Parks in urban centers, where there is likely to be greater intensity of use, should adopt more hard landscape materials and more formal landscape design.
- Parkland in suburban or city edge areas should incorporate more informal and natural landscape and design touches, as well as integrate ecological systems and wildlife corridors.

Singapore: Suburban parkland footpath with more natural materials

Photo Credit: Mike Sharrocks

Integrate utility planning into urban design. Utility and infrastructure subproject planning should be integrated into strategic urban design and planning approaches. This could include the following examples:

- utilizing riverside embankments as a way of accommodating landscaped pedestrian routes and linear parks, and also by incorporating planting into retaining walls and slopes;
- enhancing balancing ponds and bioswales as landscape and ecological features within an urban parkland area;
- utilizing energy-saving devices as part of surface materials, such as by incorporating solar power cells into bicycle ways and footpaths so as to provide lighting for the facility or to generate extra electricity; and
- transforming completed landfill sites into parkland, which would be integrated with the surrounding natural environment for recreational and wildlife benefits.

Photo Credit: Mike Sharrocks

Viet Nam: High density, mixed, and fine grain of uses in Hoan Kiem in Ha Noi

Adopt energy-efficient technology into building design. New development should incorporate energy-efficient technologies into building design; by using solar heating, climate control technology, water recycling and rainwater collection systems, as well as natural heating and cooling mechanisms. The inclusion of planting and landscape into building design can also help to cool structures using rooftop gardens, terraced planting, and also flower and/or horticultural planting embedded into building facades. Vest-pocket parks, water features, and atrium gardens can also be created between and within buildings. These examples could also be applied to other structures such as elevated roads and bridges.

Photo Credit: Mike Sharrocks

Singapore: Rooftop grass at Marina Bay Barrage

Photo Credits: Mike Sharrocks (*left*); Renard Teipelke (*right*)

Singapore: Building facade planting

Encourage pedestrian activity, public transport use, and cycling. Planning and urban design for cities should encourage walking, cycling, and public transport use (for bus, rail, and light-rail networks), thereby reducing road construction and private vehicle use. Mixed uses, a variety of facilities, and higher-density development will help support this. There should also be a focus on transit-oriented development, whereby public transport services are integrated with, or close to, higher-density and mixed-use development. Combined bicycle and pedestrian paths need to be aligned along the more attractive, scenic, as well as direct routes to encourage users. Traffic calming measures should be adopted in quiet neighborhood areas and in busy city centers.

United States: Use of natural materials for residential street traffic calming in Charleston

Singapore: Pedestrian table crossing

Photo Credit: Mike Sharrocks

Design for a hierarchy of functions and activities. There needs to be a focus on the hierarchical importance of functions (and activity needs) for the type and size of parks, roads, and pathways. Thus, this would include appropriate road and pavement widths, together with planting for specific road functions and traffic capacity needs. Where there is likely to be a greater intensity of use, footpaths should be broader with greater use of durable materials. Routes through suburban environments should incorporate more natural environmental features.

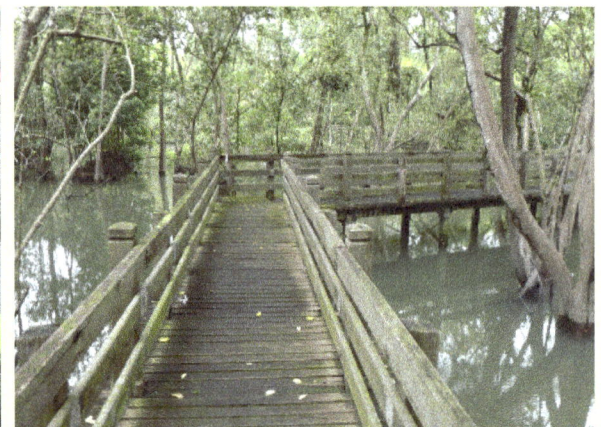

Different pedestrian routes for varied waterside functions: Harbor front (*left*) and mangrove boardwalk (*right*), both in Singapore

Photo Credit: Mike Sharrocks

People's Republic of China: Tianjin riverside walk

Malaysia: Riverside walk in Melaka

Photo Credit: Mike Sharrocks

Promote a sense of place and livability. It is important to promote a sense of place, through the application of design quality and cultural sensitivity for each city, to improve livability and the quality of life for residents, as well as to support the city's tourism appeal. There should be an emphasis on character differentiation. This could be done by incorporating genuine local features into urban design, such as incorporating aspects of heritage or culture through the use of typical and/or traditional building materials and design touches for each city and its parts. A sense of place will also be generated by the way people occupy and use spaces and how they are allowed to "personalize" buildings.

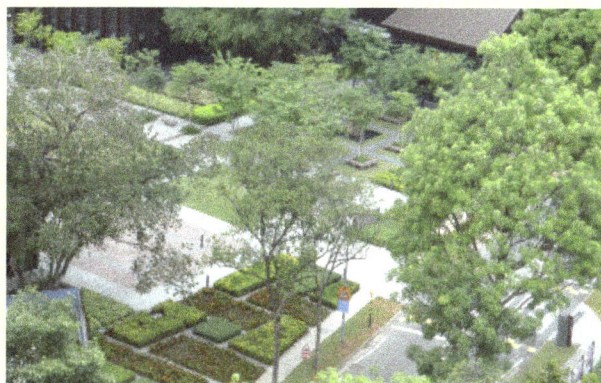

Photo Credit: Mike Sharrocks

Key spaces with a different sense of place. *Clockwise from top left:* Fatahillah Square in Jakarta (Indonesia), Secretariat Area in New Delhi (India), Federation Square in Melbourne (Australia), and Zhongshan Park (Singapore)

Photo Credit: Mike Sharrocks

Art and sculptures: Building murals in Melaka (Malaysia) and heritage sculpture in Singapore

Reduce management and maintenance costs. Efforts to reduce landscape and/or streetscape management and maintenance costs are often linked to the use of higher-quality materials, good design, and the integration of the natural environment into design approaches. Similarly, the design of landscape and urban spaces must be linked to appropriate use and viability rather than the provision of tree planting for the sake of it, for example, which is likely to lead to disuse or high maintenance costs.

Source: M. Sharrocks. 2015. Urban Design Sustainability and Liveability Principles. Background write-up.

E for Environment

Key elements in unbundling the E for environment concern natural resource management and low-carbon technologies to increase efficiency, as well as climate resilience of infrastructure, including planning and construction standards, and disaster risk management to increase the protection of communities and assets.

GrEEEn projects aim to make explicit use of the opportunities to improve environmental conditions and enhance ecological assets. The quality and optimal use of ecological assets identified as a unique selling point of a city should be improved through public works, regulations, or incentives for behavioral change, among other means.

Greening Infrastructure

Infrastructure forms the skeleton of a network of functions in a city. However, the built environment is not independent from a city's natural environment. Therefore, a key concern is to design infrastructure projects in a way that can realize their effectiveness and efficiency, while sustaining and—ideally—enhancing natural assets. The following examples combine two concepts of green infrastructure, which have been primarily common in Europe and North America, respectively: green infrastructure as physical interlinkages between natural systems within a city (green hubs and links) and green infrastructure as environmentally designed systems (low-impact development). Merging these two concepts, green infrastructure promotes an integrated design approach. Natural interlinkages are sustained and natural assets are enhanced through infrastructure, which is required for the development of urban areas—ecosystem services are integrated with the built environment.[13]

Photo Credit: Andrey Terekhov

While growing cities need new infrastructure, eight-lane highways promoting private car use do not represent a low-carbon development path

---

[13]   Examples of practical low-impact design solutions in the field of flood control and water management include rain gardens, street storage, bioretention, permeable pavement, vegetated roof cover, bioswales, rainwater harvesting, and green streets (Beauchamp, Adamowski, and Beausejour 2015).

Principles for greening infrastructure systems are well documented in many sources (World Bank 2010b, ICEM 2015). Resource flows are mapped to understand where efficiencies can be achieved. Resource "cascading" is one powerful technique. In typical water systems, water fit for human consumption is currently also being used for other purposes, such as washing cars or watering gardens, making inefficient use of a valuable resource. Through resource cascading, resource quality can be matched more evenly with the needs of the user. For example, "gray water" can be reused for toilet flushing, and wastewater can be used to water public landscaping.

Initiatives formulated as part of the GrEEEn City Action Plan (GCAP) will focus on natural resource efficiency, for example in the reduction of carbon emissions in one or more sectors. A project may focus, for example, on public transport (to reduce the use of private cars) and green buildings (to conserve energy used for heating or air-conditioning).[14] Since one project can hardly address all the ways that a city contributes to climate change, however, a broader city wide tracking mechanism can be useful for monitoring the cumulative changes that come from many different actions and initiatives in industry, utilities, transport, etc.

Resource-Efficient Systems

Reducing carbon footprints and conserving resources can also be achieved through "distributed infrastructure systems." Moving water, heat, power, etc. long distances along distribution pipes always causes resource losses. Rather than having large systems where end users are far from the source, it is possible to size systems to a more local scale and capture the associated efficiency gains. Multiple wastewater treatment plants (especially operating in separate minibasins in the city, with gravity flow) is one example.

A variant on the theme is "looping," in which resources are cycled or passed back and forth among different users. For example, the heat by-product from industrial production processes is used to heat water, which flows to neighboring residences and through some form of radiator. The cool water flows back to the factory for reheating, and the cycle repeats itself. "Looped" resource flows are also examples of distributed (localized) systems. Separate small systems can be connected at key points to ensure service in the case of breakdown, which increases resilience. Studies show that distributed energy systems can boost efficiency by 55%–80% (World Bank 2010b, p. 70). These principles can be applied by designers of grEEEn projects that include water, wastewater, stormwater, district heating, and district cooling components.

Applying grEEEn project design for a transformation toward resource-efficient infrastructure systems, the pollution hierarchy is an important concept (US EPA 2015b). The hierarchy comprises avoidance, reduction, recycling (including recovery), treatment, and disposal. Avoiding pollution in the first place is always preferable; if that is not possible, then ways to reduce the extent of pollution at the source should be explored and implemented. From the waste that is produced at the source, usable materials should be recovered and recycled. Finally, the remaining waste should be treated and disposed of in compliance with local environmental conditions and regulatory requirements.

---

[14]   On the energy use or demand side, switching to nonmotorized transport will reduce fuel use and hence carbon emissions. The other large energy use is in buildings. Improving energy efficiency in buildings will reduce carbon emissions if the supply is from fossil-based sources. However, to make a city a zero-carbon city, it is necessary to constantly increase the proportion of renewable energy in the overall energy supply mix. Some cities are already fortunate to be solely dependent on renewable energy, particularly hydropower (GIZonlineTV 2015).

Photo Credit: ADB/Ahmed Zahid

Waste recycling can be an income source for communities, but it requires a thorough assessment of its direct and indirect environmental and social implications

Different initiatives based on this pollution hierarchy need to be considered in the planning, design, implementation, and operation stages. Pollution should be addressed at the appropriate stage through the most effective initiative. Each initiative should be analyzed from economic and equity perspectives, and possible externalities should be suitably addressed as a part of designing the initiative itself. For instance, if the initiative is meant to reduce recyclable plastic waste at the source, then the absence of recyclables will have an impact on the waste-picking communities and the informal recycling chain. In taking such an initiative forward, such social and/or equity considerations would also need to be considered.

Green Technologies

While the term "technology" refers to the application of knowledge for practical purposes, the field of "green technology" encompasses continuously evolving methods and/or techniques that are intended to mitigate or reverse the effects of human activity on the environment. Alternatively, green technology is the application of one or more among environmental science, green chemistry, environmental monitoring, and electronic devices to monitor, model, and conserve the natural environment and resources, and to curb the negative human impacts, particularly on the local environment.

Examples of green technologies include those pertaining to air pollution abatement and monitoring, water supply quality and conservation, wastewater (both sewage and stormwater) treatment, land and/or soil remediation, solid waste treatment and management, recycling and recovery, and energy conservation. Given the focus on climate change abatement, there are a number of other greenhouse gas (GHG)-reducing technologies that are also promoted under green technologies. These are classified as low-carbon technologies and are covered in the subsequent section.

While these are traditional green technologies, green infrastructure designs for cities are increasingly being considered and are a part of grEEEn solutions. These designs could pertain to expanding the tree cover or incorporating engineered structures and/or facilities such as

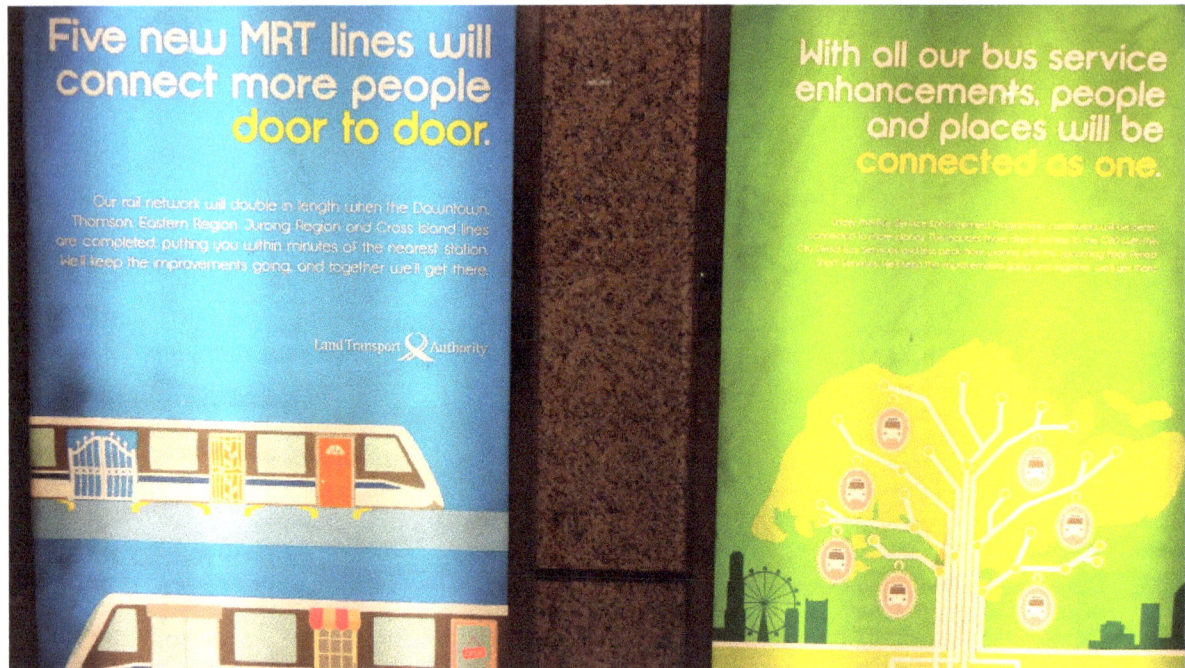

Singapore: A comprehensive public transport system based on long-term demand planning can help cities in reducing humankind's carbon footprint

Photo Credit: Renard Teipelke

parks, bioretention, rain gardens, trees, and swales into the city's infrastructure. This takes different forms in different cities and cultures. In Asia, one focus in on the introduction of parks and gardens into existing cities. In Singapore, water recycling is being applied due to shortages in the water supply. In Australia, the concept of water-sensitive urban design offers opportunities for urban design, landscape architecture, and stormwater infrastructure.

GrEEEn solutions need to consider both traditional green technologies and green infrastructure designs. In supporting city governments to apply grEEEn solutions, technology centers should be identified and nurtured to perform research and development on potential technologies. These centers should conduct research on the conceptual, laboratory, and pilot and/or demonstration scales, and also support the dissemination of the possibilities on the commercial scale. They should carry out their activities in a collaborative manner with the government, the private sector, and community groups. International agencies (funding, development, and others) should also offer support so that a platform for global cooperation is established. For instance, the Green Technology Center in the Republic of Korea is contributing in this direction (Kang 2014). It has initiated a smart grid project on Jeju Island, a river restoration pilot project for Indonesia's Ciliwung River, and a technology transfer initiative on new carbon capture (KIERSOL), among others. While these technologies are not solely directed toward cities' needs, similar initiatives catering to urban needs are required.

As one form of green technology, low-carbon technologies are increasingly becoming the focus given the important challenge of climate change mitigation. In addition to green measures that contribute to improved natural resource efficiency through improved design of infrastructure projects, the use of low-carbon technologies to produce positive environmental impacts can also be considered part of grEEEn project design. In a city context, low-carbon

Viet Nam: Lighting solutions for public infrastructure, such as this bridge in Ha Giang, can provide several benefits regarding functionality, public safety, and place enhancement.

technologies include energy-efficient technologies (particularly in buildings), no-carbon power such as using renewables, and low-carbon fuel. They also include technologies that reduce GHG emissions, such as carbon capture and storage technologies.

Cities have a major role to play in reducing humankind's carbon footprint. They consume 78% of the world's energy and contribute more than 60% of all carbon dioxide and significant amounts of other GHG emissions—while covering less than 2% of the earth's surface (UN-Habitat 2015a). It is understood that urban activities related to buildings, transport, energy, and industry all generate GHGs, which erode the ozone layer and cause climate change (Global Commission on the Economy and Climate 2014). A fundamental aspect of designing grEEEn projects is determining how to reduce GHG emissions on an economically sustainable basis.

In order to measure the impact of low-carbon technologies on emissions, establishing baselines is critical: GHG emission estimates can be done on a project basis for individual urban projects that have a mitigation potential, or for the whole city as part of a citywide GHG inventory, which will allow for credible, analysis-based determinations of the magnitude of carbon-related impacts of specific activities, projects, and/or subsectors (World Bank 2013). Citywide GHG inventories are encouraged as part of urban profiling under the GrEEEn Cities Operational Framework (GCOF). Recent case studies reviewed by ADB provide evidence that GHG inventories enable cities to drive green investments, leverage and access climate financing, and raise public awareness (Sandhu and Kamal 2015). While low-carbon technologies tend to produce positive environmental impacts and can be an important part of grEEEn project design, the institutional dimensions (regulations, policies, and incentives) of their application should also be considered. Solar power, for example, can help reduce

Photo Credit: ADB

Philippines: With the installation of solar panels, which provide about 50,000 kilowatt-hours monthly, and geothermal power supply, the Asian Development Bank has switched to 100% renewable energy and targets a 50% decrease in its annual corporate carbon footprint, which is equivalent to a reduction of more than 9,500 tons of carbon dioxide emissions.

carbon footprints, but, in some cities, the institutional capacity to maintain solar technology is not in place, so economically it will not be a sound investment. The economics tend to depend on the national and/or federal and provincial and/or state policies which are intended to promote solar power across a larger geographical area and not specific to a city.

Institutional capacity building may be used to fill the gap and make solar technology viable. In another city (due to national or state policies), the cost of developing solar power facilities may be prohibitive in comparison to the revenue from selling the power to the grid. Here a solar feed-in tariff—essentially a subsidized price—could be effective in catalyzing more private investment in solar power in the short to medium term, while production costs continue to decline. These institutional and financial measures are examples of "enablers" that can be used to make green technology viable. GrEEEn project design requires widening the lens to increase the chances of successful introduction of green technology.

Another aspect of grEEEn project design is exploring the possibility of preserving and enhancing the environment as a secondary feature of the proposed intervention. Consider a proposal to build new bus stops (sheds) as part of a public transport project. What environmental enhancements can be built into the project design? The bus stops could include solar panels on the roof that generate power for street lighting. Similarly, green roofs can be considered for large warehousing developments. Streetscape improvements can incorporate green infrastructure for stormwater retention as well as low-energy lightbulbs for streetlights (Development Finance International 2014). An illustrative example of energy-efficient lighting action plan is given in Insert B.

Urban Form and Spatial Planning

Going beyond the optimization of individual subsystems, the harmonization of urban development patterns and urban infrastructure is the biggest opportunity for improving environmental impacts. And yet, this is often not considered in urbanization decisions. Planners and engineers sit in different meetings at different times and ask different questions. GrEEEn Cities need to start changing that.

Compactness of urban form is the key to sustainability (UCCRN 2011). First, absolute size matters: small apartments and row houses consume fewer resources in construction and generate fewer GHGs during operation than large freestanding houses. Second, most highly efficient urban infrastructure technologies can only be introduced at high development densities. For example, district heating, which is less energy-intensive than individual boilers in every building, generally requires a minimum development density of 40 dwelling units per hectare to be cost-effective. Development density also correlates strongly with energy consumption in transport (ADB and GIZ 2011). Third, the replication of low footprint building typologies becomes possible as economic viability becomes achievable due to the possible scale of implementation.

The arrangements of buildings on the ground and the extent to which they are attached to each other also have a major impact on energy performance. Buildings produce more GHGs than any other element of the urban system (about 25% of total on average) (World Bank 2010b, p. 17). Party-wall construction (buildings that are attached) is more energy-efficient than detached, freestanding buildings. Buildings should be oriented and designed to take advantage of passive solar heating and ventilation.

Another aspect of development patterns—the land-use mix—can also greatly reduce GHG emissions. The colocation of work, living, and play activities reduces travel distances and give people the opportunity to walk and ride bicycles more often to their destinations. The associated resource savings are substantial.

At the city and district level, decisions about where to urbanize need to reflect infrastructure development and operation requirements. Development should be built downhill from water reservoirs to take advantage of "free" transmission by gravity. New development should be located close to existing water and wastewater mains to minimize transmission distances. Planners should use any excess capacity in existing infrastructure systems before building new systems. Infill sites, vacant land within existing urbanized areas, should be developed as a priority before greenfield sites. Taken together, these decisions can reduce infrastructure operating costs by 30% or more (World Bank 2010b, p. 74).

Existing development plans in a given city may already include mixed-use development patterns that are good for the environment. GrEEEn projects can use these plans as is, strengthening the infrastructure delivery and management aspects. Where required, grEEEn projects can include an updating of existing urban development plans to introduce greener development patterns, which can then be combined with green infrastructure and management practices. Often, the whole plan does not have to be updated; it may be sufficient to introduce greener development patterns in a few select districts that are likely to generate a large share of the GHGs in the city. While greening cities is urgent, it will be most successful if it is done incrementally through existing planning and growth management systems.

GrEEEn Cities Energy-Efficient Lighting Action Plan

Trial results in a number of cities demonstrate that light-emitting diode (LED) lighting is an effective, energy-efficient, and mature technology ready for mass deployment. A growing number of cities around the globe are already experiencing the benefits of LEDs, including Buenos Aires and New York City, both of which recently announced full-scale plans to upgrade their road lighting infrastructure to LEDs. Conversion to energy-efficient LED lighting poses a good opportunity to make a city greener and financially healthier as it reduces demand on electricity and consequently contributes to carbon dioxide (CO_2) emission reduction targets. At the same time, well-planned LED lighting decreases lighting pollution in urban areas, improves safety and produces a sense of security among citizens, and helps create a city identity.

ACTION 1: Solutions for Urban Roads – Retrofit and Greenfield LED Street Lighting

LEDs are the most energy-efficient option for road lighting today and can help municipalities achieve energy savings of 50%–70% over conventional road lighting technologies and reach up to 80% savings when coupled with smart controls. Good road lighting also promotes security among its citizens, better aesthetics, efficient use of the road network, and road safety by reducing road-related accidents. In addition, the shift to a low-carbon lighting technology such as LEDs would help reduce greenhouse gas emissions and generate significant budgetary savings that could be reinvested in other citizen services such as education, health care, or infrastructure.

LED street lighting can also be deployed around commercial infrastructure, for example, in eco-industrial parks such as Ascendas Tech Park in Viet Nam.

ADB Metro Manila LED Street Lighting Retrofit Project

- In Metro Manila, 1,484 lamps were replaced with LEDs in major thoroughfares and flyovers.

ACTION 1A: Funded Solutions

Implementing LED street lighting projects funded by international finance institutions.

LED Road Lighting Retrofit Project with the Government of Malaysia

- A lighting retrofit project for the expressways of Kuala Lumpur to help the government reduce CO_2 emissions by 40% by 2020.
- Across 63.1 kilometers of roads, 3,145 high pressure sodium vapor lamps were replaced with LEDs, resulting in average energy savings of 62%.
- This was financed through a commercial bank with a sovereign guarantee from the government.

ACTION 1B: Innovative Solutions to Address Viability Gap

Innovative solutions can be designed to address challenges in financing energy efficiency projects. One example is a project with sovereign or microfinance institution guarantee to mitigate banks' risk. Another model could be a funded pilot to demonstrate project bankability, energy savings, and tangible benefits, intended for replication via financed or funded scale-ups. This is done through close collaboration with stakeholders during the pilot phase to conduct surveys, complete energy audits, and develop the most efficient and cost-effective lighting solutions for the city.

ADB Promoting Energy Efficiency in the Pacific (Phase 2)

- Energy-efficient lighting was installed through a mix of outdoor and indoor lighting technologies (LEDs, solar LEDs, and T5 sets)
- The project (majority composed of lighting) is set to deliver $1.75 million in annual energy savings in the Pacific or 3.49 gigawatt-hours and 2,818 tons of CO_2 avoided per year.

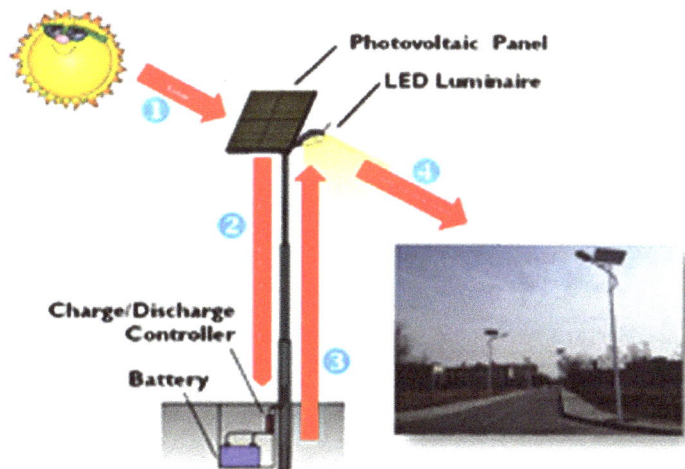

Action 2: Solutions for Locations with Unstable Power Supply or Off-Grid Locations – Solar LED Street Lighting

For urban areas with highly fluctuating power supply or rural communities with limited or no access to electricity or the grid, solar LED street lighting can make a significant impact by providing lighting with an integrated source of electricity.

Action 3: Solutions for Commercial Offices, Public Offices, and Residential Retrofits – Indoor Energy-Efficient Lighting

Apart from the outdoor opportunity, efficient indoor lighting solutions play a key role in moving toward "green buildings." Comprehensive energy audits and close collaboration with stakeholders will identify key points of energy efficiency improvements through lighting in commercial and public offices as well as residential areas.

In some countries, energy audits and/or conversion to energy-efficient lighting are being supported through special incentive programs.

Action 4: Solutions for Community and Livelihood – Night Markets and Community Centers

Extended daylight hours in communal areas and properly lit roads enable business, education, community, and employment-related activities at night; promote social cohesion by bringing members of the community together; and make the areas safer at night. Philips provides solar-powered indoor systems, mobile streetlights, minigrids, and charging stations to promote community identity and continuity of livelihood options well into the night.

Off-Grid Lighting in Viet Nam's Rural Thanh Son Village

- To improve the lives of people living in 288 households in Thanh Son, 928 lights were installed in households, a community center, and a kindergarten.
- Solar home systems and solar road lights were installed in this off-grid area to leverage the extensive solar energy available.

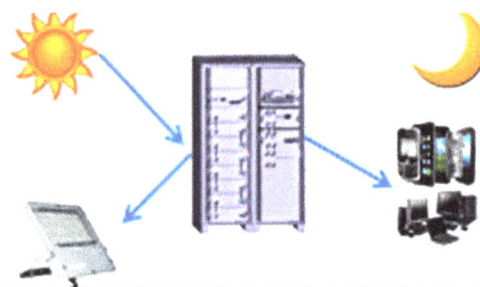

Action 5: Solutions for City Branding – Building the City Image as a Leader in Sustainability and City Ambiance

As cities move toward building identity and positioning themselves as attractive places to visit, connected LED lighting can perfectly show off the architectural details of the cities' major sights while slashing energy consumption by 85% compared with previous lighting systems.

Da Nang Dragon Bridge

- The city of Da Nang required a lighting solution that was not only energy efficient, but would also beautify and highlight the steel bridge as an iconic landmark of Da Nang.
- A full turnkey package of LED lighting fixtures, lighting design with controls, installation of lighting and controls, commissioning, and maintenance was provided. About 2,500 energy-efficient LED light points were installed, including LED road lighting solutions.

Action 6: Solutions for the Smart City – Intelligent Lighting to Promote Sustainability and Livability

Cities want to provide safety and security for citizens in the most efficient and cost-effective way. Lighting controls provide a dynamic, intelligent, and flexible solution to bring city lighting to life. Intelligent lighting optimizes a city's lighting operations and manages the light levels according to the city's needs—increasing a Smart City's green credentials in the process.

Through intelligent lighting, lighting is adjusted to the right levels at the right times and can be based on pedestrian and vehicle presence. Real-time system information and operation reports also enable optimization of maintenance activities.

Astana, Kazakhstan

- The city illuminated its most famous monuments with cutting-edge connected lighting technology in preparation to host the EXPO 2017 International Exhibition which has as its main theme "Future Energy."
- The LEDs are linked up to a wireless control system, enabling their color and brightness to be customized from a central monitor. The controls also permit a range of different effects such as ripples, cross-fades, sparkles, strobes, and bursts.

Photo Credits: Philips Lighting/Development Finance International

Note: This insert was prepared by Development Finance International supported by Philips Lighting (2015) to share examples of possible actions that can be taken to accelerate the adoption of LED lighting and thereby achieve tangible outcomes toward GrEEEn Cities.

Climate Resilience and Disaster Risk Management

These interventions all contribute to climate change mitigation by reducing GHG emissions. GrEEEn projects can also help cities adapt to climate change, a slow process that is expected to continue for decades if not centuries. Settlement patterns, infrastructure improvements, and behavioral changes can all help cities tackle the challenges posed by (i) climate-induced events such as floods or cyclones, and (ii) other climate-induced changes such as increased incidences of vector-borne diseases.

A resilient city is "a city that has managed to successfully support measures to strengthen individuals, communities, and institutions to (a) Reduce or avoid current and future hazards; (b) reduce current and future susceptibility to withstand hazards; (c) establish functioning mechanisms and structure for disaster response; and (d) establish functioning mechanisms and structures for disaster recovery" (Wamsler, Brink, and Rivera 2013, p. 71). This definition is aligned with ADB's Operational Plan for Integrated Disaster Risk Management 2014–2020 that aims at enhanced disaster resilience, which does not come at the cost of socioeconomic development (ADB 2014k). This integrated approach requires the integration of disaster risk reduction into development, the double perspective of disaster risk management and climate change adaptation, and the development of adequate (which most often means higher) disaster risk financing capabilities. Experiences from the Greater Mekong Subregion have, however, already proven that resilience-improving green solutions can be implemented in a variety of conditions, if natural systems are reintegrated into the planning process through the design of green infrastructure (ICEM 2015).

ADB's Jiangxi Pingxiang Integrated Rural–Urban Infrastructure Development Project is an example where the concept of the "Sponge City" is piloted through an integrated disaster risk management approach, which does not apply isolated "gray" infrastructure fixes such as concrete dikes, but combines flood risk management with ecological river rehabilitation to protect floodplains, create green riverbanks, and rehabilitate embankments and wetlands to make use of natural water flows (ADB 2015g). In addition to such approaches, traditional practices for resource conservation can also add to resilience by blending local knowledge with advanced technology to cope with climate and disaster risks and to increase environmental quality in urban communities. Examples are traditional rainwater harvesting techniques, as revived in dry regions such as Rajasthan, India (Pareek 2015), or the use of aerated lagoon systems for improved wastewater management, as applied in the city of Dong Hoi in Viet Nam (World Bank 2015a).

Moving from the project level to the policy level, cities can apply a variety of strategies to achieve improved resilience through integrated planning mechanisms (Figure 4.1).

In order to get the initial assessment of climate and disaster risks right and to build up resilience in urban areas, there are a number of tool kits city managers can use for improved analysis and planning. One example is the ICLEI Asian Cities Climate Change Resilience Network (ACCCRN) Process (Box 4.2).

Figure 4.1: Strategies for Climate- and Disaster-Resilient Cities

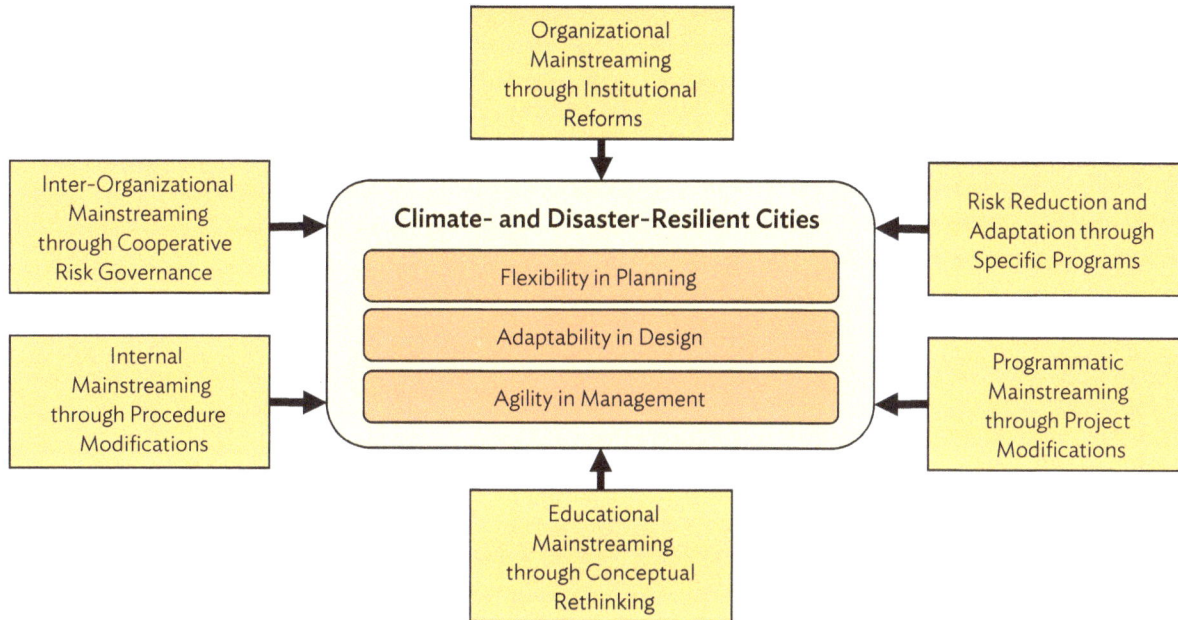

Sources: Adapted from C. Wamsler, E. Brink, and C. Rivera. 2013. Planning for Climate Change in Urban Areas: From Theory to Practice. *Journal of Cleaner Production*. 50. pp. 68–81; K.C. Desouza and T.H. Flanery. 2013. Designing, Planning, and Managing Resilient Cities: A Conceptual Framework. *Cities*. 35. pp. 89–99.

Box 4.2: ICLEI ACCCRN Process

ICLEI – Local Governments for Sustainability and Rockefeller Foundation, through its Asian Cities Climate Change Resilience Network (ACCCRN) program, developed a comprehensive tool kit for the assessment of climate-related risks to urban areas and the development of corresponding strategies toward increased resilience of cities. The tool kit identifies six phases: (i) engagement – to get the process started, (ii) climate research and impacts assessment – to thoroughly assess the status quo, (iii) vulnerabilities assessment – to identify places and groups particularly exposed to negative climate impacts, (iv) city resilience strategy – to formulate resilience building measures, (v) implementation – to prepare and execute measures, and (vi) monitoring and review – to accompany the implementation and to readjust based on performance evaluation. Besides a number of useful tools, the key focus in the application of the ICLEI ACCCRN Process is on engaging and building resilient communities. Therefore, this tool kit is one example of support for the GrEEEn Cities Operational Framework, particularly by stressing the integration of resilience aspects and strategies into the overall planning process of a city.

Source: ICLEI and Rockefeller Foundation. 2015. *ICLEI ACCCRN Process: Building Urban Climate Change Resilience: A Toolkit for Local Governments*. New Delhi: ICLEI South Asia.

Another example of tools for strengthening resilience through urban planning is ADB's (forthcoming) *Guidance Notes on Reducing Disaster Risk in Urban Areas through Land Use Management*. ADB has developed these guidance notes to support developing member countries officials in integrating disaster risk considerations in urban land-use management processes. Figure 4.2 illustrates a basic approach as concerns land-use planning. The first line of defense is to avoid locating new development in high-risk areas. The second action is to enhance the resilience of vulnerable areas (flood-prone areas and steep slopes) in which people live or valuable economic assets are located. Finally, cities should try to guide future development to areas of low disaster and climate risk. These principles should be applied in the design of grEEEn projects.

The principle of redundancy also informs grEEEn project design. Urban subsystems are often put out of commission by natural hazards. To recover quickly and safeguard human life and property, a backup system is required. Redundancy can be achieved, for example, by linking distributed energy systems together, so that when one breaks down the other can provide the services.

Automation of infrastructure systems also helps deliver services to users that need it during regular service periods and disaster events. Smart City attributes and techniques can contribute directly to GrEEEn Cities goals and objectives (Vogl 2012, pp. 373-405).

Figure 4.2: An Approach to Disaster Risk-Sensitive Land-Use Planning

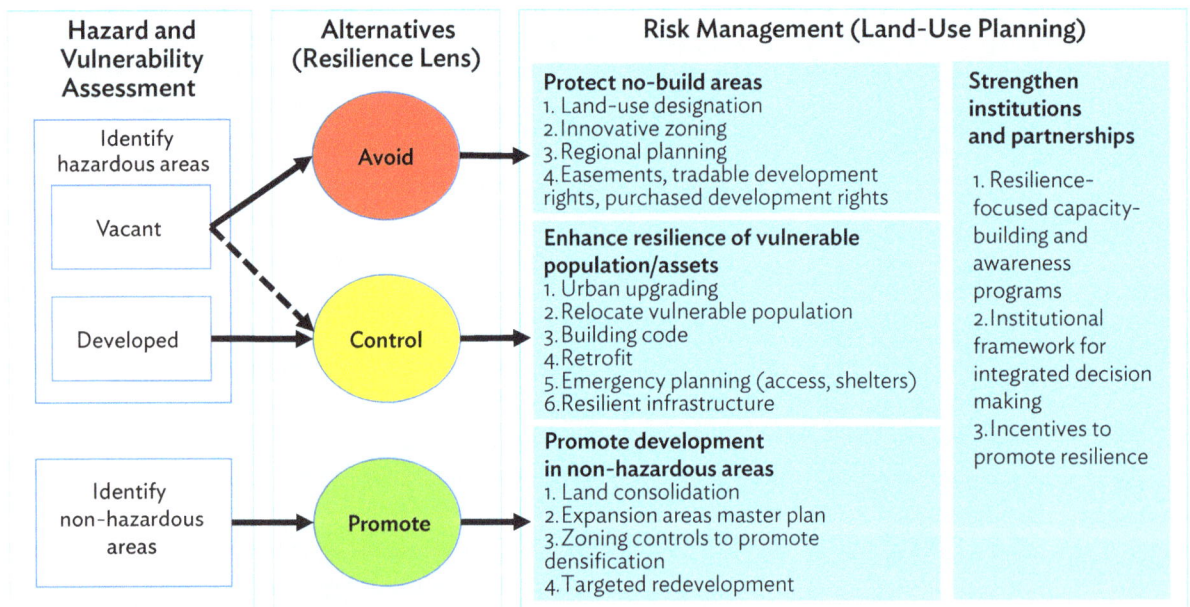

Source: Adapted from AECOM 2015. Graphic prepared as part of ADB Technical Assistance for Addressing Disaster Risks through Improved Indicators and Land Use Management. Manila (TA 7929-REG).

Photo Credit: Ramola Naik Singru

Myanmar: Riverboat communities, such as in Mandalay, require a risk-sensitive planning approach toward resilience that also provides affordable and accessible basic urban services

E for Equity

The equity pillar emphasizes the role of social and human capital in urban development. It refers to the equity of access to key services among all citizens (particularly poor and marginalized communities), the distribution of development benefits and access to those benefits, and the opportunity to participate equally in consultation and development processes.

Urban investment projects have the potential to reduce poverty. They provide short- and long-term employment opportunities, including skills enhancement. Improved infrastructure, services, land-use management, and connectivity with transport facilities create economic opportunities and improve the environment for microenterprises as well as small and medium-sized enterprises (SMEs) to grow their businesses (ADB 2014j). Services, which are accessible and affordable for the poor, contribute to equity.

ADB and other development institutions are working with local and national governments in Asia to strengthen this link between urban investment and poverty reduction (ADB 2003a). ADB's overarching approach to poverty reduction and promoting social benefits of urban projects is set out in its guidance note on poverty and social dimensions in urban projects (ADB 2014g). Additional methodological guidance is provided in the tool kit on inclusive urban development (Naik Singru and Lindfield, forthcoming). The Inclusive Urban Development Framework sets out the underlying principles of accessibility, affordability, resilience, and sustainability for an integrated approach to inclusive urban development. "Inclusive" urban infrastructure development is defined as an integrated approach encompassing sustainable, resilient, accessible, and affordable solutions to the challenges faced by the urban poor and vulnerable groups by enhancing their access to urban services and infrastructure through targeted investments. This integrated approach encourages an institutional delivery mechanism that brings together all institutions and stakeholders—

Improvements in the transport or sanitation sector can have cobenefits in other areas, resulting, for instance, in increasing business for shopowners in Kobuleti, Georgia *(left)* or higher school attendance rates and improved health of children on Ebeye island, Marshall Islands *(right)*.

government, the private sector, and civil society—who have the capacity to deliver systems for inclusive urban service delivery. The approach proposes that the capacity of the urban poor communities, slum networks, and nongovernment organizations (NGOs) should be effectively used in conjunction with the city government and the private sector, as applied in the Neighborhood Upgrading and Shelter Project in Indonesia (Box 4.3).

Taking the needs of the poor and other vulnerable groups into account when designing urban infrastructure projects includes using social safeguards to mitigate any negative impacts of urban development projects. For instance in Bangladesh, community resilience was increased by strengthening community-level disaster preparedness through community awareness raising performed in conjunction with community-level hazard mapping and planning (ADB 2014a).

GrEEEn Cities build on these elements of equity by focusing on the main ingredients of cities: people and places.

Cities for People

GrEEEn Cities put people first. They embrace a holistic view of prosperity, creating an environment for all citizens to flourish and thrive. There is an imperative to create GrEEEn Cities in Asia to provide a better quality of life for residents. Making such cities work requires the engagement and involvement of a full cross section of society. This can be done in an open and inclusive manner using some of the guiding principles outlined in Box 4.4.

Citizen ownership is built through a process of communication, consultation, consensus, and involvement. Cities must emphasize engagement and ownership of residents in planning and managing the transformation of a city. This entails various approaches and tools for community engagement throughout the project cycle, including (i) stakeholder consultation and consensus-building through participatory planning, (ii) stakeholder involvement during the project design stage through charettes and focus group discussions,

Indonesia: Promoting pro-poor city planning through neighborhood upgrading and low-cost housing projects

Box 4.3: ADB Neighborhood Upgrading and Shelter Project, Indonesia

The Asian Development Bank supported the Government of Indonesia in implementing a comprehensive participatory slum upgrading program as part of the "Cities without Slums" and the "One Million Houses" programs to meet the Millennium Development Goals. In addition to infrastructure upgrading and site development, pro-poor city development plans and improved living conditions in urban slums have been targeted. In particular, strengthening planning and management capacities of local governments and sustainable mechanisms for community engagement, as well as launching public–private partnerships for affordable housing, have been key aspects of the implementation.

As part of the first project phase, approved in 2003, urban assets, residents' well-being, and their income opportunities were improved through expanded access of informal settlers to microcredit for shelter finance and increased provision of shelter for urban poor in 32 cities and districts of 17 provinces. The project implemented a participatory community-driven planning approach to strengthen both the capacity and role of governments and communities in meeting their responsibilities.

To further strengthen pro-poor spatial planning and related capacities of concerned communities and sector institutions, a second phase of the project was approved in 2013. Neighborhoods within 20 project cities have been selected for project implementation through a community implementation organization. In addition to infrastructure upgrading and new settlements areas, to be financed and constructed under public–private partnership schemes, the project includes the formulation of community-driven neighborhood upgrading plans in alignment with overall city development plans as well as operation and maintenance plans to ensure the sustainability of investments.

Sources: ADB. 2003. *Neighborhood Upgrading and Shelter Sector Project.* Manila (IDN 35143-013); ADB. 2014. *Neighborhood Upgrading and Shelter Project (Phase 2).* Manila (IDN 46094-001).

Box 4.4: Guiding Principles for Open and Inclusive Citizens' Involvement in the GrEEEn City Action Plan Process

1. **Commitment:** Leadership and strong commitment to open and inclusive policy making is needed at all levels—politicians, senior managers, and public officials.

2. **Rights:** Citizens' rights to information, consultation, and public participation in policy making and service delivery must be firmly grounded in law or policy. Government obligations to respond to citizens must be clearly stated. Independent oversight arrangements are essential to enforcing these rights.

3. **Clarity:** Objectives for, and limits to, information, consultation, and public participation should be well defined from the outset. The roles and responsibilities of all parties must be clear. Government information should be complete, objective, reliable, relevant, and easy to find and understand.

4. **Time:** Public engagement should be undertaken as early in the policy process as possible to allow a greater range of solutions and to raise the chances of successful implementation. Adequate time must be available for consultation and participation to be effective.

5. **Inclusion:** All citizens should have equal opportunities and multiple channels to access information, be consulted, and participate. Every reasonable effort should be made to engage with as wide a variety of people as possible.

6. **Resources:** Adequate financial, human, and technical resources are needed for effective public information, consultation, and participation. Government officials must have access to appropriate skills, guidance, and training as well as an organizational culture that supports both traditional and online tools.

7. **Coordination:** Initiatives to inform, consult, and engage civil society should be coordinated within and across levels of government to ensure policy coherence, avoid duplication, and reduce the risk of "consultation fatigue." Coordination efforts should not stifle initiative and innovation but should leverage the power of knowledge networks and communities of practice within and beyond government.

8. **Accountability:** Governments have an obligation to inform participants how they use inputs received through public consultation and participation. Measures to ensure that the policy-making process is open, transparent, and amenable to external scrutiny can help increase accountability of, and trust in, government.

9. **Evaluation:** Governments need to evaluate their own performance. To do so effectively will require efforts to build the demand, capacity, culture, and tools for evaluating public participation.

10. **Active citizenship:** Societies benefit from dynamic civil society, and governments can facilitate access to information, encourage participation, raise awareness, strengthen citizens' civic education and skills, as well as support capacity building among civil society organizations. Governments need to explore new roles to effectively support autonomous problem solving by citizens, civil society organizations, and businesses.

Source: Organisation for Economic Co-operation and Development (OECD). 2009. *Focus on Citizens: Public Engagement for Better Policy and Services. OECD Studies on Public Engagement.* Paris. http://www.oecd-ilibrary.org/governance/focus-on-citizens_9789264048874-en;jsessionid=10pkqk4u34xgs.x-oecd-live-03

(iii) stakeholder involvement during implementation through citizens committees and partnership mechanisms, and (iv) continued citizens' monitoring during the operation and maintenance stage through citizen scorecards and social media channels (see section "Tools for Accountability in Urban Service Delivery"). The goal is for people to recognize that they have a stake in their city's development, and to contribute toward the transformation required. An example of a formal institutional mechanism for enabling stakeholder involvement and citizens' ownership is described in Box 4.5.

As noted in Chapter 2, the GrEEEn Cities Operational Framework (GCOF) takes advantage of a city's unique selling point. The assets of a city are not limited to their temples, waterways, and vistas; they also include the character, vitality, and creativity of the people that live in it. In some cities, people gladly welcome visitors and show them around; in others, people mix freely across ethnic and religious lines, bonding as one; in others still, local people are gifted creators of fine art, music, or cuisine. These talents are part and parcel of the identity of the city, and should be central to any plans for its future development.

Box 4.5: Institutional Mechanism for Equity and Multistakeholder Participation in Colombo, Sri Lanka

The city consultation process for the provision of services in low-income settlements in Colombo, Sri Lanka, underscores the importance of having an institutional structure in place to facilitate stakeholder participation and bridge the gaps between local government and local communities.

The Colombo City Consultation was started in November 1998, through an agreement signed among the Colombo City Council, an indigenous nongovernment organization, Sevanatha Urban Resource Centre, and the Urban Management Programme. The process aimed to strengthen the existing community development council (CDC) system, which originally comprised around 600 community councils, to enhance community participation, strengthen the capacity for revenue mobilization, and decentralize municipal services. It sought to build goodwill and trust among citizens, government, and development partners.

Key to this was the establishment of a multistakeholder forum that was actively participated in by municipal officials and CDC leaders. The output of this forum was a draft action plan (including policy reforms to be made by the Colombo City Council to recognize the CDCs, and strengthening the institutional and financial components of the CDCs) to leverage the CDC as the primary institution for ensuring that communities continue to meaningfully participate in the development process. The process also highlighted the need for timely, visible improvements in service delivery to demonstrate the effectiveness of the CDC system and city consultation process as an instrument for joint decision making.

Source: E. Pieterse. 2000. Participatory Urban Governance: Practical Approaches, Regional Trends and UMP Experiences. Research paper prepared for Urban Management Program of United Nations Development Programme (UNDP), United Nations Centre for Human Settlements (UNCHS), and the World Bank. http://isandla.org.za/publications/72/

Social and cultural development is surely broader than the physical planning and management of the city, but the shape and functioning of the city facilitates (or inhibits) to some degree the social and cultural life of a city. A public plaza creates an opportunity to mingle; a bike trail or shuttle service connects cultural dots across the urban fabric; a summer event program showcases the young talent, rejuvenating local cultural assets. GrEEEn City Action Plans (GCAPs) identify and elaborate on initiatives and actions that support the social and cultural development of local people, including for the poor. This approach leads to more dynamic and vibrant cities.

GrEEEn Cities also look at the distributional efforts of basic urban development processes. Fundamentally, cities grow by urbanizing peripheral lands and constructing buildings and infrastructure on them. But what is the distribution of these "products" of urbanization? What share of land, housing, and services go to the poor, semi-poor, and middle class? These questions are fundamental to the degree of equity that a society attains. The processes by which urban assets get distributed within society are governed by local institutions and can be impacted by urban planning, infrastructure delivery, and development control activities. This is one of the reasons that inclusive approaches to urban development emphasize the assessment of the needs of vulnerable groups, willingness-to-pay studies, appropriate standards, redistributional instruments such as subsidies (where required), and other features of socially sound urban development (Salzman et al. 2014).

A systematic approach to determine the extent to which urban infrastructure and services are equitable was undertaken in the City Project in Los Angeles, United States. This project identified and addressed disparities in the access to urban recreation and social services. Specifically, the City Project involved conducting numerous studies on the inequitable access to green space in Southern California by race, ethnicity, and class. It initiated actions for "healthy green land use" and participatory community planning processes (The City Project 2015).

Generating Social Benefits through Place-Based Urban Projects

GrEEEn Cities are concerned with making great urban places. It is not enough to build networks of urban roads. This is very helpful in connecting people, including the urban poor, to employment and service areas. It is not enough to deliver affordable water and power services, although these are needed to satisfy basic needs and to engage in productive economic activity. The social aspirations of GrEEEn Cities go further: to make being in the city more rewarding.

GrEEEn Cities explicitly seek to create a high-quality public realm that all residents can enjoy. What is the experience of walking down this street, through this low-income neighborhood, along this river? The Landscape Urbanism concept, for instance, uses networks of open spaces as the organizing principle for developing a city (Rouse and Bunster-Ossa 2013). Neighborhoods are connected to each other and to city center(s) through a network of parks, paths, and other open spaces. This approach improves access to urban open spaces in low-income communities, enhances connections to employment areas, and improves the quality of life (Box 4.6).

Box 4.6: Strengthening Inclusive Growth through Regionally Balanced Urbanization of Secondary Cities Development

Focusing on rural–urban poverty linkages and the rapid urbanization in Southeast Asia, the inclusive development of second-tier cities and secondary towns is crucial. Case studies from Myanmar, Viet Nam, and the Greater Mekong Subregion exemplify this point.

Myanmar: The Capacity Building Support of the Asian Development Bank (ADB) to the Ministry of Construction enabled the preparation of a scoping study for the Strategic Development Plan for Green Mandalay, as a potential model for the management of urban development in Myanmar. Forming a baseline understanding of Mandalay's issues concerning quality of life, the study identified GrEEEn City actions for a clustered city development, as Mandalay features townships that originally emerged from rural villages, making the city into a cluster of urban, peri-urban, and rural areas. The actions include strengthening of spatial planning and building regulations; the building of institutional capacity for that; decreased carbon footprint from human settlements development, transport, and solid waste; lower flood risks through proper management of new developments and solid waste collection; lower groundwater supply pressure; lower risks of soil and water pollution; and improved access to basic services for Mandalay's poor.

Viet Nam: Secondary cities development is a key goal in the Framework Master Plan for Urban Development in Viet Nam to 2025 and Vision to 2050. Supporting the master plan's implementation, ADB's Secondary Cities Development Program (Green Cities) supports Ha Giang, Hue, and Vinh Yen in combining urban development and environmental planning through integrated infrastructure and services improvements, which preserve environmental resources, foster climate and disaster resilience, increase economic competitiveness, and enhance social equity within these secondary cities. GrEEEn City Action Plans developed under this GrEEEn Cities Initiative guide the following investment loan, which features a results-based lending modality for improved urban management and implementation performance.

Greater Mekong Subregion: ADB's Corridor Towns Development Projects and Livelihood Support for Corridor Towns Project in Cambodia, the Lao People's Democratic Republic, and Viet Nam aim at a regionally balanced development from which the selected towns can benefit from increased traffic and trade flows along the Greater Mekong Subregion corridors. Corresponding environmental and economic infrastructure investments are oriented toward green growth and climate resilience, with a particular focus on poor communities. This is connected to potentials concerning tourism, as well as local products and value chains. Different types of urban, peri-urban, and rural settlements are to be connected in a transport system, which strengthens regional integration and local development objectives.

Strategic policy options for such urban–rural integration cases are straightforward: rural–urban spatial planning and policies need to be integrated; local action and decentralized planning should be promoted; economic competitiveness has to be promoted; improved connectivity can be used to unlock rural economies; and existing assets and skills should be built upon. In order to realize these options, partnerships with the private sector and civil society are crucial in project design and development, implementation and monitoring, as well as capacity building.

Source: R. Naik Singru. 2015. Regional Balanced Urbanization for Inclusive Cities Development: Urban–Rural Poverty Linkages in Secondary Cities Development in Southeast Asia. *Southeast Asia Working Paper Series*. No. 11, July. Manila: Asian Development Bank.

People's Republic of China: Redevelopment for housing for the elderly in Shaoxing, Zhejiang

The place-based approach can also be used to focus resources explicitly on poor or marginalized districts of the city. Many previous urban development paradigms have tried to do this. The best ones have used land tenure and other measures to make sure that local residents become stakeholders in their own community (Mahadevia 2002, Banerjee 1999). With actual ownership comes the sense of responsibility in the fate and greater likelihood of taking positive action. A version of this approach is used in the upgrading of informal neighborhoods in many Asian cities.

Land readjustment is another place-based approach that can give people a bigger stake in urban development. Originated in post-World War II Japan and Republic of Korea, land readjustment (including land pooling and land sharing) is used to make infrastructure improvements to an existing (often unplanned) community (Metropolitan Area Planning Council and Lincoln Institute of Land Policy 2011). Rather than relocating the residents, they give up a share of their land for the infrastructure easements and road rights-of-way. In exchange for the land, they get service improvements and a higher-quality urban environment. While difficult to apply without the proper legal framework, land readjustment has enjoyed a resurgence of late, including as part of an ambitious new ADB-financed project to redevelop multiple informal areas in Ulaanbaatar, Mongolia (ADB 2013f). Box 4.7 presents a recent experience of an urban upgrading project in Ho Chi Minh City, Viet Nam, which combined infrastructure improvements with housing construction and regularization of land tenure.

Community gardens are a powerful tool to turn run-down, unproductive urban spaces into community assets (Box 4.8). Community gardens have been found to increase neighboring property values (Urban Gateway 2015). New York City's more than 800 gardens have since the 1970s helped engage the community, decrease crime, improve diets, and create cleaner environments in the city.

The community garden is also a way to address unused spaces in the city. As a result of disinvestment and out-migration, Detroit had approximately 80,000 vacant buildings and lots in 2013. Residents, nonprofit organizations, and corporations joined together to repurpose vacant lots as community gardens, creating more livable areas while reducing blight. In Montreal, unused areas such as the tops of water reservoirs and the spaces below expressway overpasses are used as community gardens.

Box 4.7: Urban Upgrading Project in Ho Chi Minh City, Viet Nam

The Tan Hoa–Lo Gom Canal is typical of many canals in Ho Chi Minh City, where poor people, clustered in dense informal settlements, are highly vulnerable to flooding. The neighborhood along the canal has flooded an average of five times per year since 2010. The Tan Hoa–Lo Gom Canal Sanitation and Urban Upgrading Project sought to address this by combining infrastructure improvements (dredging, stormwater, and sewerage) with housing construction and regularization of land tenure. The waterfront was also redeveloped, creating usable public open spaces and contributing further to increased property values. The project achieved cobenefits such as better access to services for low-income households and avoided losses resulting from natural hazards.

A twofold approach was taken with respect to housing and resettlement: (i) upgrading of existing low-cost housing and (ii) resettlement of some residents in new apartment buildings. Families participating in the upgrading component were offered low-interest loans for individual septic tanks and house rehabilitation, and given incentive grants to cover installation costs of electricity and water meters. For households relocated due to the canal widening, in situ relocation in three-story apartment blocks was preferred to preserve existing livelihood and social networks.

Due to its integrated approach, its clear identification of interrelated social and environmental problems, and the participation of residents, the project provided tangible benefits to the local residents. The project also demonstrated that in situ relocation is possible by using some remaining large plots of land occupied by obsolete industries that still exist within the city. However, low-rise apartment buildings appear to perform poorly in a context of high land value in the central districts of Ho Chi Minh City. Such an approach was found to be replicable for small areas, but may be more challenging for large-scale applications.

Source: Belgian Development Agency. 2014. Urban Upgrading in Ho Chi Minh City. Reflection paper. January 2014/002. http://www.btcctb.org/files/web/publication/002_Urban%20upgrading%20in%20Ho%20Chi%20Minh%20City_Tan_Hoa_Lo_Gom_Canal_EN.pdf

The community garden should not be for temporary use waiting for more intensive urban development; rather, it should be for planned or adapted use that achieves permanent status under the local zoning code. In Montreal, the city designates community gardens as public parks to protect them from commercial speculation.

The community garden can also be a way to promote social cohesion in local communities. A study of five informal settlements in South Africa found that while community garden only modestly contributed to food security and increased income, they had a wide range of other benefits for women that included reducing social alienation and family disintegration (Van Averbeke 2007).

Tools for Accountability in Urban Service Delivery

A key aspect of equity is ensuring distribution of development benefits and access to those benefits, and the opportunity to participate equally in consultation and development processes. Social accountability in the delivery of urban services is critical. When service providers are more accountable to their clients, including low-income households, service quality and affordability tend to improve.

Box 4.8: Community Gardening Program in Montreal, Canada

Responding to its citizens' requests, the city of Montreal has created 97 community gardens and 8,195 allotments since 1975—an approach that has since been adopted by many other cities in Canada and worldwide. The Montreal community gardens serve about 10,000 people a year, which makes the program one of the most significant in North America. The objective of the program is to allow the citizens of Montreal to garden in a specific location to support an activity which contributes to improving the well-being of the community by stimulating social interaction, contributing to city beautification, and producing healthy and nutritive food at little cost.

The city provides the land, the equipment, and the materials necessary for the program to function efficiently. It also repairs the equipment, provides water, collects garden refuse, and offers the services of horticultural animators. Gardening committees, elected by the members' gardeners, supervise daily activities in the garden sites and manage the distribution of plots.

Some gardens are situated on city-owned land that is eventually destined for the construction of apartment buildings. Others occupy land owned by either government or by religious institutions.

The gardens give cohesiveness to the community life of the neighborhood. Gardening activities enable gardeners to fraternize, to fulfill their need for contact with nature, and, in the case of those who take part in the voluntary garden committees, to take an official role in society. Some garden sites organize events to which the whole neighborhood is invited.

Canada: Community gardens in Montreal (*left*) and Vancouver (*right*)

Source: City of Montreal. 2015. Community Gardens. http://ville.montreal.qc.ca/portal/page?_pageid=5977,68887600&_dad=portal&_schema=PORTAL

The first step is to strengthen communication links among service providers and their customers. This gives people the opportunity to express their opinion on service quality and value-for-money, and, in particular, to lodge complaints about inadequate services. Some of the tools that can be used to improve social accountability in service delivery are the following (World Bank 2010a, Sheikh 2011):

- **Participatory planning and budgeting:** provide mechanisms for incorporating stakeholder priorities, identifying differing agendas of different stakeholders, and seeking compromise and consensus

- **Citizen charter:** enhances accountability by providing citizens with a clear understanding of service delivery standards, including timetables, user fees for services, and options for grievance redress
- **Citizen monitoring tools and committees:** promote transparency and accountability by providing a formal mechanism to verify local government performance in service delivery or plan implementation (Box 4.9)
- **Citizen report card:** allows service users the opportunity to provide input on service coverage and quality and to identify priority service needs
- **Community scorecard:** empowers service users by giving them a line of communication to the service provider and delivers valuable feedback on service quality

Recent examples for how social accountability has been applied to urban water systems are discussed in the Phnom Penh Water Supply case study (Box 4.10) and the application of the GrEEEn Cities Operational Framework (GCOF) to Urban Water Systems (Insert C).

Box 4.9: GrEEEn City Scorecard for Environmental Improvements in Vinh Yen, Viet Nam

What is the purpose of the scorecard?	The scorecard aims to monitor the improvement of the Dam Vac Lake environment (i.e., water quality, public access, timeliness of development of infrastructure, etc.) following the implementation of Initiative 2 of the GrEEEn City Action Plan (GCAP) to improve the urban environment, including Dam Vac Lake
Where will the scorecard be implemented?	The scorecard will be implemented in the Dam Vac Lake area and along the main tributaries
Who will implement the scorecard?	• A Dam Vac Lake protection committee will be created. It will gather (i) representatives of communities living around the lake, (ii) representatives of the civil society (e.g., youth and women's unions, nongovernment organizations), (iii) representatives of the private sector (e.g., businesses involved in lake-related recreation and tourism as well as real estate developers) • A facilitator such as a nongovernment organization (e.g., GRET) will assist the committee

What are the steps to implement the scorecard?

1. Planning and preparation
- Establish the committee by Vinh Yen City People's Committee
- Identify and train lead facilitators
- Contact and secure cooperation of the relevant service providers (i.e., water supply and drainage company and environment company of Vinh Phuc Province and/or Vinh Yen City)
- Identify the main groups who may have an interest in the protection and development of the Dam Vac Lake
- Develop a work plan and budget for the full scorecard exercise

continued on next page

Box 4.9. *continued*

2. Implement the scorecard
- The committee will develop the GrEEEn City Scorecard by generating and prioritizing issues (i.e., cleanup environment water quality, infrastructure development, tree planting, tourism development, public access, etc.)
- Input and/or indicators will be developed (e.g., individual, public, and industrial outlets discharging directly in the lake, public area around the lake, area covered with trees, water quality parameters, timeliness of construction, etc.)

3. Develop an input tracking matrix: example of such a matrix is presented below

Input/Indicator	Entitlement/Plan Budget	Existing Situation	Remark/Comments
Number of public outlets discharging in the lake	Only public storm sewers to discharge in the lake	Xx combined outlets (waste/stormwater still discharging)	
Area planted with trees	12 hectares	6 hectares	Delay in planting
Shoreline cleanup	Cleanup every week	Cleanup not regularly done	Lack of employees
Expenditure on sewage system	$4 million	$3 million	Delay in hiring contractor

4. Develop a matrix for scoring the performance: could be done by subgroups (women, businesses, etc.)

	Community Criteria	Score (1–5)	Reasons/Comments
A	Quality of environment		
A-1	Shoreline cleanliness	2	Presence of waste at different location; no regular cleanup
A-2	Water quality for bathing	3	Improving but still under national criteria;
A-3	...		
B	Transparency and efficiency of construction		
B-1	Timeliness of wastewater sewage system	3	Delay in construction
B-2	...		

5. Develop the scorecard for the service providers
- The water supply and drainage company and other relevant services will carry out a self-evaluation of the services provided under the GCAP; it will help the committee to assess the performance from the supply side.
- The steps are almost identical to the generation of the community scorecard as presented above and involves facilitated brainstorming on criteria for self-evaluation and scoring done in small groups of providers.

6. Interface meeting
The main purpose of the interface meeting is to share the scores generated by the committee and by the service providers to ensure that feedback from the community is taken into account, and that concrete measures are taken to improve services and/or maintain good practices. The meeting should provide an opportunity for the committee to provide feedback to service providers and the GCAP Implementation Committee and to negotiate agreements on improving the services under the GCAP together with relevant stakeholders.

Source: ADB. 2015. *Enabling GrEEEn Cities: Vinh Yen GrEEEn City Action Plan.* Manila.

Box 4.10: Phnom Penh Water Supply Authority, Cambodia

The Phnom Penh Water Supply Authority (PPWSA) is the water utility that serves Cambodia's capital city, Phnom Penh, and its surrounding areas. In 1992, it provided poor-quality piped water at a very low pressure (0.2 bar) for only 10 hours a day to only 20% of the city's residents. Nonrevenue water was extremely high at 72% due to illegal connections, manipulation of bills, and physical leakage. Tariffs were extremely low, there was no metering, and less than half of the amounts billed were collected. Staff were underpaid and demoralized. The utility then underwent a dramatic turnaround: staff engaged in corrupt activities were fired, bill payment was enforced, illegal connections were regularized, metering was introduced, and the utility gained autonomy from the municipality in financial and personnel matters. In the next 14 years, the customer base multiplied ninefold to reach over 90% of residents, service quality improved from intermittent to continuous supply of safe drinking water at a good pressure of 2 bar, and nonrevenue water was cut to only 6%. Tariffs were increased and the utility went from being bankrupt to making a modest profit. It now has motivated, well-paid staff.

In order to reach the poorest, the PPWSA established a revolving fund to finance domestic connections to help the poorest connect to the network. The utility now serves more than 27,000 families (14% of all customers) in more than 123 urban poor communities at subsidized tariffs and connection fees, which can be paid in installments. Poor households are entitled to receive subsidies of 30%, 50%, 70%, or 100% of the connection fee, depending upon their financial conditions. These conditions are jointly evaluated by a committee of the utility and local communities, with results being published.

The main lessons from the PPWSA experience are the following:

Water doesn't have to be free
The PPWSA demonstrates that access to water does not mean that it has to be free and that the urban poor will be considerably better off paying for safe, piped water than they would be buying water of questionable quality from private vendors. For instance, Phnom Penh's unconnected residents used to pay KR1,000 a day for water bought from private water vendors; today, they only spend about KR5,000 per month for PPWSA-supplied water.

Cost recovery is vital
By developing a tariff structure where the utility fully recovers its cost of water production and transmission, the utility has become financially viable and is now able to invest in the water infrastructure.

Civil society must be involved
The PPWSA developed a close relationship with its customers. For example, it provided incentives to members of the public who reported illegal connections, and it has set up an effective system to register and resolve complaints.

The remarkable increase in bill collection and the reduction in illegal connections have also highlighted the importance of involving users and civil society in a service that they want and are willing to pay for. The key has been to develop a utility–customer relationship, based on long-term community building rather than short-term contractual relationships. Effective awareness campaigns also enabled the PPWSA to increase tariffs with broad public support.

The PPWSA has shown that through a transparent environment where water utilities have sufficient autonomy, where tariffs can cover costs, where service is equitable to all, and where there is the active involvement of staff and civil society, clean water targets can be met.

Source: Cambodia Water Action: Phnom Penh Water Supply Authority: An Exemplary Water Utility in Asia. http://www.scribd.com/doc/103537906/Cambodia-Water-Action-Phnom-Penh-Water-Supply-Authority-An-Exemplary-Water-Utility-in-Asia

Social accountability can be fostered by giving specific stakeholder groups a voice, such as women in a meeting on a planned transport project in Uzbekistan *(left)* and members of Thuy Xuan commune in Hue City in a public consultation on resettlement sites *(right)*.

Photo Credits: Narendra Singru (left); Pierre Arnoux (right)

City Inclusiveness

City inclusiveness is about promoting equity; it is about creating cities where all can participate in their social, economic, and political life (Box 4.11). This means considering the needs of all users (age, gender, economic status, etc.).

This includes especially the children. World Vision (2014) in a recent report analyzes the ways in which children are able to contribute to safe, healthy, resilient, and prosperous cities by influencing urban policies, processes, and institutions that better reflect the diverse needs of children. It also addresses questions about children's abilities to participate, and how this engagement takes into account their evolving capacities and vulnerabilities.

It proposes the following Guiding Principles for Child Participation:
1. Participation is a right and works to fulfill other rights.
2. Participation is ethical and safe.
3. Participation is meaningful and sustainable.
4. Participation strengthens familial, community, and societal relationships.
5. Participation is a process and method across different sectors.

Box 4.11: How Inclusive Is Your City?

- How informed are citizens about the municipal budget?
- Do people in your city have equal access to clean water, clean neighborhoods, and other services?
- How attractive is your city to investors?
- How safe is your city to live and work in?
- How often do the elected representatives meet their constituencies?
- Are all ethnic groups given equal opportunities?
- How much are women involved in citywide decision making?
- How participatory is the decision-making process?
- Are the poor given proper consideration?

Source: UN-Habitat. 2000. Global Campaign on Good Urban Governance. Concept paper. Nairobi.

The report also makes recommendations for improving children's participation in urban contexts. Through meaningful participation, children are able to become actively involved in social and cultural development and to bring positive social change among their peers and communities (also see Box 4.12).

Another example of children's involvement in the planning of the city is the Humara Bachpan campaign in India (Sturgis 2015, Humara Bachpan 2014). This campaign calls for the inclusion of child-friendly components in urban policies. As part of this campaign, children are organized into child clubs. Through this structure, children from slums have found a voice to

Box 4.12: Greater Mekong Subregion Youth Caravan Visits Hue

During the 2014 Greater Mekong Subregion (GMS) Youth Caravan, a group of 36 youths from the six GMS countries spent 8 days traveling through the region to see regional integration and visiting projects financed by the Asian Development Bank. One of the stops was in Hue, Viet Nam, where the Provincial People's Committee hosted the group and the Department of Planning and Investment presented its GrEEEn City project to the youth. The project made a strong impression on the participants. "Hue Green City is [an] unprecedented project in Viet Nam [whose] aims are not simply about protecting the environment but are local people-oriented and ensure the sustainable development of regional economy," remembers Minh Duc, a student from Ha Noi University who joined the caravan. Vu Ngoc Bich, who is studying in Ho Chi Minh City, recounts that "the project has a very clear vision for considerable and long-term benefits to Hue," especially in light of the impact climate change may have on Viet Nam. Thac Thu Trang from Ha Noi recalls the many actions the Provincial People's Committee suggested to improve the city and plans the local authority has made, such as promoting bicycle use in the city center through bike lanes and bike sharing. The project inspired Tan Tien Le from Viet Nam University to suggest initiatives from other cities that Hue could take on, such as setting up a 360-degree cinema in the Citadel to help tourists better understand its history. A project that can inspire the youth has a much stronger potential for long-term sustainability and impact through its broader base of support.

Viet Nam: GMS Youth Caravan on their tour through the Greater Mekong Subregion

Photo Credit: Dang Huu Cu

Source: This box was provided by Lainie Thomas, social development specialist (civil society and participation), Human and Social Development Division, Southeast Asia Department, Asian Development Bank, who consolidated inputs provided by young participants of the GMS Youth Caravan visit to Hue, Viet Nam.

The key to an inclusive approach is the context-specific identification of a project's stakeholders, such as children or ethnic minority populations, in order to design solutions that meet these groups' specific needs.

articulate their concerns about issues affecting their lives. Through these child clubs, groups of children are creating detailed "social maps" of their marginalized neighborhoods to voice their concerns about public spaces. The "young mappers," together with adult facilitators, traverse the slums and learn to understand their neighborhoods' shape, street connectivity, and density of houses. Based on this information, the skeleton of the map is formed and further specific information added. The children then identify their needs regarding public areas that could be potential spaces for playing, equipped with urban street furniture. These maps are presented to local officials by the child clubs to inform the planning process.

Inclusive Resettlement

Investment programs often involve land acquisition and the relocation of population. Thus, the displacement of the population may create social impacts and social disruption. Vulnerable groups are likely to be disproportionately affected or at risk of further impoverishment due to the impact of resettlement.

The GrEEEn Cities Operational Framework (GCOF) provides a conduit for minimizing conflicts during resettlement and land acquisition. This can promote and contribute to equity, inclusiveness, and poverty reduction. This application also furthers quality of life by providing a clean, safe, and healthy living environment for relocated households.

Resettlement is inclusive when there is equitable access for the entire relocated population, including the poorest and most vulnerable, to urban infrastructure, land, housing, social services, and livelihood opportunities. Inclusive resettlement is particularly built through a participatory planning and decision-making process shared between various levels of government, relocated communities, and civil society (UN-Habitat 2013a). Resettlement is not only about rebuilding houses for all people, but also about reviving livelihoods and rebuilding the community and the environment. In that sense, inclusive resettlement has to be sustainable, resilient, and affordable.

Sustainable. Resettlement will be sustainable if it can maintain the community structure, preserve the social networks, and allow relocated households to continue their livelihood

Photo Credit: Sushma Kotagiri

People's Republic of China: Resettlement area in Shaoxing, Zhejiang

or to create new livelihood opportunities. Without sustainable resettlement, the relocated population may abandon the new sites. Sustainability is also built through a proactive community, government, and civil society, maximizing the potentials of the community's or city's available resources for its development. Assessing the needs and vulnerabilities of affected populations, with particular attention to livelihoods, is essential during resettlement planning.

Resilient. Resilience could be, in specific cases, an alternative to resettlement. The question of relocating or not relocating may be pertinent to populations living in disaster-prone areas. They are often the most vulnerable and their livelihoods are site-specific; relocation may impoverish them. Building safe and resistant houses and infrastructure and training the population on how to build resiliency to future disasters may be a more sustainable option.

Affordable. Land, housing, and urban services should be affordable to all relocated households. Adequate compensation and assistance and financial mechanisms should be proposed to allow the poor and vulnerable to have access to land, housing, and urban services.

The implementation of the GCOF contributes to successful relocation. The following are lessons learned from successful resettlement practices, which follow this approach:

Consultation and participation. Successful resettlement includes obligatory broad community consultation and participation. Affected communities have to be involved in critical relocation and implementation decisions (i.e., site selection, identification of basic need, house design, and implementation). The presence of an institutional structure in place to facilitate stakeholder participation and bridge the gaps between local governments and local communities should be considered to build goodwill and trust between the citizens, government, and development partners (see the case of the city consultation process in Colombo, Sri Lanka, Box 4.5). Close coordination among various stakeholders, including citizens, from the early stages of the planning process is also a key ingredient of success. It can be done through the creation of community development committees (see the case of the Lunawa Environmental Improvement and Community Development Project, Box 4.13).

Box 4.13: GrEEEn Resettlement Example in Colombo, Sri Lanka

Colombo, Sri Lanka is vulnerable to floods during the monsoon season, since most areas are less than 6 meters above sea level. Frequent flood damage persisted in certain areas, including those surrounding Lunawa Lake where there was an inadequate drainage system with continuous heavy industrial wastewater discharge into the lake. The people living in the Lunawa Lake catchment area suffered from habitual flooding 4–6 times per year. The Lunawa Lake, which had once significantly supported the fisheries industry and played a key role as the base for a life-supporting system, had become a biologically dead lake contaminated with toxic waste. Thus, having adequate flood control and an improved drainage system in these areas remained an urgent priority.

The Lunawa Environmental Improvement and Community Development Project was an innovative initiative signed in December 2001 between the Japan Bank for International Cooperation and the Government of Sri Lanka with two main components: (i) technical and (ii) human settlements and community development. The project improved the drainage system through the construction of new stormwater drainage systems and rehabilitation of existing canals and streams. Upgraded housing, amenities, and solid waste management created a hygienic and pleasant environment.

In order to achieve the project objective while at the same time meeting the livelihood needs of the local residents, the project focused on community mobilization. Community development committees consisting of representatives of the affected communities were formed and were closely involved in the project from the planning stage. UN-Habitat was a partner in the implementation of the project's community development component. Nongovernment organizations and Japan Overseas Cooperation Volunteers worked in partnership to improve the living conditions of the people. Close coordination among various stakeholders, including citizens, from the early planning stages was significant in achieving the success of the project.

The project has broken ground in many significant ways. One feature of the project was the solid partnership among different stakeholders—the Ministry of Urban Development and Sacred Area Development, local authorities, and local nongovernment organizations. The latter were instrumental in the social marketing (through multiple home visits and follow-up interactions) of proposed interventions to increase the trust of affected communities in the project team and government agencies. This was done in combination with strong community mobilization (establishment of community development committees comprising representatives of affected communities), development of an innovative community consultation mechanism in the form of neighborhood development forums (these extended and maintained the communication links between resettled households, residents of host communities, and concerned stakeholder agencies), and establishment of the community information center.

The Lunawa catchment area was home to around 18,000 households, 883 of whom were resettled. The project was able to ensure the security of tenure of former slum dwellers who had to relocate to make way for the project. Damaged houses had to be either refurbished, or the households had to relocate. There were three options for resettlement: (i) resettlement in one of four resettlement sites prepared by the project, (ii) resettlement in land purchased by project-affected persons (self-relocation), or (iii) settle in the original site after regularizing the plots if possible (on-site resettlement). The project undertook several additional tasks with the active participation of all stakeholders and with the objective of making all affected people voluntary partners and beneficiaries of the project, such as creating links between the formal banking sector and urban poor households (bank accounts were opened initially for project-affected persons to receive entitlements), as well as creating numerous community-based organization and strengthening existing community-based organizations that received community contracts to build drains, service roads, community centers, etc. within the resettlement sites and other parts of the project area. Apart from providing a sense of ownership to the communities, these

continued on next page

Box 4.13. *continued*

activities have contributed significantly toward livelihood restoration among the project-affected people. In many cases, affected individuals and families were able to improve upon their previous situation by tapping into opportunities provided by the project.

The project is a replicable model which attempted to strike a balance between the needs and interests of heterogeneous types of people—the illiterate and the literate, rich and poor, and landless and landowners—by building innovative partnerships and ensuring the participation of all stakeholders from planning until implementation.

Source: UN-Habitat. 2009. *Innovative Approaches for Involuntary Resettlement: Lunawa Environmental Improvement & Community Development Project*. Nairobi.

Photo Credit: Pierre Arnoux

Viet Nam: Resettlement of boat people in Phu Mau commune of Thua Thien Hue province provided them with fully serviced houses along a canal, assuring continued access to their boats as their main source of livelihood

Importance of planning. Planning is essential in the development of new relocation sites. Making arrangements with government and public utilities to provide infrastructure services (e.g., water, sewerage, electricity, and solid waste collection) and social services (e.g., schools, transport, and health clinics) on a timely basis is essential. These services also have to be affordable. The roles and contributions of each stakeholder have to be clearly defined. The case of urban environmental planning and management in Phuket City, where guidelines for environmental planning and management were drafted by a highly inclusive body (Urban Environmental Policy Drafting Subcommittee), illustrates the importance of planning in successful resettlement (Box 4.14).

Box 4.14: Inclusiveness, Participation, and Cohesion in Urban Governance in Phuket, Thailand

The urban environmental planning and management approach implemented in the Municipality of Phuket, Thailand, demonstrates the GrEEEn Cities Operational Framework elements of economic competitiveness (public–private dialogue) and equity (inclusiveness), as well as several enabling factors (strategies, governance, institutions, civil society, and the private sector).

Guidelines for environmental planning and management in Phuket were drafted by a highly inclusive body (the Urban Environmental Policy Drafting Subcommittee), which comprised representatives of local communities, the academe, nongovernment organizations, local governments, and the business sector. Each sector had concrete roles and contributions: the academe was involved in environmental and social impact assessments, nongovernment organizations worked closely with community-based organizations in raising awareness of ecotourism and broader environmental awareness in everyday life, while the municipal government functioned mainly as a leader and/or facilitator.

The city consultation process involved a mix of several interventions at various levels. Recycling and prudent use of resources were encouraged at the community level. A fund was started to encourage recycling and was used to support capacity-building initiatives in low-income neighborhoods. The organization of youth into waste management teams allowed them to increase their income while learning about proper waste management. Policy frameworks were developed and pushed at a provincial level to guarantee consistency between localities, and action plans were developed through a local and participatory process. Such coordination and planning arrangements strengthened the linkages between local, provincial, and national infrastructure development initiatives.

The most distinguishing aspect of the Phuket process was the level of cohesion between the different stakeholders and its broad-based inclusiveness. Each stakeholder had a well-defined and concrete role and contribution. The city consultation approach was thus effectively used to develop a common understanding and vocabulary across stakeholders. Additionally, the approach enabled the municipality to implement a participatory approach to environmental management, explore innovative approaches to urban governance in the context of national decentralization, and put in place an enabling environment for participatory governance.

Source: E. Pieterse. 2000. Participatory Urban Governance: Practical Approaches, Regional Trends and UMP Experiences. Research paper prepared for the Urban Management Programme of the United Nations Development Programme, United Nations Centre for Human Settlements, and the World Bank. http://isandla.org.za/publications/72/

Favor in situ relocation. Projects that favor in situ relocation often have better results as they preserve the social network and current livelihoods of the population. At a minimum, relocation should take place as close to the original community as possible. A key cause for unsustainable relocation is the distance of the new site from vital resources (productive land and food sources), relatives, social networks, livelihoods, and markets (see the cases of Urban Upgrading Project in Ho Chi Minh City [Box 4.7] and Habitat for Humanity in Viet Nam [Box 4.15]).

Preserve community structure. People belonging to the same community have to be resettled together to a new site to preserve social networks. Housing designs, settlement layouts, and community facilities also have to reflect the community's values in order to facilitate ownership of the new site (see Boxes 4.7 and 4.15).

Box 4.15: Recovery and Resilience in Habitat for Humanity Housing Project, Viet Nam

The floods in September 2011 in the Mekong Delta affected the lives of about 80,600 households, putting more than 200,000 children at risk and destroying up to 1,600 homes. Families were desperate to return to their homes after the flooding, so that children could go back to school and adults could resume their livelihoods. Six months after the disaster, Habitat for Humanity had helped 290 families, or approximately 1,450 people, return to and repair their homes through the distribution of emergency cleaning kits and emergency shelter kits. In addition, the households received training from construction supervisors on how to build resiliency to future disasters. Manjeet Panesar, program officer at Habitat for Humanity, said, "These households now have the knowledge to protect and repair their homes, therefore reducing their own vulnerability to future disasters. A project like this has positive impacts on whole communities as people share these new skills with their neighbors and family members who also live in disaster-prone areas. It's really important to build disaster resilience into people's homes so that their homes continue to provide protection and security."

Source: Habitat for Humanity. 2012. Recovery and Resilience in Vietnam.* 24 April. http://www.habitatforhumanity. uk/page.aspx?pid=1108

* ADB recognizes "Vietnam" as Viet Nam.

The past initiatives described in this chapter demonstrate the applicability of the GCOF, emphasizing equity, inclusiveness, and stakeholder partnership including Urban Management Partnerships in urban and peri-urban areas.

Cobenefits by Interconnecting the 3Es

In designing grEEEn solutions, a cobenefits approach is applied. This approach has helped in its basic form to assess the cumulative benefits of green infrastructure and inclusive green growth initiatives proposed by Vinh Yen and Hue during the formulation of their GrEEEn City Action Plans (GCAPs).

The cobenefits approach has evolved as a means to facilitate climate change mitigation, including green growth, as part of the broader sustainable development agenda. Progress has so far been insufficient on the integration of the three pillars of sustainable development: economic, environmental, and social. For many countries, achieving sustainable development has been sidelined by many challenges on the economic, financial, food, and energy fronts (Santucci et al. 2015, pp. 18–19). Green growth, which has emerged in recent years in response to climate change risks, focused on two of the pillars only—environment and the economy— until policy makers asked for more inclusiveness and social consciousness (Hammer et al. 2011, pp. 14–17). Among developing countries, resource constraints and rapidly changing demographics seriously limit their ability to pursue sustainable development. In this context, climate change mitigation, including green growth, often does not become the overarching goal. Economic development, basic service delivery, and poverty reduction constitute the more pressing sustainable development priorities. The cobenefits approach offers a way by which countries can capitalize on the synergies between climate change mitigation and development priorities, enabling them to advance simultaneously on all fronts of sustainable development. The cobenefits approach is about multiple benefits in different sectors or subsectors resulting from one policy, strategy, or initiative. It refers to the implementation of initiatives, policies, or projects that simultaneously contribute to reducing the impacts from climate variation and disaster risks while solving local environmental problems in cities and, in turn, potentially having other positive developmental impacts such as improvements in public health, energy security, and income generation as well as distribution (Figure 4.3).

Cities lead the path toward an inclusive green global economy within the sustainable development framework and will benefit most from the application of the cobenefits approach. At the city level, the interlinkages between the environment, economic, and social inclusion policies have never been so evident. As the pace of urbanization accelerates, cities in the developing world are driving economic growth, creating jobs and stimulating investments as well as innovations. In the process, however, they are contributing vastly to global warming and environmental degradation leading to unprecedented levels of greenhouse gas (GHG) emissions, loss of biodiversity, water scarcity, and various forms of pollution. Moreover, they primarily attract millions of migrants from the rural areas, many of them unskilled, each lured by the prospect of a better job and higher income. Without adequate infrastructure, housing, and employment opportunities, these migrants become socially excluded, confined to a life of deprivation and urban poverty. However, amid the myriad of pressures they confront, the cities are ideally placed to demonstrate how the cobenefits approach to climate change, including green growth, can contribute to improving the environment, economy, and social inclusiveness of their metropolitan areas and urban centers. There is also a growing realization that climate change initiatives on their own, without being linked to waste, transport, housing,

Figure 4.3: Cobenefits Approach to Climate Change Mitigation and Inclusive Green Growth

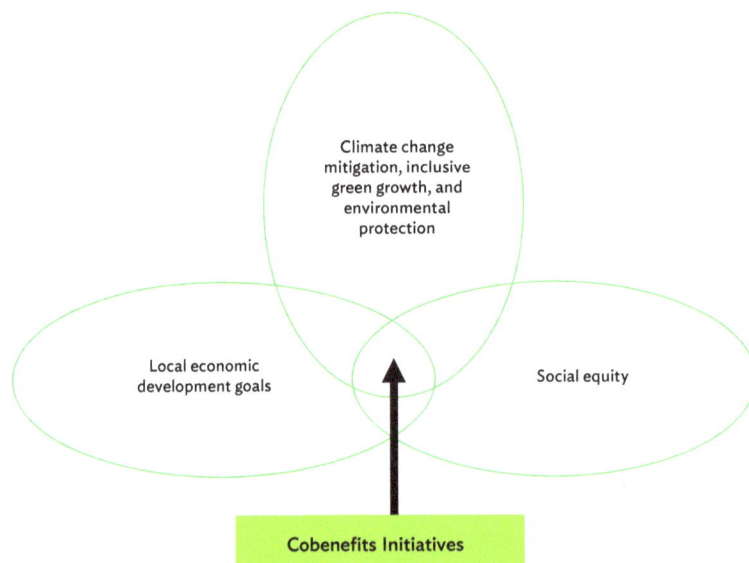

Source: Adapted from J. Puppim de Oliveira, C.N.H. Doll, and A. Suwa. 2013. Urban Development with Climate Co-Benefits: Aligning Climate, Environmental and Other Development Goals in Cities. *UNU-IAS Policy Report*. Yokohama: UNU-IAS. p. 7, Figure: Framework of Co-Benefits Approach for Cities. http://archive.ias.unu.edu/resource_centre/urban_development_with_climate_cobenefits-e.pdf

and energy, run the risk of weaker political support and effectiveness. Countries such as Brazil, the People's Republic of China, India, Indonesia, and Japan are demonstrating that it is possible to promote win–win strategies in climate change mitigation, environmental quality, and socially inclusive local development through the cobenefits approach (Box 4.16).

Applying the cobenefits approach to developing GrEEEn Cities entails, first and foremost, a thorough understanding of the direct and indirect environmental, economic, and equity impacts of proposed green infrastructure or green growth initiatives. A climate change-induced initiative, such as inclusive green growth, impacts both producers and consumers in the city. The direct impacts include all the changes in the producers' and consumers' activities as a direct consequence of the initiative. There are also broader indirect or induced impacts that follow from the direct impacts. In the cobenefits approach, both direct and indirect impacts are analyzed to show the aggregate impacts of a proposed initiative, program, or project. The Organisation for Economic Co-operation and Development (OECD) distinguished between the direct and indirect impacts to measure the cumulative benefits of green growth initiatives. The direct impacts come from (i) changes in input use resulting in altered costs, (ii) changes in waste or pollution output levels resulting in altered costs, or (iii) changes in asset value of individual properties or areas attributable to the environmental initiatives. The indirect or induced impacts may be traced to improved city attractiveness due to changed environmental quality or amenities that may influence both personal and business relocation or expansion decisions. Or they may be ascribed

Box 4.16: Cobenefits of Community-Based Solid Waste Management in Yogyakarta, Indonesia

Indonesia is a country that has experienced rapid economic growth in the last 10 years. Accompanying this has been an increased level of urbanization. Inadequate urban infrastructure and basic services have intensified environmental pollution in many cities. In the city of Yogyakarta, an organized community-based initiative for solid waste management has been gaining popularity since 2005. The first community to initiate this was Sukunan Village in 2003 and since then other neighborhoods in the region have replicated the scheme. Disseminated further through newspapers and electronic media, as well as governments, schools, nongovernment organizations, and by word of mouth, Community-Based Solid Waste Management (CBSWM) has spread, prompting the Environment Agency of the Province of Yogyakarta to establish the Association of Yogyakarta CBSWM. It currently has more than 150 community members throughout the province.

The growth of CBSWM in Yogyakarta had led to a decrease in solid waste by as much as 28% in 2008–2010 in the participating areas, possibly contributing to savings in public health with fewer reported cases of dengue fever. Communities also became cleaner as the number of open dumps and open burning sites decreased. Many economic benefits have also been associated with the growth of CBSWM in the province. These include savings in transport costs for collection and increased income generated from recycling through a socially inclusive, community-based approach. For example, the economic value of reused and recycled products, mostly from handicraft production using plastic solid waste as raw materials, was estimated at $430,000 in 2010.

Source: Based on work by Widodo Pramono in J. Puppim de Oliveira, C.N.H. Doll, and A. Suwa. 2013. Urban Development with Climate Co-Benefits: Aligning Climate, Environmental and Other Development Goals in Cities. *UNU-IAS Policy Report*. Yokohama: UNU-IAS. http://archive.ias.unu.edu/resource_centre/urban_development_with_climate_cobenefits-e.pdf

to the changes in pollution or emission levels or other policies and/or programs that may influence employee productivity because of reduced absenteeism due to illnesses (Hammer et al. 2011, p. 16). Zhou and Parves Rana (2012) cite the indirect social impacts of urban green space to individuals as (i) providing recreational opportunities, (ii) promoting physical health, (iii) enhancing social ties, and (iv) offering educational opportunities. For the city, urban green space can bolster regional identity and competitiveness, boosting tourism performance.

Cobenefits valuation is not a straightforward task, and the methodology applied to GrEEEn Cities must consider local conditions and the nature (direct or indirect) as well as beneficiaries of the cobenefits (governments, communities, individuals, or project developers). There is abundant literature on the cobenefits of climate change mitigation and low-emission development strategies. Not many studies, however, quantify cobenefits and even fewer have done so in a systematic way. The cobenefits extensively discussed are those that link climate change mitigation and air pollution policies with improved public health, specifically the avoided costs resulting from the synergy between these policies. The Netherlands Environmental Assessment Agency conducted a study for the OECD, for instance, and found that measures to reduce GHGs to 50% of 2005 levels by 2050 can reduce the number of premature deaths from chronic exposure to air pollution by 20%–40% (PBL 2009). While the cobenefits approach is growing in importance with respect to reducing GHGs to support sustainable development, there are others who assert that actions based on the approach should be measurable, reportable, and verifiable. In further developing and applying methods for the quantitative valuation of the cobenefits of climate change mitigation, the Ministry of the Environment of Japan (2009) has produced a framework with three major classifications taking into account local conditions, and the nature as well as beneficiaries of the cobenefits (Table 4.1).

Table 4.1: Levels of Valuation Methodologies for the Cobenefits Approach to Climate Change

Level	Description of Valuation Methodology	Explanation
1	No calculation is made. The valuation is done based on criteria corresponding to the actual details of the initiative.	In cases when it is difficult to quantify and calculate the cobenefits, data are difficult to obtain, and quantitative evaluation is difficult, one option is to evaluate the benefits using predetermined criteria for qualitative assessment. This approach is the easiest to implement.
2	A quantitative valuation is conducted to the extent possible using predetermined equation(s) and the available measurement data.	This is a simple method to implement a quantitative valuation of cobenefits. Data permitting, it uses actual measurements for a quantitative calculation of the cobenefits. Where no measurement data are available, default or proxy values are used.
3	A rigorous quantitative valuation is conducted using measurement data for initiatives and using specific equations.	This is a more robust method to implement a quantitative valuation of cobenefits. It generally uses actual measurement data and specific equations. Because this method requires data measurements and the formulation of equations, this is the most difficult of the valuation methodologies.

Source: Government of Japan, Ministry of the Environment. 2009. *Manual for Quantitative Evaluation of the Co-Benefits Approach to Climate Change Projects.* https://www.env.go.jp/en/earth/cc/manual_qecba.pdf

For developing countries, Levels 1 and 2 will likely apply more often given the lack of relevant data; unless grants are used to build models with the specific equations and, subsequently, to collect the data for calculating the cobenefits under Level 3. To illustrate that the valuation methodologies used will differ depending on the nature and recipient of the benefits, data availability, and ease or difficulty of measurement in a given country, a comparative summary can be prepared (Table 4.2). In the GCAPs formulated for the secondary cities of Hue and Vinh Yen under the GCOF, a Level 1 valuation methodology of cobenefits has been used to identify and discuss the cumulative benefits of proposed green infrastructure interventions.

Quantifying cobenefits is challenging, but there are existing valuation methodologies that can be applied to present a more coherent and organized approach for developing GrEEEn Cities. In the United Kingdom, well-designed, planned, and managed green infrastructure has brought about a wide range of benefits to local communities and places, underpinning sustainable development. Cognizant of the difficulties associated with identifying and quantifying the cobenefits of green infrastructure or green assets, the United Kingdom based Green Infrastructure Valuation Network has developed a green infrastructure valuation tool kit (GIVaN 2013). The tool kit identified some of the valuation techniques that may be applied in capturing the cobenefits or wide range of benefits (Table 4.3). Some of these valuation techniques are already used in developing countries such as Viet Nam, particularly for projects under official development assistance. ADB's guidelines for economic analysis of projects also cover these valuation techniques and prescribe their use as and when

Table 4.2: Examples of Key Areas and Valuation Methodologies for the Cobenefits Approach to Climate Change

Initiative Using Cobenefits Approach	Details of Cobenefits	Recommended Valuation Methodology	Target Development Goal
Aerobic treatment of domestic wastewater	• Prevented leakage of methane otherwise generated from oxidation pond • Improved public health and economic productivity	Level 2 or 3	• Environmental protection • Economic growth
Improvement of public transport systems and introduction of light-rail transit and other public transport systems	• Reduced air pollution and emissions due to reduced use of fossil fuels • Greater activity of people, goods, services, and local economy stimulation	Level 2 or 3 Level 1 or 2	• Environmental protection • Economic growth, social equity
Methane gas recovery and reuse from municipal solid waste management	• Reduction of waste • Improved income streams for businesses involved • Prevented generation of offensive odors	Level 2	• Environmental protection • Economic growth • Social equity

Source: Government of Japan, Ministry of the Environment. 2009. *Manual for Quantitative Evaluation of the Co-Benefits Approach to Climate Change Projects.* https://www.env.go.jp/en/earth/cc/manual_qecba.pdf

Table 4.3: Approaches to the Valuation of Green Infrastructure and Environmental Goods

Valuation Methodology	Description
Contingent valuation	A survey method that aims to capture individual preferences for a change in the provision of a good or service through assessing willingness to pay or willingness to accept compensation.
Hedonic pricing	This method relates the price of a marketed good to a nonmarketed good, the most common of which are property and labor. The property value approach is the most commonly used. It consists of observing differences in the values of property between locations and isolating the effect of an ambient environmental quality on the property values.
Travel cost method	This takes the cost of getting to a site as the value attributed to the good or service. The value people place on a good or environmental space is inferred from the time and cost they incur in traveling to it.
Effect on production	This measures the effects an initiative or project may have on the output, cost, or profitability of producers through its effects on their environment and the welfare of consumers.
Preventative expenditure	This is typically used when comparing the benefits provided by green infrastructure to the costs of providing engineering solutions (e.g., flood protection) and/or replacement cost approaches.
Benefit transfer	Effectively adopts or adapts information from valuation studies elsewhere, using a variety of techniques, and applies them in a new context.
Specific values	This value is effectively a shadow price required by the government to adopt in a public sector cost–benefit analysis.

Source: Green Infrastructure Valuation Network. 2013. *Building Natural Value for Sustainable Economic Development: The Green Infrastructure Valuation Toolkit User Guide.* http://www.greengrowth.org/?q=publication/green-infrastructure-valuation-tool-kit-user-guide

applicable. In addition, there are sector-specific ADB guidelines for economic analysis which can be applied in conducting a more systematic and rigorous Level 3 valuation of cobenefits.[15] Bringing these techniques together will go a long way in formulating a coherent framework for the cobenefits valuation of climate change mitigation including green growth initiatives in the rapidly urbanizing cities of the developing world.

Bringing together the 3Es and bearing in mind the potential for cobenefits, Insert C illustrates the integrated application of the GCOF to urban water systems as a concluding example for this chapter.

---

[15]   See, for example, ADB (1997, 1998, 2000, 2007a, 2007d, 2013b).

Introduction

The integrated urban development and environmental planning principles central to the GrEEEn Cities Operational Framework (GCOF) are critical for developing sustainable urban water systems.[a] Many of the great cities and city-states in history—Rome, Carthage, Constantinople, Baghdad, London, New York City, Beijing, and Tokyo—developed around water bodies. The built environment of cities has, with time, hindered the natural flows of water bodies that these cities sought to utilize and harness. The mismatch between these natural flows and the administrative boundaries of cities has meant that extensive distribution systems have been developed to enable water from watersheds outside a city's administrative boundaries to be transported into the city. As cities worldwide seek to cope with growing demands for water, future solutions will rely at least as much on more improved water resources management as on further augmenting water supply sources. Thus, an integrated approach that includes a special focus on urban watersheds is critical.

New York and Beijing provide examples of how two very different megacities have addressed urban water infrastructure and services through integrated solutions, multitiered decision making, and watershed planning. In New York, the water supply was historically sourced from two available water reservoirs outside the city—the Croton Watershed and the mountainous area near the Hudson River. Water from these two large watersheds was transported through huge underground pipes. In about 2000, the water coming from these watersheds became increasingly polluted due to the discharges from industrial and agricultural activities near the two watersheds. The city considered two alternatives to address this problem: (i) to build a multibillion-dollar water treatment plant that would keep the water clean and safe or (ii) to develop financial incentives to reduce the pollution from these activities at source. Following a comprehensive decision-making process, the second option was selected, whereby the city arranged for a financial transfer to these watershed areas to compensate for cutting back on some of the more polluting processes. The city saved billions of dollars by avoiding expensive capital investments, whereas those receiving the financial transfers in the watershed areas were compensated for reducing profitable economic activities that they were previously undertaking. The solution was politically acceptable to key stakeholders, including the residents in New York City and in the two outlying areas (NRC 2000).

In Beijing, per capita water availability of about 120 cubic meters (m^3) in 2013 is less than a tenth of the country's national average (which is itself a third of the world average). Despite a rapidly growing economy and population, Beijing was able to reduce total water demand from around 4.0 billion m^3 in the 1990s to 3.5 billion m^3 in the 2000s through a combination of measures including legislation, regulation, improved water use efficiencies, diversified water supplies, and environmental protection (UNESCAP 2015). The government has played an active role in managing water quotas by establishing benchmarks for water use efficiency for industries and publishing annual technology catalogs to encourage the adoption of promising technologies. Economic instruments such as household user water fees (that have been raised 10 times in the previous 2 decades) have encouraged water conservation. Since

Photo Credit: ADB/Raul Del Rosario

People's Republic of China: A view of white water-river rapids

the 1980s, a conscious effort to diversify water supplies, including utilizing unconventional sources such as reclaimed wastewater and harvested stormwater have paid off—in 2013, reclaimed wastewater accounted for just under a quarter of total water consumption for the year. To address the mismatch between administrative and watershed boundaries, a regional compensation mechanism was introduced whereby monetary compensation would be required from districts and counties that failed to achieve water quality requirements at transboundary monitoring sections.

The evolution of urban water supplies in both these cases relied on a comprehensive, integrated approach, resulting in improvements to water quality on the supply side in New York City, and reductions in water quantity on the demand side in Beijing. Similar thinking is encouraged in the GCOF, where solutions are developed from a wide scoping of available options, without limiting these only to specific sectors or to specific place-bound locations.

The following sections explore some recent case studies that demonstrate the types of initiatives that give insight on grEEEn design, organized around the 3E pillars (economic, environment, and equity) of the GCOF. These examples of "doing things differently," drawn from global experiences, include the use of green infrastructure, unique partnerships (including with the private sector), Smart City and information and communication technology (ICT) solutions, social accountability, and payments for environmental services.[a]

Economy

As part of the economy pillar, GrEEEn Cities are encouraged to identify ways to achieve competitive, resilient growth, including through efficiencies in service delivery, asset management, public–private partnerships (PPPs), revenue generation, and financial innovations. Recent case studies demonstrate interesting and promising ways to engage the private sector in supporting economic growth through the provision of urban services.

In Australia, legislation passed in 2006 has enabled innovative PPPs for urban water management in the state of New South Wales. The Water Industry Competition Act allowed for the development of a competitive private water market through licensing private utilities overseen by the Minister for Water and the Independent Pricing and Regulatory Tribunal (IWCAN 2014). In Sydney, the act has allowed for the development of private water utilities licensed to provide drinking water, refined water, and wastewater services to 20,000 people in homes, shops, and offices in the upcoming Central Park development (Central Park Water 2015). Central Park Water will own, operate, and maintain all water-related infrastructure within Central Park. Through extensive water recycling utilizing membrane bioreactors and reverse osmosis technologies, it will manage water through the full water cycle within the precinct and will allow residents to reduce their drinking water usage by about a half. This water network leverages as many as seven different water sources (including rainwater, stormwater, groundwater, sewage from different sources, irrigation water, and drinking water from the public main) to create both a drinking water supply and a recycled water supply (for nonpotable purposes, identified with color-coded taps).

Flow Systems (2015), which will run the private water utility in Central Park Sydney as well as seven other communities, is also working with developers and the government to develop new multiutility servicing models that bring together energy and water infrastructure and services to reduce costs and improve environmental and livability outcomes. Such multiutility servicing models have been developed in other parts of the world, such as San Francisco, where the San Francisco Public Utilities Commission is composed of three 24–7 service utilities (water, wastewater, and power) and provides retail drinking water and wastewater services to San Francisco, wholesale water to three of the area's counties, and green hydroelectric and solar power to the city's municipal departments (San Francisco Water Power Sewer 2015).

In the Netherlands, the Digital Delta program, which commenced in 2013, provides an interesting model of how cities can partner with academic institutions and the private sector to deliver solutions for the water sector. The program is a partnership between IBM, Rijkswaterstaat (Dutch Ministry for Water), local water authority Delfland, Deltares Science Institute, and the University of Delft, and will allow for the integration and analysis of water data from a wide range of sources through a cloud-based, real-time water management system (IBM 2013). In a country in which more than half of the population is located in areas prone to large-scale flooding, the system can analyze data on weather conditions, water levels, tides, levee integrity, runoff, and other factors, and share it immediately across organizations and agencies. The program has been developed through a number of subprojects focusing on specific issues. For example, data shared with the Delft University of Technology would be used to make timely decisions on maintenance schedules, save costs, and prevent flooding of key assets (tunnels, buildings, and streets). The program hopes to demonstrate that such a Smart City approach (including utilizing big data, analytics, and optimization) to managing the water cycle can be replicated in other cities in the world.

The partnership builds on the advanced water governance model in the Netherlands, which includes 23 regional water authorities that are responsible for regional and local water management in the country. The regional authorities are responsible for areas determined on the basis of subcatchment basins (i.e., watersheds) that cut across municipal boundaries.

The authorities have been effective due to (i) a strong system of legal instruments that support their mandate; (ii) a "stakeholder democracy" whereby authorities consist of farmers, businesses, and managers of natural areas in addition to residents; and (iii) financial independence by having their own tax area where they can charge levees and fees for water supply, waste treatment, and surface water pollution (Dutch Water Authorities 2015).

Another example of innovative partnerships to deliver urban water services is one between Veolia Water, a global water services provider, and Orange, one of Europe's leading telecommunications group, m2ocity, launched in 2011 in France, is an operator specialized in remote environmental data and water meter-reading services. m2ocity allows for water metering service to be established over machine-to-machine (M2M) networks, which can improve the quality of the service for consumers, optimize the water service's performance, and better safeguard water resources (Orange Business Services 2011). At present, an estimated 1,400,000 water meters and other smart sensors are connected to m2ocity's telecommunications infrastructure in France, where 1,500 towns and 25% of the population are now in range (m2ocity 2015). In Paris, water service customers can now follow their daily water consumption online, be automatically alerted in case of leakage, and set up short messaging service (SMS) or e-mail alerts for certain levels of consumption. In addition to automating the water metering and billing process, this approach also educates consumers about their water consumption and habits.

As these case studies demonstrate, PPPs enable cities to harness and utilize technology, data, research, and skills in powerful ways that help to make cities, and their water systems, "smart." At present, a number of initiatives are under way in Asia and globally to develop Smart Cities. In India, Prime Minister Narendra Modi promised 100 Smart Cities by 2022 so as to utilize technology to accelerate economic development and address challenges associated with a growing urban population. In the Republic of Korea, K-Water's Smart Water Management Initiative aims to integrate and manage water through the full water cycle, enabled by advanced ICT (Figure C.1). This includes developing networks of intelligent sensors that allow for two-way communication and utilizing automated systems and models that provide predictions on precipitation, floods, reservoir levels, and operation and maintenance needs. This approach operationalizes the premise that water is an important "asset" for cities that requires proactive management, as opposed to a resource that can be utilized relatively freely.

Environment

The environment pillar is centered on incorporating environmental management into urban planning. For urban water, the key is for cities to recognize the importance of using water resources efficiently through the 3R (reduce, reuse, and recycle) approach.

With the increasing pressure on urban land, the natural areas within the city are frequently at great risk. Public parks and green spaces often provide a refuge from the built environment, serving as the city's "lungs" and also as a means to recharge a city's groundwater. Covering these natural areas with concrete buildings results in greater surface water runoff, preventing this natural recharge from occurring.

In response to this, the concept of "green infrastructure" is becoming increasingly important in urban planning and design (Beauchamp, Adamowski, and Beauséjour 2015). In Europe, this

Figure C.1: Smart Water Management Initiative, Republic of Korea

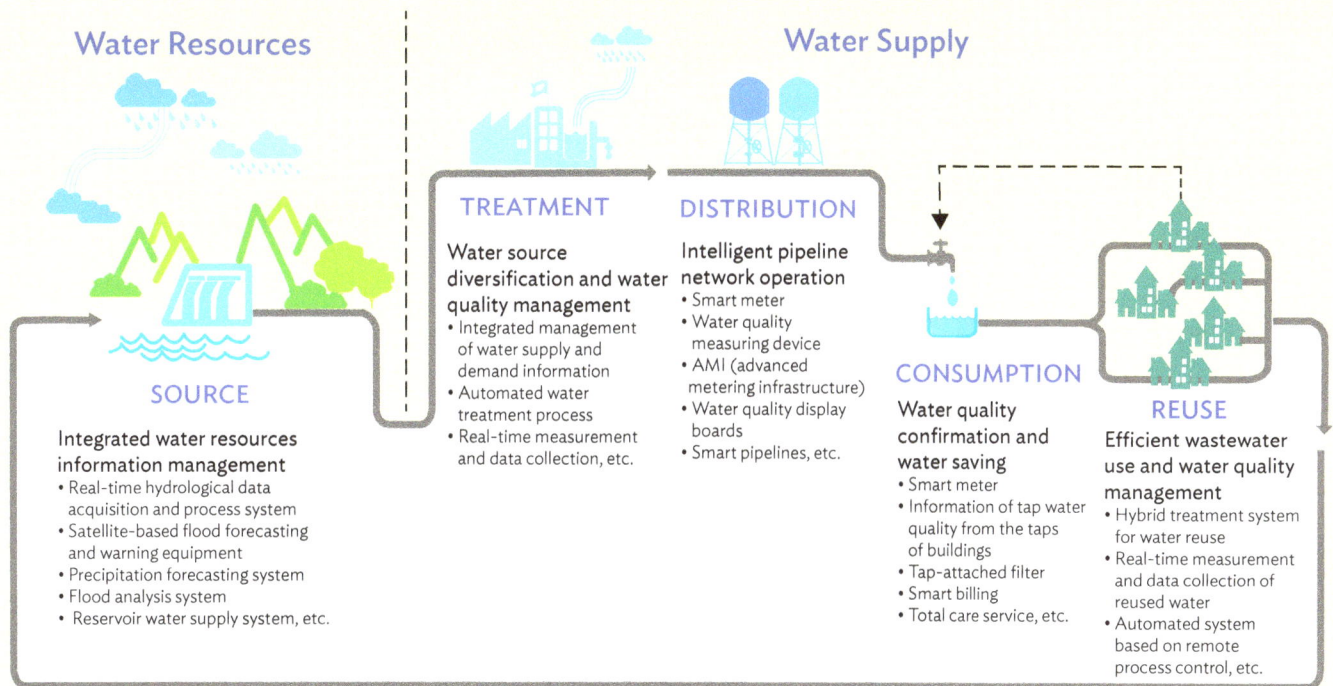

Water Resources

Water Supply

SOURCE

Integrated water resources information management
- Real-time hydrological data acquisition and process system
- Satellite-based flood forecasting and warning equipment
- Precipitation forecasting system
- Flood analysis system
- Reservoir water supply system, etc.

TREATMENT

Water source diversification and water quality management
- Integrated management of water supply and demand information
- Automated water treatment process
- Real-time measurement and data collection, etc.

DISTRIBUTION

Intelligent pipeline network operation
- Smart meter
- Water quality measuring device
- AMI (advanced metering infrastructure)
- Water quality display boards
- Smart pipelines, etc.

CONSUMPTION

Water quality confirmation and water saving
- Smart meter
- Information of tap water quality from the taps of buildings
- Tap-attached filter
- Smart billing
- Total care service, etc.

REUSE

Efficient wastewater use and water quality management
- Hybrid treatment system for water reuse
- Real-time measurement and data collection of reused water
- Automated system based on remote process control, etc.

Source: K-Water. 2015. SWMI. http://english.kwater.or.kr/eng/busi/SWMIPage.do?s_mid=1552

concept focuses more on strategically planning and managing networks of multifunctional green spaces (Natural England 2009). In the United States, this concept focuses more on the environment-friendly network of engineered structures (e.g., green roofs and rainwater collection systems) that, while supporting urban and rural development, also protect natural habitats and reduce the impact of development (US EPA 2015). The benefits of "green infrastructure" are becoming increasingly evident, particularly with respect to urban heat. Recent research in Australia suggests that a 10% increase in vegetation cover can contribute to a reduction in land-surface temperature during the day (Coutts and Harris 2013, p.64).

An important aspect of "green infrastructure" involves the design of integrated water cycle systems (Figure C.2) and the management of water during flood and drought events, and how this can be incorporated into urban design. A visual representation of this concept is the recently constructed Water Square in Rotterdam, The Netherlands (De Urbanisten 2015).

The Water Square resulted from the idea to develop a multifunctional space in the city (which is highly urbanized and located in a high flood-risk district with no natural relief system) that could store and address stormwater runoff during peak rainfall events but also serve as a center of community activity during the remainder of the year. The tiered, multicolored square can collect 1.7 million liters of water from paved surfaces as well as surrounding roofs, and then slowly release that runoff back into the groundwater and nearby canal. When the weather is dry, the square acts as a recreation area, with opportunities for sports, urban theater, and socializing. The square was designed following a participatory process, which included consultations with the local school, church, and gym.

Photo Credit: Berry Gersonius, UNESCO-IHE, The Netherlands

The Netherlands: The Water Square in Rotterdam is a prime example of multifunctional space for flood management and community activities

A flood bypass system along the Segget River in Iskandar, Malaysia, provides another case study of how stormwater can be utilized and managed in an urban setting (Dr Nik and Associates 2015). As part of a national initiative to strengthen the economy and enhance the quality of life in major corridors and cities in Malaysia, flood mitigation measures are being developed in Iskandar to ensure that the Johor Bahru central business district will be protected against 100-year return period floods. At the same time, it was decided an existing water channel (presently covered by a road due to poor water quality, odor, and debris) would be incorporated as a revitalized, central feature of the central business district, with water quality that is suitable for body contact (i.e., Class IIB). To address these goals, a proposal was developed to recycle water for the 1-kilometer stretch between the interchange and coastline, by filtering and pumping water collected at the downstream sump back upstream, ensuring that a base flow is maintained during the dry season. Water lost from evaporation and other means would be replenished from groundwater as well as rainfall harvested from surrounding buildings. The proposal would allow for stormwater to overflow to the sea during storm events, and also for the flexibility to divert water from the Segget River to the channel if the water quality of the river in the future reaches Class IIB.

Perhaps the most well-known example of green infrastructure is the urban renewal project for the Cheonggyecheon stream in Seoul, Republic of Korea, where a 5.8-kilometer long, 10-lane elevated concrete highway was taken down to restore the natural stream underneath. The restoration of the stream, completed in 2005 at a cost of several hundred million dollars, created a green corridor and public recreation space in the postindustrial center of Seoul. Despite the high operational costs associated with pumping nearly all of its water from a nearby river, the project has been considered a success, with multiple environmental and economic benefits. The project is credited with reducing air temperatures in the area, improved biodiversity (including fish and insect species), improved air quality, and improved tourism, with as many as 90,000 visitors per day (Revkin 2009). As a flagship project of the

Figure C.2: Water Recirculation Concept for Green Cities

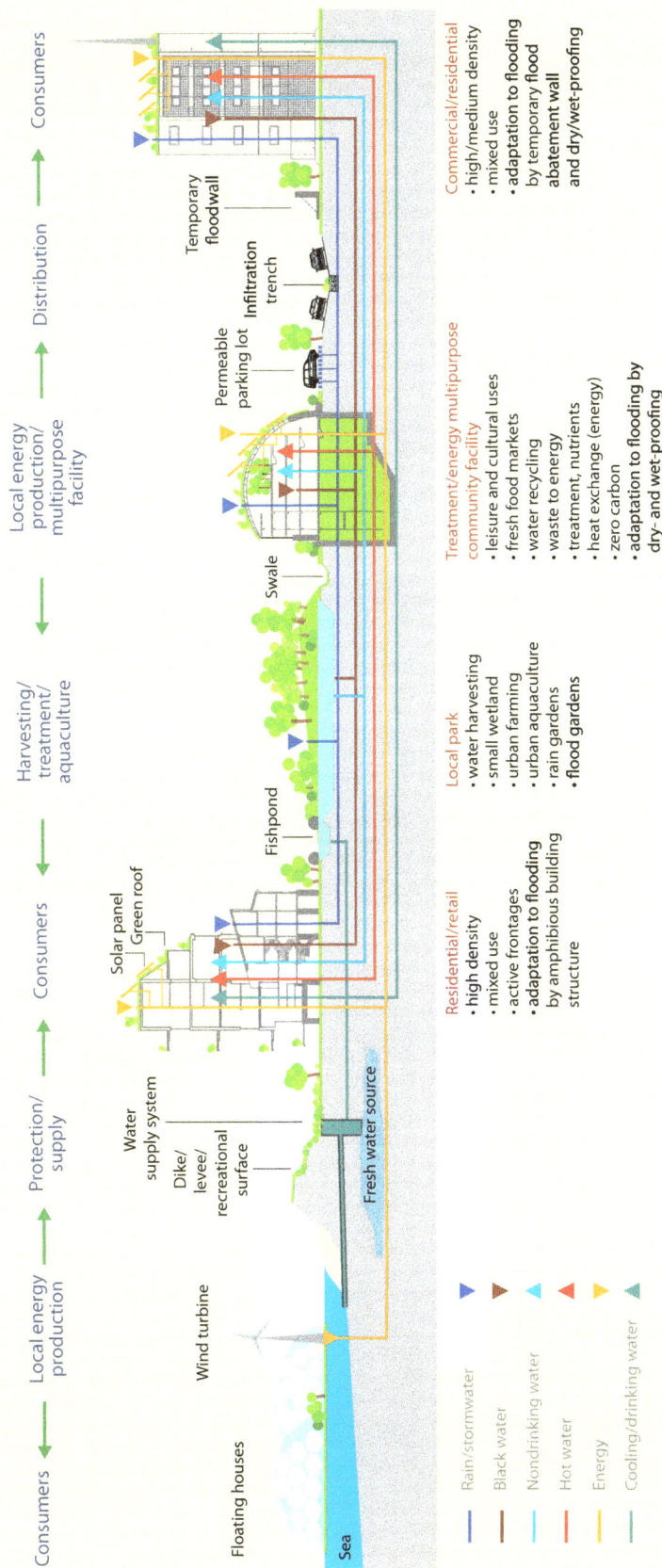

Consumers — Local energy production — Protection/supply — Consumers — Harvesting/treatment/aquaculture — Local energy production/multipurpose facility — Distribution — Consumers

Floating houses

Wind turbine

Water supply system

Dike/levee/recreational surface

Solar panel

Green roof

Fishpond

Swale

Permeable parking lot

Infiltration trench

Temporary floodwall

Fresh water source

Sea

Rain-/stormwater
Black water
Nondrinking water
Hot water
Energy
Cooling/drinking water

Residential/retail
• high density
• mixed use
• adaptation to flooding by amphibious building structure

Local park
• water harvesting
• small wetland
• urban farming
• urban aquaculture
• rain gardens
• flood gardens

Treatment/energy multipurpose community facility
• leisure and cultural uses
• fresh food markets
• water recycling
• waste to energy
• treatment, nutrients
• heat exchange (energy)
• zero carbon
• adaptation to flooding by dry- and wet-proofing

Commercial/residential
• high/medium density
• mixed use
• adaptation to flooding by temporary flood abatement wall and dry/wet-proofing

Source: Z. Vojinovic and J. Huang. 2014. *Unflooding Asia: The Green Cities Way.* London: IWA Publishing for the Asian Development Bank. pp. 41–42. http://www.adb.org/sites/default/files/publication/149304/unflooding-asia.pdf

Photo Credit: Ramola Naik Singru

Republic of Korea: The Cheonggyecheon stream urban renewal project in Seoul is a well-known example of multipurpose green infrastructure solutions

then-mayor of Seoul, the project is seen to have contributed to his election as the country's president a few years later.

These experiences have shown how existing urban infrastructure has been modified or retrofitted, often at significant expense, to become more "green" as cities have developed and their citizens' needs have evolved.[b] Seen from the lens of urban water management, a city's focus shifts from provision of the most essential services (starting with water supply, moving to sanitation and flood protection) toward social amenities and to resilience in the face of climate change.[c] This requires a corresponding shift from infrastructure focused on discrete functions to "green" infrastructure that is sustainable, adaptive, and multifunctional. The need to recognize and plan for this development trajectory is increasingly recognized, particularly in the context of urban areas that are still developing and where costs of "retrofitting" may be more manageable. ADB's ongoing work in Viet Nam considers how to integrate green infrastructure in developing urban spaces in three secondary cities by linking green spaces (to establish "green corridors" that support biodiversity) and designing infrastructure in a way that protects, links, and utilizes these natural hubs (ADB 2014). Current proposals include incorporating or protecting green corridors alongside proposed road developments (as a means to both encourage biodiversity and promote stormwater collection and treatment), and developing or utilizing wetlands or marshes to reinforce embankments and promote natural filtering of stormwater.

Equity

The equity pillar emphasizes the role of social and human capital in urban development, and refers to the equity of access to key services among all citizens, distribution of development benefits and access to those benefits, and the opportunity to participate equally in consultation and development processes.

The more direct aspect of ensuring equity in urban water supply is ensuring equity of access to water services. One particularly successful case of how this has been done is in Phnom Penh, Cambodia, where a number of pro-poor policies were introduced to dramatically increase the number of poor households connected to the water supply system from 101 household connections in 1999 to more than 17,500 connections over the next decade (Biswas and Tortajada 2010). This expansion of access to the poor was part of a wider "metamorphosis" of the Phnom Penh Water Supply Authority (PPWSA), which saw dramatic increases in annual water production, the distribution network, and its customer base between 1993 and 2008. After some initial struggles, the PPWSA's pro-poor scheme (supported by grants from the International Development Association and the City of Paris) was able to establish the financial conditions of poor households with direct help from the local communities and to apply subsidies of 30%, 50%, 70%, or 100% of the connection fee for poor households depending upon their financial conditions. In addition, households that consumed a maximum of 7 m^3 per month would pay a tariff that was substantially (i.e., 40%) lower than the real cost of providing water, helping poor households save KR130,000–KR380,000 (about $25–$75) per year. The utility has not only expanded water services to the poor but has both remained profitable and gradually increased its profitability, one of the few publicly managed water utilities in the developing world to do so.

In general, urban water users, who are often far-removed from the actual sources of their water supply, are not aware or engaged with "water." Historically, water has remained in the technical domain of city engineers. As the need for management solutions increases, the proactive involvement of citizens in the protection of their water resources becomes vital.

Social accountability processes allow citizens to be engaged with ensuring equity of access to information, services, and development benefits associated with urban water. These processes rely on civic engagement from ordinary citizens and/or civil society organizations that participate directly or indirectly in demanding accountability, including through promoting transparency, monitoring and evaluation, and participation in decision making.

One way to do this is to engage citizens in public finance processes around water. In the municipality of Sibagat in the Philippines, a group of citizens have formed the Integrity Watch for Water Anti-Corruption Group (IWAG) to monitor the finances of water projects in their region (Water Integrity Network 2013). In a municipality in which an estimated 20% of the water-related budget was lost due to governance issues, IWAG brought together volunteers with different backgrounds and expertise to strengthen the integrity of processes around the provision of water and sanitation services in the municipality. After receiving capacity building and training on the full cycle of public financing, IWAG was able to play a constructive, preventive role by identifying potential issues and vulnerabilities so that these could be addressed by the local government and water providers. A key feature is a Guidebook to Citizen's Monitoring, which explains the processes, procedures, and critical entry points for citizen monitoring in the public finance cycle. Since the initiative began a few years ago, it has enhanced the representation of marginalized groups during policy making and built capacity of citizens in areas such as procurement laws and expenditure processes. With time, IWAG's recommendations have become increasingly accepted, and there is an institutional commitment to scale up and replicate these experiences in other areas.

Crowdsourcing, the process of gathering ideas or content from a large group of people (often users) rather than from traditional employees or information suppliers, can be used to overcome geographic or logistical boundaries that may otherwise prevent citizens' participation in planning processes or access to key services. In India, ongoing research led by the Georgia Institute of Technology (2014) is exploring how crowdsourcing can be used for environmental modeling. The research relies on the use of 53-cent test kits and the high-penetration mobile phone coverage and access in the country. The research allows for residents to use the test kits to check their own water quality in areas where routine water testing is not possible. The test kits consist of a test tube that changes color in the presence of *E. coli*. At home, volunteers fill the tubes with water, allow it to incubate in the test tube overnight, and then text a series of numbers corresponding to the color of the test material (which turns purple in the presence of *E. coli*). These SMS messages are sent to a smartphone that has been preprogrammed to automatically receive, analyze, and aggregate the overall water quality data for different areas. Pilot phases of this research, which targeted eight areas near the city of Nagpur in India, demonstrated that this approach provided a dramatic, visual way to communicate water quality issues directly to users. The initial phase also helped improve the researchers' methodology, such as simplifying the sequence of numbers that users needed to text. The approach is now being scaled up for a wider evaluation in 2015, which will include a comparison of the results produced by crowdsourcing against results obtained by conventional sampling.

Crowdsourcing can also be used to engage citizens in urban planning, providing a platform for citizens' ideas, opinions, and expectations of a city. In Hamburg, Germany, the Nexthamburg (2015) initiative is seen as the citizens' City Lab, open to all citizens who want to contribute to shaping the future of the city. Nexthamburg gathers ideas for the city through multiple online (including social media) and off-line platforms and then supports citizens in determining the technical and political feasibility of project ideas, including through interactions with politicians, public administrators, subject area experts, and sponsors. The initiative hopes to serve as a citizen-driven planning process that can complement the more formal master planning process undertaken by the city. Similarly, the United Kingdom Water Industry Research group used crowdsourcing to gain fresh insights and ideas from the public on challenges facing water operators (Crowdicity 2015). The project, which began in February 2015, used an online platform called Water Talkers to engage and educate citizens from different backgrounds, offering prizes such as gift certificates and water-saving devices for top contributors (UK Water Industry Research 2015). In 6 weeks, the platform brought together hundreds of ideas on issues including new ways to express water usage (such as a clicker on taps that click for every liter of water use) or prevent litter from being disposed in the toilet (such as stickers and slogans to stick on the toilet lid).

Another key aspect of equity is to ensure equity across generations, meaning that future generations should not be disadvantaged by activities of the current generation. In Peru, the Water Utility Regulator (SUNASS, or Superintendencia Nacional de Servicios de Saneamiento), works with companies (including 50 utilities), users, and the state to ensure compliance with legal obligations and efficient tariffs that recover the economic costs of providing water.[d] In recent years, it observed that the increasing watershed degradation resulted in the increasing cost of supplying drinking water in many parts of the country. In particular, costs related to treatment chemicals, pretreatment facilities, interruption of services during national disasters, and deterioration of infrastructure were increasing.

Sri Lanka: Access to clean water has been a key factor to decrease water-related health issues in Batticaloa

Photo Credit: ADB/James Hutchison

In response to this, in 2012, SUNASS promoted a new law which stated that SUNASS, in coordination with the utilities, must include in the tariff mechanisms for ecosystem services intended to promote efficiency in water use. This process entails identifying potential ecosystem measures, assessing their impacts on drinking water costs, comparing these measures with other alternatives (such as additional treatment or developing alternative sources), and estimating a net present value with a horizon of 25 years. If necessary, the "net social benefits" were also assessed. Noting that utilities do not typically work in watersheds or rural communities, concrete partnerships with local nongovernment organizations (NGOs) and communities was a big part of this approach. In Lima, where the water supply system serviced 1.5 million households, these ecosystem services were facilitated by an investment of $112 million through two newly established funds (focusing on green investments) and a range of adaptation and disaster risk reduction activities with a strong focus on the restoration of the watershed. Water users paid for these environmental services through a tariff increase of about 5%, which ensured the financing flows needed for these conservation projects.

Lessons Learned

These global experiences demonstrate the different facets of managing urban water, drawing from multiple disciplines and focusing on solutions-based approaches. They offer some key lessons for future cities in the rapidly urbanizing Southeast Asia region.

The first concerns partnerships. Innovative partnerships with the private sector, NGOs, and academe, as well as city-to-city partnerships allow cities to harness technology, data, research, and skills to tackle their urban water challenges. Such partnerships facilitate access to the latest research and technical skills (e.g., through academe), technology and efficiency (e.g., through the private sector), best practice and peer learning (e.g., through other cities), and communities (e.g., through NGOs and civil society).

The second concerns planning ahead with respect to the future needs of citizens and building resilience to climate change. This includes a focus on developing adaptive and sustainable infrastructure, including "green" infrastructure that yields multiple environmental benefits and protection against flooding. Recent "retrofits" of such infrastructure in both the developed and developing world, often at significant expense, highlight the need to weigh and consider these aspects early in a city's development trajectory.

The third concerns the use of emerging technologies, particularly ICT (Siemens 2015). Just over 90% of households in Asia and the Pacific have access to mobile phones, with 38% using the internet (ITU-D 2015). Just 5 years ago, these figures stood at about 66% and 22%, respectively. This exponential growth provides opportunities to increasingly employ ICT-enabled solutions, particularly for Smart City planning and for ensuring equity of access to information and participation. This is particularly true in Southeast Asia, where telecommunication infrastructure and services are advanced and continue to grow.

Notes:

[a] Sameer A. Kamal provided this insert as a background write-up (2015) on applying the GrEEEn Cities Operational Framework to Urban Water Systems.

[b] Another interesting example is the Projekt Flussbad initiative in Berlin, Germany, where there are plans to turn a 840-meter stretch of a canal of the Spree River into a public swimming pool with water being filtered from the upper part of the 1.8-kilometer stretch of the Spree Canal. This resulting renaturalized habitat would also function as a purifier for overflow from Berlin's inner-city mixed wastewater system, which currently causes the pollution of the Spree River during heavy rains (Flussbad Berlin 2015).

[c] An interesting framework of how the focus of urban water management changes as a city develops is presented in Brown, Keath, and Wong (2009).

[d] This case study is drawn from presentations given by the president of SUNASS, Fernando Momiy, at the 7th World Water Forum held in Daegu and Gyeongbuk, Republic of Korea, on 12–17 April 2015.

Sources:

ADB. 2014. Secondary Cities Development Program (Green Cities): Project Data Sheet. http://adb.org/projects/details?page=details&proj_id=47274-001

P. Beauchamp, J. Adamowski, and J. Beauséjour. 2015. A Water-Centric Approach to Develop Green Infrastructure. Background write-up.

A.K. Biswas and C. Tortajada. 2010. Water Supply of Phnom Penh: An Example of Good Governance. *International Journal of Water Resources Development.* 26 (2). pp. 157–172.

R. Brown, N. Keath, and T. Wong. 2009. Urban Water Management in Cities: Historical, Current and Future Regimes. *Water Science and Technology.* 59 (5). pp. 847–855

Central Park Water. 2015. A Sustainable Water Community. http://centralparkwater.com.au/

A. M. Coutts and R. Harris. 2013. A Multi-Scale Assessment of Urban Heating in Melbourne during an Extreme Heat Event and Policy Approaches for Adaptation. Technical report. Melbourne: Victorian Centre for Climate Change and Adaptation Research.

Crowdicity. 2015. UK Water Industry Use Crowdsourcing to Gain Insight into Important Issues. http://crowdicity.com/en/news/uk-water-industry-use-crowdsourcing-to-gain-insight-into-important-issues/

De Urbanisten. 2015. Water Squares. http://www.urbanisten.nl/wp/?portfolio=waterpleinen

Dr Nik and Associates. 2015. Iskandar Malaysia Corridor and City Transformation Programme. Segget River Flood Mitigation and Rehabilitation Study. Project summary for ADB.

Dutch Water Authorities. 2015. *Water Governance: The Dutch Water Authority Model.* The Hague.

Flow Systems. 2015. Energy: Unlocking Benefits. http://flowsystems.com.au/energy/water-energy/unlocking-benefits/

Flussbad Berlin. 2015. Projekt Flussbad Berlin – Idee. http://www.flussbad-berlin.de/flussbad/idee/

Georgia Tech. 2014. Crowdsourcing Could Lead to Better Water in Rural India. http://www.news.gatech.edu/2014/09/17/crowdsourcing-could-lead-better-water-rural-india

IBM. 2013. IBM Harnesses Power of Big Data to Improve Dutch Flood Control and Water Management Systems. https://www-03.ibm.com/press/us/en/pressrelease/41385.wss

International Telecommunication Union, Telecommunication Development Sector (ITU-D). 2015. ITU Statistics: Aggregate 2005–2015 ICT Data. http://www.itu.int/en/ITU-D/Statistics/Pages/stat/default.aspx

International Water Centre Alumni Network. 2014. Public–Private Partnership for Urban Water Management (Australia). http://iwcan.org/public-private-partnership-australia/

K-Water. 2015. SWMI. http://english.kwater.or.kr/eng/busi/SWMIPage.do?s_mid=1552

m2ocity. 2015. Introduction. http://www.m2ocity.com/presentation/introduction.html

National Research Council (NRC), Committee to Review the New York City Watershed Management Strategy. 2000. *Watershed Management for Potable Water Supply: Assessing the New York City Strategy*. Washington, DC: National Academy Press.

Natural England. 2009. Green Infrastructure Guidance. www.naturalengland.org.uk/publications

Nexthamburg. 2015. Nexthamburg. www.nexthamburg.de/en/

Orange Business Services. 2011. Veolia Water and Orange Launch m2o city, a Smart Metering Operator. http://www.orange-business.com/en/press/veolia-water-and-orange-launch-m2o-city-a-smart-metering-operator

A.C. Revkin. 2009. Peeling Back Pavement to Expose Watery Havens. *The New York Times*. 17 July.

San Francisco Water Power Sewer. 2015. High Quality, Efficient and Reliable Water, Power and Sewer Services. http://sfwater.org/index.aspx?page=161

Siemens. 2015. Resilience Cities: Infographics – Water Management System. http://w3.siemens.com/topics/global/en/sustainable-cities/resilience/pages/home.aspx#w2gHTM-900x725-/topics/global/en/sustainable-cities/resilience/Documents/resilience-appetizer/index.html?tab=tab1_4

United Kingdom Water Industry Research. 2015. Water Talkers. https://watertalkers.crowdicity.com/

United Nations Economic and Social Commission for Asia and the Pacific (UNESCAP). 2015. *Water and Green Growth: Case Studies from Asia and the Pacific*. Bangkok.

United States Environmental Protection Agency. What Is Green Infrastructure? http://water.epa.gov/infrastructure/greeninfrastructure/gi_what.cfm

Water Integrity Network. 2013. Citizen Monitoring of Public Finances for Water Projects. http://www.waterintegritynetwork.net/2013/07/17/instilling-water-integrity-in-sibagat-the-philippines/

新日本製鐵（株）八幡製鐵所の副生水素

パイプラインによる水素供給

5 Creating Urban Management Partnerships

The Power of Partnerships

A partnership is a cooperative relationship between parties for advancing their mutual interests, often for achieving specific goals. Cooperation increases the knowledge, skills, and resource (including finance) base for achieving such goals, and therefore it is clear that partnerships can provide benefits in the management or implementation of any plan, initiative, or project. However, it is important when considering partnering that specific, useful, and tangible contributions can be provided by all parties and that the responsibility for delivery is properly assigned and accepted.

The complexity of a city intensifies the power of partnerships. There are many potential partners (stakeholders), and a high degree of independence among them. Michael Porter (1990) and his colleagues argue that the competitiveness of a company and the health of the communities around it are mutually dependent. The people need the investment and the jobs that are best provided by the private sector, while the companies need a safe, efficient environment that requires local government stewardship. Moving an urban economy up the value chain requires additional cultural and recreational amenities that can be provided, for instance, by nonprofit organizations.

Successful partnerships allow each party to achieve an attractive mix of benefits and costs, thereby generating value for the group as a whole. The potential to generate value lies fundamentally in the differing capacities of the parties to make certain types of contributions and shoulder certain kinds of risk. The realization of that potential depends on the appropriate allocation of costs and risks to the different parties. The formality of the partnership builds confidence among the partners and facilitates more substantial commitments and contributions.

The Urban Management Partnership (UMP), as it is proposed in this book, is a formal vehicle for engaging local stakeholders and creating social, economic, and environmental value. The UMP is a forum in which roles are rationalized and commitments are made. The complexity of the urban realm and the large number of interconnected partners make the use of a partnership vehicle particularly critical to success. Even though the typical roles of public, private, and civil society partners are widely known, all cities—and indeed all partners—are different. A forum for cooperation allows for the negotiations to unfold, trade-offs to be made, and packages of risks and rewards to be tailored to suit the needs of each participant.

Partnerships are efficient tools of learning leading to mutual gains, particularly for cities where "demonstrations" lead to significant long lasting positive impacts.

Papua New Guinea (PNG): Mentors from Hunter Water of Australia explain nonrevenue water management practices to Water PNG in Lae

The bonds that develop during this process form the foundation for implementing joint activities, for which the partners provide financial and nonfinancial resources. Since cities take a long time to be developed and are constantly evolving, there is plenty of time for partnerships to mature and grow strong. The UMP is not a one-shot initiative—it is better understood as a process of building a cooperative forum for tackling a city's challenges and jointly realizing its potentials.

The UMP builds on a long line of predecessor efforts to get urban stakeholders to work together, including downtown redevelopment associations or business improvement districts in countries such as Australia, the United Kingdom, or the United States (Houston 2003, Göktug et al. 2008). While often including the business community, UMPs sometimes have a less explicit focus on businesses than these efforts. Some UMPs intentionally incorporate all of the major stakeholders in a given locality for the purpose of coordinating with a view to achieving a specific development goal. UMPs are also unique in that they always involve an *external* partner, usually from another country, which brings specific relevant experience or expertise; for example, a water utility in Viet Nam partnering with a renowned and successful water utility such as Singapore Water. Such partnerships may have a kind of mentor–mentee flavor. The international component adds extra caché to UMPs, as city managers often show a natural curiosity to hear and learn about how foreign city managers solve problems similar to theirs (In Asia 2015). More recently, findings from related projects by the Asian Development Bank (ADB) have shown that the interest for such learning, for example, by city managers and decision makers in Viet Nam, Malaysia, India, or Indonesia, is more pronounced with regard to the immediate subregion and similar development contexts

(ADB 2014c). This idea has previously been conceptualized as South–South learning across larger regions such as Latin America, Africa, or Asia. Now, there is growing interest among developing member countries whether a concept has been tried and tested within Asia and their particular subregion.

This chapter introduces the UMP approach to implementing integrated urban development plans. The approach is based on the idea that, through effective collaboration and definition of responsibilities, the multitude of agencies and bodies (both governmental and nongovernmental) working at a variety of levels within the city planning and development system, can more effectively achieve their mutually dependent sustainable development goals through UMPs. The chapter outlines different kinds of UMPs, sets out the process for building and maintaining a UMP, and highlights some successful UMP examples.

The Urban Management Partnership Approach

The UMP is an approach to implementing integrated urban investment plans or any integrated urban development plan, which promotes partnerships and has wider application besides the implementation of a GrEEEn City Action Plan (GCAP). It is a means for establishing a multilayered (vertical and horizontal) platform that integrates and delineates the roles and responsibilities for the implementation of a wide range of projects (in terms of both scale and technical focus) over a variety of time frames to achieve sustainable results. It is a means of project delivery (coordination, implementation, operations, management, monitoring, and evaluation and accountability), but also a means for pooling resources and accessing external knowledge to improve outcomes, create win–win scenarios, and build sustained capacity. The UMP implies going beyond mere coordination between policies and consultation in planning and design, but encompasses joint work among sectors and disciplines.

The GCAPs that have been produced to date, both through ADB's work and under the initiative of a city, are relatively concise documents outlining a broad framework of necessary actions to deliver the grEEEn targets of the city (under an integrated strategy) and therefore realize its grEEEn vision. Often, within a GCAP, these grEEEn actions can be grouped, particularly if a spatial and/or asset approach (as described in Chapter 6) is used. As a result, a GCAP will include a selective number of initiatives, each with multiple hard-side and soft-side actions, which require different actors for planning, implementation, and management.

While a GCAP sets out a framework for delivering the grEEEn vision as a whole, it does not provide details of the steps required to coordinate and implement each action (which may constitute a number of separate projects). It may provide details on finance or enabling actions, but it will not set out in detail the institutional mechanisms for implementation. Each action identified under a GCAP will vary and will involve a range of stakeholders. Some actions and projects will involve many stakeholders and thus will require different types of UMPs to make progress and ensure that actions are delivered in an efficient and cost-effective way. There will be complex actions and initiatives which will require a corresponding partnership approach involving numerous stakeholders, and there will be less complex or sector actions which will require no partnerships—that is not to say it will be implemented without engaging any other stakeholders.

The UMP approach enables the "core" implementing agencies, or the city and/or regional government or council, to jointly establish the appropriate level of partnership for implementing GCAP actions. As urban systems are complex, involving multiple sectors, administrative boundaries, and jurisdictions, the approach needs to be flexible and adaptive to local settings and specificities.

Benefits of Urban Management Partnerships

UMPs provide clear benefits for implementing projects in terms of consultation and coordination, but they offer more to agencies implementing urban development projects by

- creating win–win projects that have multiple positive outputs for related sectors and/or agencies with clear cost and time efficiency benefits;
- avoiding negative impacts on other related sectors' and/or agencies' goals and avoiding repetition or duplication across sectors and/or agencies;
- increasing political and community acceptance and/or approval by leveraging combined influence;
- providing access to finance by pooling government budgets and/or partnering with external agencies (including international financial institutions), the private sector, or local community groups;
- providing lasting skills and capacity development through a mentor–mentee relationship; and
- meeting broader global objectives such as the conservation of natural resources, for example, by reducing nonrevenue water.

Types of Urban Management Partnerships

The following different types of UMPs described should not be considered independent of one another or exclusive. While they have been separated for descriptive purposes, this should not imply that only one type of partnership should be used to address a single action and/or initiative. Indeed, a single action or initiative could greatly benefit from several types of partnerships. Essentially, the creation of UMPs should be encouraged in whatever form necessary and feasible.[16]

Intragovernmental Urban Management Partnerships

Intragovernmental UMPs are essential in bringing together two or more government agencies that have a vested interest in achieving a GCAP action and/or initiative. These partnerships should be applied to the vast majority of projects as win–win conditions can be created by pooling partners' capacity, funding, and knowledge resources together, as has been proven in West Melbourne in the United States (Box 5.1).

Although the process of setting up and negotiating the terms of an intragovernmental UMP may be lengthy, it delivers greater benefits during the implementation period, resulting in better outcomes. Therefore, intragovernmental UMPs can save overall funding, resources,

---

[16]   See ADB video (2014h).

Box 5.1: Intragovernmental Coordination Element in West Melbourne, United States

The City of West Melbourne in Florida, United States, has enshrined an intragovernmental type of partnership into policy with the purpose of "fostering and utilizing intergovernmental partnerships to accomplish the city's community planning vision, public service standards, and land development priorities" through planning directives. West Melbourne's intragovernmental partnership system comprises a range of projects and priorities. These include, for instance, a comprehensive coordination, management, and redevelopment scheme of its transport, water planning, and public schools systems. In the case of water planning for example, the city has brought together a range of government agencies involved in providing the city's potable water. The city has formed intragovernmental partnerships among all agencies to better coordinate and delineate their scope of work as part of a revitalized water planning system. This includes better contract management and procurement between the authorities while creating a level standard to track water quality. This has all been coordinated at the city level while seeking to pool the resources of all the government agencies to ensure better and faster results.

Source: City of West Melbourne. 2010. Intergovernmental Coordination Element Goals, Objectives, and Policies. Horizon 2030 Comprehensive Plan. http://www.westmelbourne.org/DocumentCenter/Home/View/937

and time invested into an action and/or initiative. Essentially, they allow the partners to do more with less.

While a single agency may want to undertake work on its own (as they most naturally are used to doing), the outcome of the action and/or initiative will almost always be improved by establishing intragovernmental UMPs. This underlines the necessity of implementing these types of partnerships (particularly in developing countries) where government agencies often have little experience in sharing their knowledge, capacity, and funding. For example, the Ministry of Construction in Viet Nam possesses a disproportionate level of capacity and funding compared with local level government agencies. This often leads to a strong top-down planning and implementation process that rarely receives third-party input, resulting in projects that insufficiently pay due attention to citizens' interests and needs.

Intragovernmental UMPs therefore seek to remedy these problems by fostering a collaborative working environment within a group where resources from different government agencies can be pooled and outcomes are improved.

In order to establish an effective UMP, a road map should be drawn up detailing the tangible contributions each partner will make. As previously stated, these contributions should be composed of funding, capacity, or knowledge exchange. It is important that the partnership road map clearly delineate the scope of work and budget each government agency will contribute to the action and/or initiative. Failure to do so puts the partnership in jeopardy and risks derailing the success of the project early on. The road map must be negotiated by all the contributing parties to ensure an equitable and satisfactory outcome.

Philippines: Staff of the Khulna Water and Sewerage Authority from Bangladesh observe operations of Maynilad Water Services in Manila

Establishing an effective road map is facilitated by a series of focused workshops that allow all the participants to contribute their own ideas and to negotiate accordingly. It is important that these workshops create consensus among all the involved parties who agree to contribute their resources. Once the UMP agreements and road map are in place, periodic meetings among all the partners should be organized to touch base on their developments and amend the road map, if necessary.

Mentor–Mentee Urban Management Partnerships

Mentor–mentee UMPs are suitable when a working group has sufficient financing to implement an action and/or initiative but not sufficient capacity to implement a project. This closely resembles the more classic form of a partnership where the use of an external partner is necessary to address capacity shortfalls in an organization.

These types of partnerships have taken place around the world in both developed and developing countries and have involved partnering between institutions such as government agencies, the private sector, nongovernment organizations, and higher education institutions. Mentor–mentee UMPs create a two-way process of learning and exchange that can give smaller government agencies the opportunity to gain additional expertise in their field of operations. This also permits more advanced or larger government agencies to better understand the work processes of smaller agencies.

The role of the mentor should be to guide the mentee through any technical or financial shortfalls that may arise during the project. The mentor may also guide the mentee on the application of good practices or frameworks to accomplish the action and/or initiative successfully. A government agency or working group may seek out a mentor to help cover any aspect of an action and/or initiative that they are not familiar with or that has already been carried out elsewhere. As with intragovernmental UMPs, the role of the mentor and the nature of the mentor's relationship with the mentee must be clearly defined in a partnership agreement to limit any misunderstandings that may arise at a later stage.

The mentor should meet a range of criteria directly related to the action and/or initiative and should ideally be from a similar context as the mentee. This allows the mentor to understand

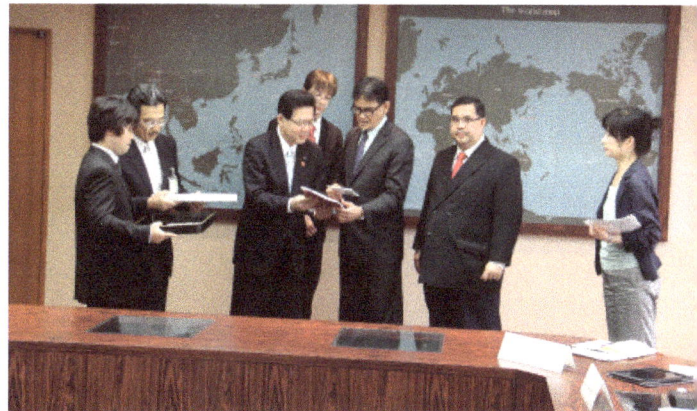

Photo Credit: Amit Prothi

Japan: As part of a mentor–mentee exchange visit, a delegation from Melaka, Malaysia, inspected smart infrastructure solutions in Kitakyushu Eco-Town

the setting of the work environment along with any political, social, or economic disruptions that may arise during implementation. Essentially, the closer the action and/or initiative previously undertaken by the mentor reflects the current one, the more effective the UMP will be.

The level of interaction and support between the mentor and mentee should also be determined in advance between the parties. This could range from the mentor's participation on a daily, weekly, or monthly basis depending on the need of the mentee. The mentor may also accompany the mentee during specific events which the mentee may need guidance on.

The mentors in ADB's Water Operators Partnerships (WOPs) Program provide their services free of charge and are only provided the cost of travel. The key reasons the mentors are enthusiastic about participating in the program is because they believe that they are providing a service that complies with their corporate social responsibilities, and it enables their staff to expand their global experience and helps build their capacity besides opening new areas of business development in the mentee's country. Unique aspects of the ADB WOPs are that they are demand driven, a business case, and people-centered (Box 5.2).

Two other examples of mentor–mentee relationships are the United Cities and Local Governments (UCLG) program set up under Cities Alliance (Box 5.3) and the City-to-City Cooperation of Yokohama's Y-Port (Box 5.4).

Box 5.2: ADB's Water Operators Partnership Program

Designed as a water utility twinning program, the Water Operators Partnerships (WOPs) of the Asian Development Bank (ADB) aim at knowledge sharing and capacity building in the water sector by matching mentors and mentees. The partnerships provide a very decisive soft component to ADB water and sanitation projects, by supporting water utilities to provide better service coverage and delivery, improved financial stability in their operations, and proper asset management by learning from their experienced mentor. The WOP program identifies six steps to improve utility performance:

1. **Identify:** ADB identifies and profiles recipient partners among its clients.
2. **Match:** ADB finds appropriate mentors and matches the partners.
3. **Agree:** ADB facilitates diagnostic visit by mentor; partners agree on work plan.
4. **Implement:** Partners carry out work plan through series of exchange visit.
5. **Adopt:** Recipient adopts best practices to improve performance.
6. **Replicate:** ADB supports replication and scale-up.

With more than 40 WOPs established since the program's start in 2007, some of the lessons learned about the relevant partnership success factors are (i) the willingness of the mentor and mentee to commit to the partnership activities through financial, human, and time resources; (ii) agreement on realistic, tangible outcomes reflected in a practical work plan; and (iii) the importance of regular visits and joint workshops for ongoing communication and knowledge exchange under the motto "seeing is believing."

Source: ADB. 2014. *Water Operators Partnerships: Twinning Utilities for Better Services.* Brochure. Manila. http://www.adb.org/sites/default/files/publication/42702/twinning-utilities-better-services.pdf

Box 5.3: United Cities and Local Governments Program

Under Cities Alliance, the United Cities and Local Governments (UCLG) program "added new depth to city partnerships by making genuine progress on capacity building and exchange of knowledge." The underlying issue targeted by UCLG is to improve the capacities of civil service employees by bringing together civil servants from developed cities and less developed cities across different countries. The program began when Lilongwe, the capital of Malawi, asked Johannesburg to assist it in creating a city development strategy in 2008. The mentor and mentee began their first session by defining what their relationship is to ensure there would be no misunderstandings later on. They also set key targets across five areas, including performance management, by-law reviews, a debt-recovery strategy, and the initiation of a long-term capital investment program. These targets were decided on in close cooperation with both the mentor and mentee and have since proved to be extremely successful. This allowed the program to be replicated in cities across the world. Similar to the Asian Development Bank's Water Operators Partnerships program, UCLG's success can be put down to the mentor and mentee's focus on specific areas where their partnership could be beneficial. This is in contrast to the classic alternative of city twinning, which has resulted in many sectors of activity being agreed on with few actual results in implementation.

Source: United Cities and Local Governments. 2011. A Very Civil Partnership. *United Cities.* March. pp. 44–46. http://www.citiesalliance.org/sites/citiesalliance.org/files/CA_Images/MENTORING%20article%20in%20united%20cities.pdf

Box 5.4: City of Yokohama's Y-PORT: City-to-City Technical Cooperation

The Yokohama Partnership of Resources and Technologies (Y-PORT) is a project by the City of Yokohama to engage in international technical cooperation to foster sustainable urban development in developing countries, particularly in Asia and the Pacific. The key rationale behind this activity is Yokohama's own experience of turning around its development path from a heavily resource-based to a low-carbon one. When shifting the focus on sustainable urban development in the 1980s–1990s, Yokohama broadly engaged its citizens and the private sector to contribute to this new policy direction. Through a myriad of policies, standards, and schemes, urban development in the metropolitan area of Yokohama was innovated into a resource-efficient low-carbon model of growth and development (e.g., city center renewal with Minato Mirai 21 becoming the new central business district, development of a model transit-oriented neighborhood in Kohoku New Town, UNESCO-recognized extensive cultural heritage conservation, and Yokohama Smart City Project).

As a member of the Regional Network of Local Authorities for the Management of Human Settlements (CITYNET) in Asia and the Pacific, Yokohama signed the 2012 agreement on the Asia Smart City Conference for strengthened city-to-city cooperation. Instead of simply advertising its technology products abroad, the city government decided to offer comprehensive sustainability solutions, where technology is combined with the know-how of Yokohama's public and private sectors, as well as its research institutions. Through Y-PORT, Yokohama is cooperating with other local and metropolitan governments through four approaches:

- Advisory services for sustainable urban development (e.g., in urban growth management)
- Yokohama city promotion through its successful development model, as well as event and conference formats (e.g., the annual Asia Smart City Conference)
- Deployment of cutting-edge technologies through collaboration with companies and research institutions located in Yokohama (e.g., matchmaking sessions for private sector companies from Yokohama and its partner cities)
- Capacity building through training sessions and study tours (e.g., dispatch of experts to and/or from Yokohama on field visits)

Japan: Yokohama's new central business district Minato Mirai 21 is a flagship example of transforming a city toward a low-carbon future

Photo Credit: Hideo MORI

Thailand: Yokohama partners with the Bangkok Metropolitan Administration to tackle climate change impacts through sustainable urban development.

Photo Credit: City of Yokohama

continued on next page

Box 5.4. *continued*

Yokohama's broadened engagement in international technical cooperation has been put on stronger institutional feet through a comprehensive partnership agreement with the Japan International Cooperation Agency (JICA) in 2011, as well as a memorandum of understanding (MOU) with the Asian Development Bank in 2013 to foster sustainable urban development in developing regions through Yokohama's knowledge and technologies. Similar MOUs have been signed between Yokohama and its project partner cities and metropolitan regions, based on an existing bilateral relationship between the Japanese national government and the partner cities' national government. In the case of the Bangkok Metropolitan Administration in Thailand, JICA provides through technical assistance for the Master Plan on Climate Change together with corresponding capacity building, while Yokohama provides technical advice in various urban sectors and engages local officials, the private sector, and research institutions in training and field visits. In the case of the city of Cebu in the Philippines, Yokohama provided technical support in the drafting of the Mega Cebu Vision 2050 for the metropolitan region of Cebu. To foster civil society and private sector engagement, participatory planning was applied from the outset, and discussions between private companies from both places as well as with city officials from Cebu have taken place to scope the relevant issues of the metropolitan region's future development needs with regard to infrastructure and resource-efficient technologies. A similar technical cooperation process has been initiated with Da Nang in Viet Nam. On Yokohama's side, the city government has signed partnership agreements with leading technology firms, such as Hitachi and JFE Engineering Corporation to support the international technical cooperation.

Sources: T. Hashimoto. 2014. Urban Challenge and City Level International Technical Cooperation of Yokohama with Cebu. Presentation at the ADB Enabling GrEEEn Cities Regional Conference, 13–14 May, Manila. http://www.scribd.com/doc/226081893/City-to-City-Learning; International Technical Cooperation Division, City of Yokohama. 2011. Y-PORT Brochure; R. Teipelke. 2015. *Urban NEXUS Tools and Case Studies*. Sector Project Sustainable Development of Metropolitan Regions. Eschborn: Deutsche Gesellschaft für Internationale Zusammenarbeit (GIZ).

Developing Useful Urban Management Partnerships

The benefits of UMPs and the types of UMPs available have been discussed earlier. The process flowchart in Figure 5.1 illustrates that some kind of UMP is nearly always necessary in implementing integrated urban development projects. The figure shows that partnerships should always be established as a platform for implementing complex actions and/or initiatives. Only when actions or projects are very simple (sector)—and the implementing agency has sufficient capacity and resources—should a project be implemented by a sole agency. Even then, the implementing agency, as a check, should ask itself whether win–win scenarios can be achieved by partnering with other agencies or organizations, as these will provide benefits beyond their project. This is the nature of integrated and sustainable urban development and at the heart of the GrEEEn Cities Operational Framework.

The flowchart is established as a high-level working tool for assisting a GCAP implementing body in addressing both the simplification of a complex urban development initiative (Boxes 3.0–3.4 in Figure 5.1.) and the assignment of appropriate and useful UMPs for the implementation of actions or projects.

There are numerous ways for cities to scope opportunities to join forces with the private sector, civil society, nongovernment organizations, as well as external partners to address urban development challenges in specific sectors and places or across thematic areas and administrative boundaries. While the UMP approach is flexible in its adaptation in a certain context, it requires careful assessment of the most urgent issues to be tackled through an UMP and to identify the right partners that can add value through human, financial, time, and other resources.

The UMP approach builds on experience in developed and developing countries. When different partners come together during events, it has been apparent that these actors and organizations have much interest, commitment, and relevant expertise. It is essential to provide platforms for initiating UMPs, such as the marketplace, which has been piloted during the ADB Enabling GrEEEn Cities Regional Conference (Box 5.5). The important thing is to get started and to divert away from traditional ways of addressing urban development challenges, by working on innovative solutions planned, designed, and delivered through the most effective type of UMPs.

Figure 5.1: Decision Process Flowchart for Guiding Urban Management Partnership Development

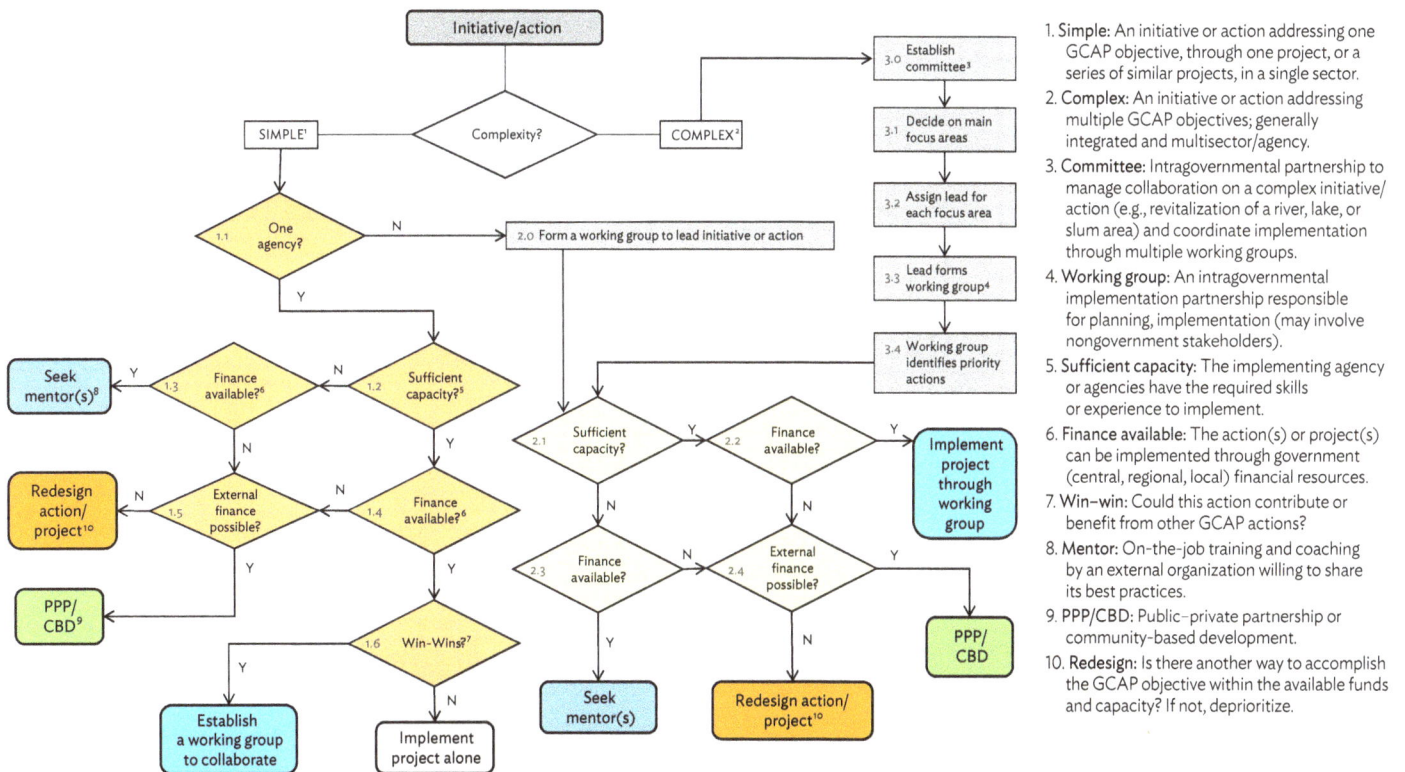

1. **Simple:** An initiative or action addressing one GCAP objective, through one project, or a series of similar projects, in a single sector.
2. **Complex:** An initiative or action addressing multiple GCAP objectives; generally integrated and multisector/agency.
3. **Committee:** Intragovernmental partnership to manage collaboration on a complex initiative/action (e.g., revitalization of a river, lake, or slum area) and coordinate implementation through multiple working groups.
4. **Working group:** An intragovernmental implementation partnership responsible for planning, implementation (may involve nongovernment stakeholders).
5. **Sufficient capacity:** The implementing agency or agencies have the required skills or experience to implement.
6. **Finance available:** The action(s) or project(s) can be implemented through government (central, regional, local) financial resources.
7. **Win–win:** Could this action contribute or benefit from other GCAP actions?
8. **Mentor:** On-the-job training and coaching by an external organization willing to share its best practices.
9. **PPP/CBD:** Public–private partnership or community-based development.
10. **Redesign:** Is there another way to accomplish the GCAP objective within the available funds and capacity? If not, deprioritize.

CBD = community-based development, GCAP = GrEEEn City Action Plan, N = no, PPP = public–private partnership, Y = yes.
Source: Authors.

Box 5.5: A Marketplace of Partners at the Enabling GrEEEn Cities Regional Conference in Manila, Philippines

In line with the GrEEEn Cities Operational Framework of enabling Urban Management Partnerships (UMPs), city managers can benefit from a diverse group of actors from the public, private, and civil society sectors—it is a true marketplace of partners. The Enabling GrEEEn Cities Regional Conference, organized by the Asian Development Bank and held in May 2014, highlighted the variety of UMP modalities by bringing together companies, development agencies, city managers, and many other groups to find synergetic solutions to shared urban development problems. It became clear to many participants during this marketplace session that the complexity of challenges in the urban realm is met by a diverse expertise in innovative project design, technologies, and financing mechanisms. Hard- and soft-side solutions are thought up and implemented together to achieve climate-resilient cities that enhance livability.

The Sustainable System Integration Model by AECOM or the Urban Simulation Model by CDM Smith are just two examples of innovative planning and design approaches that provide city managers with a range of different perspectives on their cities' development paths and options. These models are part of a variety of decision support systems, which are taken up in chapter 6. The conclusion for such models is clear: the matching of city governments' technical staff with specialized planning companies can broaden their perspective on urban development challenges and opportunities as well as make more efficient use of resources.

Cities in Asia seeking advice on linking such planning activities with actual infrastructure financing have been supported by the Cities Development Initiative for Asia (CDIA). This kind of city–development agency partnership enters at the stage between planning and project feasibility, in order to realistically assess what investment projects are feasible and most strongly aligned with a city's development needs, while having positive impacts on the economy, environment, and equity of a city. In addition to this prioritization of infrastructure investments (City Infrastructure Investment Programming and Prioritization [CIIPP] Toolkit), CDIA undertakes prefeasibility studies and advises city managers on how they can strengthen their projects' readiness for financing.

The crux between project planning and design, on the one hand, and financing, on the other, has become more crucial, because most cities can no longer fund necessary projects on their own. In order to match such public projects with possible financiers, companies such as PricewaterhouseCoopers can offer specialized project design services. Very often, public projects need to be approached and designed differently to attract private investors. The same is true for city governments finding specialized companies for providing the right technology solution. From the early visioning and planning stages to project feasibility and design, city managers in need of nonpublic investors, constructors, operators, etc., need to have a second lens on their projects: How to structure public–private partnerships, how to mitigate risks, and how to assign responsibilities—specialized services are available on the market for city managers to tap.

For this, the energy efficiency area is a case in point. The retrofitting of public buildings in Melaka, Malaysia, exemplifies how UMPs can kick-start the implementation of integrated urban development plans. Energy efficiency was one of the key focal areas to achieve the

Photo Credit: ADB/Edsel Roman

Melaka Green City vision. However, the state government was required to lead by example to show other stakeholders in the city what can be done in this area. A total of 95 public buildings were identified for potential energy efficiency gains through retrofitting. The mixture of large and small public buildings, as well as the combination of higher and lower cost options created an investment package with manageable risks and achievable results. An investment company was set up, founded by Danish Energy Management in cooperation with the Danish Investment Fund for Developing Countries. For the efficient realization of investments, a one-stop shop for the financing, design, and implementation of energy efficiency projects was created. With the government being at the forefront of energy efficiency, potential scaling-up and replication by the private sector can go hand in hand, fostering improved resource efficiency, while also creating economic opportunities for local companies in this sector.

Another partnership example in the energy efficiency area is lighting. Philips estimates a 40% reduction in energy consumption if light-emitting diode (LED) lighting replace older technologies. The saving of valuable resources already starts in the design and manufacturing of products, stretches over the operation stage, and can include the material recovery at the end of a product's life cycle. This closes the material loop, when former parts are not only properly recycled but also reused. Most relevant to urban development is street lighting in this regard. More efficient solutions can save energy and public money. Matching innovative companies with city governments and their service providers can increase livability in urban spaces through improved street lighting for greater safety and enhanced experience of public spaces.

Sources:

ADB. 2014. Enabling GrEEEn Cities Regional Conference. http://www.adb.org/news/events/enabling-grEEEn-cities-sustainable-urban-future-southeast-asia

J. Bachmann. 2014. Sustainable System Integration Model. Presentation at the ADB Enabling GrEEEn Cities Regional Conference, 13–14 May, Manila. https://www.scribd.com/doc/226085436/Sustainable-System-Integration-Model-SSIM

CDIA. 2015. City Infrastructure Investment Programming and Prioritisation Toolkit. http://cdia.asia/resources/toolkit/

Y. Noda. 2014. Building Cities and Infrastructure of the Future. Presentation at the ADB Enabling GrEEEn Cities Regional Conference, 13–14 May, Manila. https://www.scribd.com/doc/226085547/Building-Cities-and-Infrastructure-of-the-Future

L . Reid and D. Spector. 2014. Quantifying Sustainability Performance to Support Investment. Presentation at the ADB Enabling GrEEEn Cities Regional Conference, 13–14 May, Manila. https://www.scribd.com/doc/226085436/Sustainable-System-Integration-Model-SSIM

H. Rytter. 2014. Retrofitting Public Buildings for Melaka. Presentation at the ADB Enabling GrEEEn Cities Regional Conference, 13–14 May, Manila. https://www.scribd.com/doc/226085678/Retrofitting-Public-Buildings-for-Melaka-Cities-Henrik-Jensen

F. Tetteroo-Bueno. 2014. Green Innovation and Products. Presentation at the ADB Enabling GrEEEn Cities Regional Conference, 13–14 May, Manila. https://www.scribd.com/doc/226084841/Green-Innovations-and-Products

J. Van Etten. 2014. Prioritizing City Infrastructure Investments. Presentation at the ADB Enabling GrEEEn Cities Regional Conference, 13–14 May, Manila. https://www.scribd.com/doc/226085277/City-Infrastructure-Investment-Programming-and-Prioritization-CIIPP-Toolkit

Philippines: The Marketplace format of the first Enabling GrEEEn Cities Regional Conference, held at ADB headquarters in Manila on 13–14 May 2014, brought together companies, development agencies, city managers, and other groups to present integrated urban development solutions from different regions worldwide

Photo Credit: ADB/Edsel Roman

Structuring Urban Management Partnerships

This section uses an example from the implementation of the GCAP for Melaka, Malaysia, to illustrate the application of the UMP flowchart process in Figure 5.1 (ADB 2014f, Modak 2015). In Melaka, to implement a single complex action, Melaka River Cleaning and Beautification, UMPs are being created at a number of levels to both simplify a complex GCAP initiative and subsequently implement, through working groups, a number of actions (Figure 5.2).

This example also illustrates good ways of hierarchical intragovernmental UMP development in Melaka, although implementation is at an early stage and an evaluation of potential downstream partnerships with external bodies is not yet possible.

The Melaka example uses terminology that was used (and worked) in that specific government setting: a *coordinating agency* established an *executive committee* which was ultimately responsible for implementing the Melaka River Cleaning and Beautification initiative through a number of *subcommittees*. Figure 5.2 outlines key stages in the process of breaking down the complex initiative into achievable actions and assigning subcommittees (intragovernmental UMPs) with the responsibility for implementing their respective actions and/or projects and thus delivering the goals of the initiative under a GCAP. This process corresponds with Boxes 3.0–3.4 of the UMP decision process flowchart in Figure 5.1. While the process may not be so linear in reality, the Melaka case study provides a real example of how this can be achieved.

Figure 5.2: Establishing a Hierarchical Partnership Platform for Implementing Initiatives in Melaka, Malaysia

1) Coordinating agency identifies complex initiative →
2) Coordinating agency establishes executive committee composed of most important government agencies related to the initiative →
3) Executive committee breaks down into key actions →
4) Executive committee designates membership composed of all relevant government agencies formed around each action →

5) Executive committee assigns a lead agency to each action →
6) Stakeholders meet to establish initial relationship, discuss existing roles, and create subcommittees for each action →
Melaka is now at this stage →
7) Subcommittees examine whether external partnerships will be necessary and identify partners →

8) Subcommittees draw up detailed and time-bound road maps underlining responsibilities and deliverables for each subcommittee member →
9) Subcommittee report plans back to executive committee who approves plans or seeks modification →
10) Executive committee endorsed by city/state government

Source: Authors.

Photo Credit: ADB/Lester Ledesma

Malaysia: Intragovernmental Urban Management Partnerships have been identified as a key enabler to coordinate and implement activities toward the cleaning up and beautification of Melaka River

The coordinating agency should have the largest stake in the initiative and should also be responsible for overall coordination of the executive and subcommittees, which are ultimately responsible for the delivery of the initiative. In Melaka, this coordinating agency is the Melaka Economic Planning Unit (UPEN).

When initiating the implementation of complex initiatives, the coordinating agency will be responsible at the outset for identifying a wide range of relevant government stakeholders. Table 5.1 lists the agencies identified as having some role in implementing the Melaka River Cleaning and Beautification initiative.

Of the agencies in Table 5.1, through initial consultation, an executive committee was established, which includes the stakeholders with the most significant contribution to implementation. This committee, in coordination with UPEN, delineated a number of actions as follows, which together, if implemented satisfactorily, will result in attaining the objectives of the integrated urban development initiative:

- Healthy river
- Beautiful river (recreation)
- Beautiful river (tourism)
- Functional river
- River for all

UPEN and the executive committee, with assistance from ADB, then held a workshop to start an initial dialogue between government stakeholders in terms of determining their roles relevant to the selected urban development initiative (often, government agencies lack coordination to such an extent that it is unknown what the relevant responsibilities of other agencies actually are). After considering the existing roles of agencies, the workshop also provided the opportunity to establish subcommittees (partnerships), each with a lead agency, for implementing the individual actions identified under the initiative.

Table 5.1: Agencies in the Melaka River Cleaning and Beautification Initiative, Malaysia

Agency	English Agency Name	Government Level	Main Function in Relation to the Melaka River
BKSA	Water Regulatory Center	Federal/state	Raw water intake monitoring
IWK	Indah Water Konsortium	Federal/private	Sewerage and wastewater treatment
JAS	Department of Environment	Federal/state	Monitoring (ambient) water quality
JKNM	Melaka State Health Department	Federal/state	Health promotion and enforcement
JPBD Melaka	Melaka State Town and Country Planning Department	Federal/state	Spatial planning state level
JPNM	Melaka Agriculture Department	Federal/state	Agricultural practices, enforcement (?)
JPS Melaka	Melaka Drainage and Irrigation Department	Federal/state	Water catchment management, drainage and irrigation
MBMB	Melaka Historical City Council	Local	Enforcement, beautification, river cleaning
MGTC	Melaka Green Technology Council	State	Monitoring and promotion
MPAG	Alor Gajah Municipal Council	Local	Enforcement, beautification, river cleaning
MPHTJ	Jang Tuah Jaya Municipal Council	Local	Enforcement, beautification, river cleaning
MPJ	Jasin Municipal Council	Local	Enforcement, beautification, river cleaning
Perhutanan	Melaka Forestry Department	Federal/state	Forestry practices, enforcement (?)
PPNM	Melaka Fisheries State Office	Federal/state	Fishing practices, enforcement (?)
PPSPM	River and Coastal Development Corporation Melaka	State	River development and promotion, river transport
PPSPPA	Solid Waste Management and Public Cleansing Corporation	Federal/state	Solid waste management
PTG	Melaka Land and Mines Department	Federal/state	Land management, land titles
SAMB	Melaka Water Supply Company	State	Treated water supply
SPAN	National Water Services Commission	Federal	Regulation water supply
UKT	Local Government Unit	State	Policies and plans for local authorities
UPEN	Melaka Economic Planning Unit	Federal/state	Coordination

Source: Authors.

The lead agencies have executive decision-making powers and are responsible for the overall implementation, management, and coordination of their subcommittees' work. They are held directly accountable to the coordinating agency and therefore have an important responsibility toward the project. For this reason, lead agencies should only be selected from larger government agencies with sizable financial, logistical, and/or knowledge resources.

Agencies that are identified as partners in a subcommittee must have specific and identified roles in implementing projects and/or actions. They must also commit some resources to the project and have responsibility for some deliverables.

Figure 5.3: Organization Chart of the Melaka River Cleaning and Beautification Initiative, Malaysia

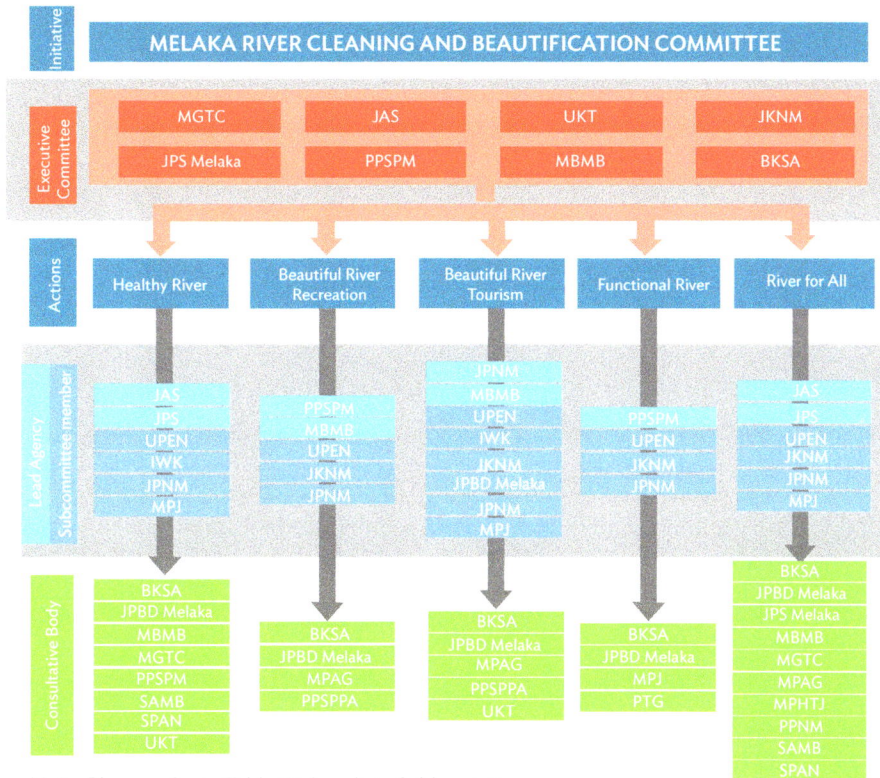

Note: Please refer to Table 5.1 for a list of abbreviations.
Source: Authors.

Stakeholders that were identified but fall outside of the subcommittees (therefore without specific responsibilities for implementation) may still provide useful contributions to the implementation of particular actions. It is therefore useful to establish a consultative group for each action as a way of committing certain agencies to making themselves available for consultation as implementation progresses. It is useful to have this wider group because (i) it expands the available knowledge base, including data capture etc., and (ii) it limits the size of the "real" implementing UMP—this is important as too many agencies may reduce implementation efficiency.

The subcommittees should then consider their options with respect to external partnerships using the UMP decision process flowchart (Figure 5.1), and subsequently draw up detailed and time-bound road maps underlining responsibilities and deliverables for each subcommittee member.

Finally, the executive committee should be endorsed by Melaka's chief minister to legitimize its work and give the necessary backing to all the government agencies involved in the initiative.

The Melaka River Cleaning and Beautification initiative has established the organizational framework (as presented in Figure 5.3) through simple coordination and a single workshop. The initiative has yet to fully define the responsibilities of each committee member and seek external partnerships for each action, but the UMP process is under way.

6

Key Enablers for Achieving Livable Cities

This chapter discusses key enablers—that is, mechanisms and systems that can help make grEEEn solutions possible. Enablers include policies, strategies, sector plans, regulations, financial incentives, technologies, governance institutions, civil society, and private sector interventions. Among others, the chapter discusses asset management tools, financing mechanisms, performance monitoring and indicators, decision support systems (DSS), and information and communication technology (ICT).

Asset Management for Sustainability and Resilience

Asset Management for Cities

The exponential pace of urbanization has increased stress on urban infrastructure, as cities continue to grow horizontally and vertically. The natural environs of a city and its physical boundaries strain to cope with the growing demands of populations aspiring for a better quality of life. Maintaining public infrastructure performance and service delivery is imperative to meet the demands of an ever-increasing urban population. The challenge of continuous and efficient service delivery for cities is exacerbated by climate variations and increased risks to natural disasters (World Economic Forum and Boston Consulting Group 2014).

Asset management has been integral to city planning and management of service delivery and is a critical element in the achievement of sustainable and inclusive development (Vanier and Rahman 2004).[17] Assets are the basis of production in the economy—whether they are productive assets held by enterprises, buildings which house these productive assets, infrastructure on which these enterprises depend to run their factories and distribute their goods, or natural assets which supply the raw materials and absorb the waste of production.

A city's assets cover (i) the physical and social infrastructure, and buildings that a city owns or administers; (ii) the natural environment of the city and its surroundings that belong to the community unless in private ownership—land, forests, rivers, lakes, and the air; and (iii) its cultural and historical heritage that can be promoted to generate income and jobs. All three categories need to be included in asset management plans for cities.

The GrEEEn Cities Operational Framework links established approaches of comprehensive asset management to include natural, social, and historical attributes as an integral part of asset inventory and maintenance costs for enhancing livability.

---

[17] See also Government of Saskatchewan video (Ministry of Government Relations 2012).

Photo Credit: Renard Teipelke

Dangerously open sewerage and environmentally hazardous landfill cover damage: Cities will not be able to achieve long-term benefits from their infrastructure investments without proper asset management

The Institute of Asset Management of the United Kingdom (2015) quotes ISO 55000 to define asset management as the "coordinated activity of an organization to realize value from assets" and an asset as "an item, thing or entity that has potential or actual value to an organization." Asset management covers two aspects—advisory services, where an advisor or financial services company provides asset management by coordinating and overseeing a client's financial portfolio; and corporate finance, the process of ensuring that a company's tangible and intangible assets are maintained, accounted for, and put to their highest and best use. This definition shows that coverage of asset management for a city is wider than that of its built assets, which in the past have been the main focus of local governments.

Asset management involves balancing costs, opportunities, and risks against the desired performance of assets, to achieve the objectives of the owning organization—or in this case, the city. Asset management enables a city to examine the need for, and performance of, assets and systems at all levels. It enables the application of analytical approaches toward managing an asset over the different stages of its life cycle—from the initial demand for the asset, through its use, to its disposal. And it includes managing any postdisposal liabilities. Furthermore, asset management involves making the right decisions and optimizing the delivery of value—to minimize the entire life costs.

Asset Management as an Enabler

Asset management is an established platform that can be used as an enabling tool to ensure the resilience of urban infrastructure. The deployment of preventive management approaches based on risk and condition assessments can be a conduit for ensuring continued operation and maintenance (O&M) and compliance with planning, design, and construction standards, and regulatory requirements for long-term asset performance and continued service delivery. Resilience is the ability of a system to withstand or accommodate stresses and shocks, such as climate change-induced variations and impacts or major disasters, while still maintaining its function. In cities, resilience will depend on the ability to maintain essential assets, and to ensure access to services and functions that support the needs of citizens and business. Some key aspects of a resilient city are summarized in Box 6.1.

Box 6.1: Understanding Urban Resilience through Asset Management

At an urban scale, resilience will depend on the ability to maintain essential assets, as well as to ensure access to services and functions that support the well-being of citizens. Cities that may be considered resilient most often exhibit the following key characteristics:

- **Flexibility and diversity.** The ability to perform essential tasks under a wide range of conditions, and to convert assets or modify structures to introduce new ways of achieving essential goals. A resilient system has key assets and functions distributed so that they are not all affected by a given event at any one time (locational diversity) and multiple ways of meeting a given need (functional diversity).
- **Redundancy and modularity.** The capacity for contingency situations, to accommodate increasing or extreme events, unexpected demand, or surge pressures; also, multiple pathways and a variety of options for service delivery, or interacting components composed of similar parts that can replace each other if one or even many fail.
- **Safe failure.** The ability to absorb shocks and the cumulative effects of slow-onset challenges in ways that avoid catastrophic failures, or where failures in one structure or linkage are unlikely to result in cascading impacts across other systems.
- **Resourcefulness.** The capacities to identify problems, establish priorities, and mobilize resources. Resourcefulness is also related to the capacity to recognize and devise strategies that relate to different incentives and operational models of different groups.
- **Responsiveness and rapidity.** The capacity to organize and reorganize, as well as to establish a function and sense of order in a timely manner both in advance of and following a failure.
- **Learning.** The ability to learn through formal and informal processes, as well as to internalize past experiences and alter strategies based on knowledge and experience.

Source: Adapted from the 2014 City Resilience Framework developed by Arup International Development and the Institute of Social and Environmental Transition under the Rockefeller Foundation-funded Asian Cities Climate Change Resilience Network project.

Asset management enables preventive and timely corrective actions to be undertaken by cities. Effective asset management ensures that investments to minimize future O&M costs are made, which increases asset life and defers financing for asset replacement. Savings generated by sound asset management can be used to improve service levels, including the extension of networks to underserved low-income areas.

The GrEEEn Cities Operational Framework (GCOF) enables improved asset management to be linked with enhanced livability and encourages a city to examine and manage its natural attributes, and its cultural and historical assets through an asset management framework (Figure 6.1). It links the qualitative value of services to asset performance and demonstrates that effective asset management is directly or indirectly related to environment improvement

Figure 6.1: Asset Management for GrEEEn Cities

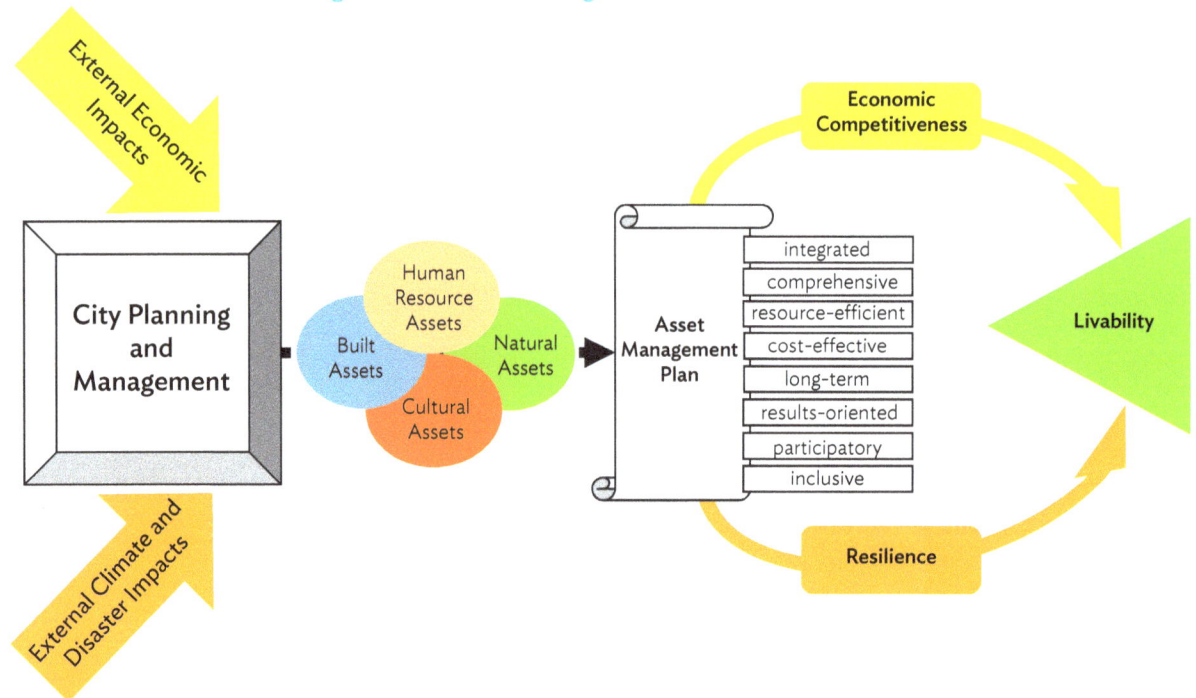

Source: Authors.

and more livable cities. For example, better management and treatment of domestic wastewater will lead to less pollution of water bodies, improved health of communities, and an enhancement of the city's livability. Under the urban profile of the GrEEEn City Action Plan (GCAP), the spatial distributions of natural, historical, and cultural assets are mapped and their operation, maintenance, and preservation are seen to be within the jurisdiction of the city government. Natural, social, historical, and cultural attributes can be integrated as "city" assets, become part of the asset inventory, and included in an integrated asset management framework and plan.

Key Elements of an Asset Management Plan

An asset management plan considers the core assets of a city to be held by households, enterprises, the community (government mainly), and the finance sector.[18] Households have human capital and housing assets. Enterprises have productive capital, land and buildings, and rights over the exploitation of natural resources. Communities—the government—have social and physical infrastructure, for example, hospitals and public transport, respectively, and control of the use of natural capital, for example, water bodies and forests—for recreation, resources, and waste sinks. Asset management is concerned with identifying, quantifying, and, where appropriate, locating these assets. They are also concerned with how city governments—and specific agencies—are able to allocate resources and meet O&M needs in relation to these assets.

---

[18]   Financial assets are not considered in this review.

Asset management plans vary in complexity in cities where they are used (two examples from Canada are presented in Boxes 6.2 and 6.3). The content, scope, and level of detail would be tailored to local contexts, driven by the resources and data available.

The following are the key elements of an asset management plan:

- **Objectives.** Describes the objectives of the plan, including guidelines on how often it should be updated, and how the plan will be monitored, evaluated, and improved. This section can also outline how the city's assets relate to its wider vision, strategy, and plans (e.g., GCAP).
- **Asset inventory.** Describes what built and natural assets the city or the agency owns and has, and the location of these assets. This could be a geographic information system (GIS)-based register of assets that draws from different datasets. It would be periodically updated, with new assets added as they are built or acquired, and old ones deleted as their useful lives end. Such an inventory would capture the different facets of a city's assets, including
  (i) *human capital*—using population, education, and income data by level of education to aggregate present value of average incomes;
  (ii) *housing, including neighborhood infrastructure*—satellite and construction cost data;
  (iii) *productive capital*—capital estimated through capital-to-output ratios and allocated by industry clusters, where possible;
  (iv) *land and buildings, including a heritage overlay*—satellite and construction cost data;
  (v) *social and physical infrastructure, for example, hospitals and public transport, respectively*—satellite, construction cost, and sector inventory data; and
  (vi) *natural capital, for example, water bodies and forests* (for recreation, resources, and waste sinks)—satellite data, supplemented with appropriate resource and/or contingent valuation methodologies.

Box 6.2: Guide for Municipal Asset Management Plans in Ontario, Canada

With a view to encouraging all municipalities to focus on improving their asset management plans, the Ministry of Infrastructure in Ontario, Canada, released its *Guide for Municipal Asset Management Plans*, which covers both asset management planning and the steps for developing a detailed asset management plan. For asset management planning, the guide focuses on innovation, integration with financial planning, and enhancement of the planning process associated with asset management. In developing a detailed asset management plan, the guide urges reviewing the state of local infrastructure, defining the desired levels of service, developing an asset management strategy keeping those in view, and providing a financing strategy.

Source: Government of Ontario, Ministry of Infrastructure. 2012. *Building Together: Guide for Municipal Asset Management Plans.* Toronto. http://www.moi.gov.on.ca/pdf/en/Municipal%20 Strategy_English_Web.pdf

Box 6.3: Asset Management in Fredericton, Canada

The City of Fredericton, the capital of the province of New Brunswick in the eastern part of Canada, is an example of a municipality that focuses on asset management as a key component of a long-term financial plan for sustainability. With a population of 56,000 (and more than 100,000 in the Greater Fredericton region), the city is known as a Smart City because of its two universities and its thriving engineering and technology sectors. In recent years, it has taken significant steps to improve its asset management program, including setting up its first asset management system in 2005.

Perhaps the most significant step in overall asset management came with the city's adoption of the Public Sector Accounting Board (PSAB) regulation 3150 in 2009. This regulation stipulates that, after 1 January 2009, local governments must account for their tangible capital assets on their financial statements.

Becoming compliant with PSAB 3150 was not easy and required considerable time commitment from the staff in all departments. The first task was to do an initial inventory of all of the city's tangible capital assets, such as water and sewer piping, treatment plants, pumping stations, municipal buildings including police and fire stations, recreational buildings, roads, and other municipal assets. This initial inventory required the staff to determine the size and location of all assets, the year the assets were built, and the initial capital cost. Because some infrastructure assets were old (more than 100 years old), costing and other information was not always available. In cases where there were gaps in cost information, it was sometimes necessary to "work backward" by establishing what it would cost if a particular asset were built today, and by estimating what the cost would have been 50 years ago, for example. In some instances where records did not exist, it was also necessary to estimate the date that a particular asset was built.

After this initial inventory, the staff determined the life cycles for each asset group. Whereas some water pipes, for example, may last for 80 years, concrete sidewalks generally last for 40 years only. With the initial valuation and the life cycles of each asset, it was possible to arrive at the current residual value of each asset. With these data, the city's financial statements could now include the value of all of the city's tangible capital assets.

Since becoming "PSAB-compliant," New Brunswick has developed a more complete understanding of its infrastructure assets, which has enabled improved coordination between departments and improved awareness among its citizens.

Source: M. Jamer. 2015. Infrastructure Asset Management: Can the Canadian Municipal Experience Help Inform Better Practices in Southeast Asia? *The Governance Brief.* Issue 21. Manila: Asian Development Bank. http://www.adb.org/sites/default/files/publication/152995/governance-brief-21-infrastructure-asset-management.pdf

- **State of local infrastructure.** This builds on the asset inventory to include information identified by the current state of the assets, such as a financial and replacement cost valuation, asset age distribution and expected useful life, and the condition of assets. This would involve an analysis of the replacement costs, depreciation, and net asset values for all assets, as well as of age, condition, and capability. Uniform data verification and condition assessment policies should be adapted to the extent possible.

- **Expected outcomes and desired level of service.** This identifies outcomes and levels of service for assets, through performance measures, targets, and time scales to achieve them. It describes the level of service expected in the future based on forecasting demand using project population and incomes, as well as any external trends or issues that may affect expected levels of service. For instance, a city's water body may serve as a containment facility for storm- or floodwater during the monsoons, and its capacity must be maintained—through desilting or expansion to ensure its role during a flood or climate-induced hazard. The "visioning" and "urban profile" aspects of the GrEEEn City approach would enable such natural assets to be recognized in building a city's resilience to climate change.

- **Asset management plan.** The main section of the plan includes the set of planned actions that will enable the assets to meet expected outcomes and the desired level of service in a sustainable way. The strategy identifies which assets are of high, medium, or low priority in the context of the level of service, costs and revenue,

Photo Credit: ADB

Photo Credits: ADB/Pushpa Kumara (*left*); ADB/Luis Ascui (*right*)

The development and implementation of an asset management plan and system require a skilled workforce whose capacities are regularly trained.

environment improvement, cultural or historical importance, and livability. The plan would include planned actions for the maintenance, repair, replacement, disposal and expansion of assets, and activities related to unexpected events. The plan also includes non-infrastructure solutions (actions or policies that can lower costs or extend asset life) and outlines procurement methods or principles.

- **Subasset management plans.** Separate plans should be produced for major subgroups, including (i) urban infrastructure—roads and sidewalks, cycling paths, water supply, wastewater collection and treatment, solid waste collection and disposal, road maintenance, and public open space management; (ii) conservation and preservation of the natural environment; and (iii) identified social, historical, and cultural attributes. These would be identified during the preparation of the urban profile and their priorities determined during the visioning exercise.

- **Financing plan.** This shows yearly expenditure forecasts broken down by non-infrastructure solutions, maintenance, renewal and rehabilitation, replacement, disposal activities, and expansion activities. Where possible, actual expenditures for the preceding 3–5 years should also be assessed. The strategy shows yearly revenues by source and discusses key assumptions. It identifies any funding shortfall that cannot be eliminated by revising service levels, asset management, and/or financing strategies, and assesses its impact and how it will be managed. It is supported by documentation that explains how the expenditure and revenue forecasts were developed, including on operating costs (including routine and periodic maintenance) and revenue (including past and projected charges levied on service users).

- **Monitoring mechanisms.** This includes the mechanisms that allow for establishing the effectiveness of actions against outcomes, applying timely corrective actions for improvement, ensuring that assets are generating sufficient revenues, and ensuring that these are maximizing returns on investments. This should involve communities, to encourage better awareness and acceptance of the constraints and challenges faced by city governments.

Mechanisms for Implementation

The successful implementation of an asset management plan requires mechanisms to ensure financial sustainability, engagement with key stakeholders, and institutional coordination. To be useful, asset management plans must be closely integrated with a city's wider strategies and plans. There is also space for engaging the private sector, to improve efficiency and bring in technical knowledge.

For financial sustainability, direct charges need to be levied on those who use or benefit from an asset to ensure that the costs of asset management are recovered, where possible. Ideally, these charges should recover all costs—depreciation, interest and other charges on debt, and operation and routine maintenance costs. At the very minimum, they should recover the costs of O&M. Nevertheless, it has to be recognized that payments for the use or benefit of some assets can be funded only out of general taxation or transfers. There are many cases, however, where user charges could be levied and are not. Options for different financing structures exist and should be broadly scoped and adjusted to a particular asset (World Economic Forum and Boston Consulting Group 2014, pp. 58–63). Without appropriate budgets and "guaranteed" sources of funds or revenue, asset management will fail.

Different asset groups will be managed by various stakeholders. Stakeholder engagement and communication is critical. Partnerships need to be built, and citizens and businesses should be encouraged to contribute to solutions rather than simply complaining about the standard of services and the condition of assets. There needs to be regular and mandated consultations between the community and businesses, on one side, and city representatives, on the other, as part of a joint responsibility to maintain assets. Sponsorship should be sought, where possible. For example, the management of public open spaces, gardens, and parks benefits from strong community ownership and business sponsorship where simple issues, such as noncollection of garbage, can spoil the area. Periodic surveys collecting views and opinions should be routine.

While the overall responsibility for asset management would generally remain with the city government, the private sector can and should play a role with respect to access to finance, technology, and efficiency in operations. This could involve adopting one or several of the modalities of private sector participation—contracting, outsourcing, franchising, leasing, public–private partnerships (PPPs), or divestiture. By far, the easiest is the outsourcing of the O&M of certain assets to the private sector to manage. The selection of assets to be outsourced should be on the basis of O&M costs to be incurred, the revenue to be realized, and the returns to the private sector. Nevertheless, it is essential to define the contracting terms carefully, with an emphasis on specifications and outcomes to ensure that the PPP is effective. This will be undertaken on a case-by-case basis and will depend on the condition of the asset, the remaining service life, the level of service required, what needs to be done to the asset, the estimated costs and revenues, the levels of risks, and the affordability of tariffs.

An appropriate institutional mechanism for implementing the asset management plan is critical. This would involve delegating roles and responsibilities within the government—and elsewhere. Responsibilities for maintaining and conserving natural and cultural assets would need to be delegated across departments with allocated expenditure lines approved by the local government, and they need to take account of what the communities and the private sector are already doing.

Finally, asset management plans should be fully integrated as part of a city's strategy and planning processes and provide a means to make the urban profiling and GCAP processes more tangible, quantifiable, and operationally relevant. The integration of asset management into the City of Vancouver's Corporate Business Plan (Box 6.4) provides an example of how this integration can be achieved in practice.

Financing for GrEEEn Cities

The Financing Challenge

Urban infrastructure worth several hundred billion dollars a year will be needed to fill prior gaps and keep pace with the unprecedented urban growth in Asia. Over the 10-year period from 2010 to 2020, the 32 developing member countries of the Asian Development Bank (ADB) require financing of $747 billion annually to meet the growing demand for energy, transport, telecommunications, water, and sanitation. About 68% of this is needed for new capacity investments in infrastructure, and about 32% is needed for the maintenance

Persistent financing gaps lead to ineffective utilization and unrealized benefits of assets, adversely impacting livability. Building capacity of the public sector to leverage private sector and innovative sources of financing in parallel to improving its fiscal position is imperative.

Box 6.4: Integrating Asset Management in City Plans and Strategies in Vancouver, Canada

The City of Vancouver, Canada, prepared its 2014 Corporate Business Plan, which provided an overview of its citizen and customer service priorities and delivery strategies. In the plan, the city outlined 10 long-term strategic goals, which included goals relating to safety, the environment, provision of services, civic amenities, and so on.

Of particular relevance is **Goal 10: Vancouver's Assets and Infrastructure Are Well-Managed and Resilient**. This is measured by (i) the share of major public works assets in poor condition, (ii) the share of civic use buildings where detailed external condition assessments have been completed, and (iii) the value of infrastructure (tangible capital assets) per capita.

In relation to this, the following short-term priorities have been identified:

• **10A: Strategy for City-Owned Property Leased to Nonprofit Agencies**
Implement an effective business strategy that establishes a centralized structure and process for managing and overseeing the city-owned property leased to nonprofit agencies.

• **10B: Capital Projects Operational Efficiency**
Enhance management and coordination of all capital projects undertaken by the city, including public works and facilities renewal and/or development, with the objectives of maximizing efficiencies and value for money as well as minimizing disruptive impacts on the public and other stakeholders, to include the development of project management protocols, expectations and training, and a center of expertise in project management for all of the city's major capital projects.

• **10C: Maintenance, Safety, and Energy Performance of City-Owned Buildings**
Optimize the management of city-owned buildings, with a focus on (i) completing and maintaining condition assessment data, (ii) developing and implementing a seismic strategy, and (iii) developing and implementing a facility energy management plan.

Source: City of Vancouver. 2015. *2015 Corporate Business Plan.* Vancouver. http://vancouver.ca/files/cov/corporate-business-plan.pdf

or replacement of existing assets (Naik Singru and Lindfield, forthcoming in 2016). The infrastructure gap increases in scale and nature, if not addressed in a timely manner. Asia has large savings, significant international reserves, and rapid accumulations of funds that could be utilized for meeting these infrastructure investment needs, but Asian markets have fallen short in using available resources to channel funding into highly needed infrastructure projects (Bhattacharyay 2010).

Financing is required for designing, implementing, and operating livability in cities. With fiscal decentralization and devolution of power, a large number of countries in Asia have divested their service provision responsibilities to local governments (Naik Singru and Lindfield, forthcoming in 2016). Local government revenues are often insufficient to meet their capital expenditure, and they are dependent on fiscal transfers from the provincial and national budgets. The operating expenditures pertaining to infrastructure assets are met through the local government's finances. Often, local governments do not have the required finances to maintain these assets. This results in ineffective asset utilization and unrealized benefits that the assets were intended to achieve.

National governments recognize that cities need to develop to continue contributing to the national economy and invest in infrastructure financing, for which an increase in the provision for capital expenditure is required.

As cities seek to improve their financial standings, national governments are also requesting multilateral banks and donors for support directly at the subnational level, including lending to provincial and local governments without sovereign guarantees. While the public sector must still improve its fiscal position, it must also be more effective in using its relatively scarce budget to leverage more private sector financing and raising it to above the 20%–30% share it currently holds (Naik Singru and Lindfield, forthcoming in 2016). This includes catalyzing the participation of domestic sources of finance, including capital markets, if sustainable systems of infrastructure financing are to be developed. Attracting such funds requires improvements in market structures, incentives, and instruments and in accountability by all participants, including governments and donor agencies. Taken together, such actions can lower costs and improve performance, making room for commercially priced finance to support a larger share of infrastructure projects, as in the more developed markets (Sood, Mays, and Lindfield 2012).

First, cities can take charge of their revenues by maximizing conventional finances such as increasing efficiency in the collection of user charges; introducing new "green" charges such as emission or effluent charges for maintaining the environment and in addition to user charges for the public service provided by the government or industry; assessing the revenue potential of tradable development rights and marketable permits.[19] Second, cities can leverage private sector finance by identifying and unbundling potentially profitable investments and funding these from the capital markets. Finally, cities can seek specialist green financing such as the Clean Development Mechanism, Global Environment Facility (GEF), Climate Investment Funds (CIF), and the ASEAN Infrastructure Fund, among others.[20] Due to the nature of the international agreements, city governments are not able to directly access these funds and need to route their requests for funding through the national governments. National governments should proactively access funds that are globally being made available, especially for climate change-related activities, such as the Green Climate Fund (GCF).[21]

---

[19] A good example is the ADB (2007c) Program Loan to the Philippines for the Local Government Financing and Budget Reform Program Cluster, which addressed more efficient national–local government fund flows; improved revenue generation at the local level; capacity development of local government units in planning, financial management, and procurement; and improved monitoring systems. Being rated *highly successful* and, furthermore, leading to a follow-on cluster program, this program was recognized through a Sustainability Award by ADB's Independent Evaluation Department in 2015.

[20] The GEF has a focus on assisting city governments to meet their capital expenditure requirements. Funds have to be accessed by the national governments.

[21] The GCF is a fund within the framework of the United Nations Framework Convention on Climate Change founded as a mechanism to make a significant and ambitious contribution to the global efforts toward attaining the goals set by the international community to combat climate change. This is to assist the developing countries in both adaptation and mitigation practices.

Nevertheless, the demand still outstrips the supply. In terms of total value, these funds tend to be small when compared with investment needs. Given that, there is a need for city governments to position and market their initiatives in such a way that it becomes attractive for these funds to support.

Increasingly, the lack of sufficient development funding to meet the growing needs of the cities is affecting the private sector and their business. The traditional approach of using public funds for creating public assets, and private funds for private assets and goods, falls short. There is a need to harness the potential of the private sector in raising finances and benefit from the efficiencies that the private sector is recognized to bring. In identifying how the private sector can contribute, it should be clearly noted that the private sector will be interested only if their profit motive is met. Risk-free financial returns comparable to or higher than the prevailing market norms are necessary conditions for private sector involvement. Wherever this is possible, city governments should engage the private sector in raising financing capital. However, the mainstay of development funding for cities will continue to remain through public funds. This can be ably supported by additional funds available from the private sector.

As part of the urban profiling exercise (see Chapter 3), the GrEEEn Cities Operational Framework (GCOF) assesses options for financing green infrastructure in cities. This is achieved through an assessment of primary and secondary data gathering and analysis by (i) understanding the municipal finance framework in cities through a review of existing laws and decrees, as well as interviews with government officials at the state and provincial levels and with officials from bilateral and multilateral agencies; (ii) assessing the private sector's perspective on subnational lending and infrastructure financing through interviews with local commercial banks and discussions with infrastructure development and private sector professionals; (iii) evaluating the potential for innovative financing and risk management tools, using prior experience, expert knowledge, and client discussions to identify innovative financing tools; and (iv) developing a prefeasibility analysis for proposed investments and the potential for private sector participation through a cross-matrix to assess the strategic importance of initiatives to enhance competitiveness and inclusiveness. Through this process, opportunities for leveraging financing from the public sector, the private sector, and international financing sources can be identified and developed. This can be done by making financing available to encourage local governments to invest in green infrastructure. There are different mechanisms for operating such facilities, and this will have to evolve based on national or provincial needs. There are examples of successful implementation experiences such as the Tamil Nadu Urban Development Fund (TNUDF) in India (Insert D), which will have to be analyzed for its relevance in the context.

Some particularly relevant mechanisms for how each of these financing sources can be developed and utilized will be discussed later.

Public Sector Financing
Traditional financial instruments, such as property taxes, congestion charges, variable parking fees, and toll lanes, are an important first step toward achieving greener urban infrastructure.

Since GrEEEn City projects take an integrated approach to development, financing for these projects should take advantage of the underlying economy of a green city. The benefits

Photo Credit: Renard Teipelke

There is a need for new financing mechanisms to meet the rising demand for infrastructure investments in rapidly growing cities

accruing should be cumulative. For example, an upgraded road generates benefits for adjacent properties; an improved stormwater system creates benefits for the users of a whole district; an investment incentive brings hotel development to a city. If the road, stormwater system, and investment incentive are all located in or focused on the same vicinity, however, they can combine to spur the redevelopment of the whole area. In such a case, the resultant economic benefits in that location can outweigh the costs of the individual investments.

When considering how such projects can be financed, the future dynamics of the real estate market become important. A successful initiative in a given place will produce increases in land value. The benefits accrue to the property owners. Most of those benefits are brought about by investments and enabling measures put into place by public sector actors. How can the public sector recover the "unearned increment" of the land property value increases? How can those funds be put to work again on the next initiative to be undertaken by the Green City?

Two ways of recovering the unearned increment are property taxes and betterment taxes. Many cities around the world do not have a modern property tax, in which property owners pay an annual tax to government based on a certain percentage (often 1%–2%) of the current market value of their property (either land or improvements—buildings, etc.— or both). This is one of the best ways to recover infrastructure development as well as O&M costs. The tax will be fair to the extent that property owners use and benefit from the urban services provided to their property and in their district. Betterment taxes are also used in a limited number of countries to recover the cost of infrastructure improvements from their main beneficiaries: the owners of nearby property. Local governments levy a one-time fee on the property owners. Every property within the designated impact area of the investment pays something; properties in closer proximity to the works typically pay a higher fee.

Other economic instruments that can be utilized include incentive pricing and risk management schemes. Block tariffs for urban services make low quantities available at low prices, while charging more per unit in the case of above-average consumption. This encourages conservation and boosts affordability for low-income households. Water and wastewater services are often priced using block tariffs. Risk management schemes include hazard insurance, in which property owners pay a small fee for an insurance policy that will refund part of their losses in the case of a severe hazard event. Flood insurance, commonly sold in more developed countries, is being considered with increasing frequency across Asia.

Another important dimension for financing, particularly for O&M of infrastructure assets, is for cities to adopt measures that minimize costs. A city's efforts must begin here, and the move to diversifying revenue sources. This is particularly relevant in cases in which an emphasis on resource conservation (to decrease the ecological footprint) leads, when successful, to a decrease in consumption of the resource (e.g., water and energy). As quantities consumed decline, service providers collect less revenue and the funding available for O&M decreases. To maintain service levels, water and energy service providers may be faced with the need to raise tariffs, which can create additional political challenges.

Cost reductions can be achieved through the use of new technologies and measures to make O&M more efficient. Cities in Australia are looking at the feasibility of tapping into alternative water sources. Analysis done by Marsden Jacob Associates (2006) shows that options like "catchment thinning" and purchasing irrigation water can lower costs, especially where it is not necessary to build long transmission pipelines.[22] The use of long-life bulbs for street lighting has been consistently successful across many Asian cities in reducing energy costs (The Climate Group 2012; Development Finance International 2014). Technology can also help reduce O&M costs, as urban utilities rely on computer tools, inspection robots, and geographic information system (GIS) to monitor the performance of underground assets (World Economic Forum and Boston Consulting Group 2014).

---

[22]   See also Organisation for Economic Co-operation and Development (OECD) (2015, p. 65).

The experience of Tamil Nadu, India, provides a comprehensive and compelling case study on how a city's demand for infrastructure can be linked with domestic financing through the establishment of an intermediary (Insert D).

Private Sector Financing

Local government funding is usually insufficient to finance the whole range of green infrastructure identified in GCAPs. A diverse set of revenue sources must be targeted. National governments can provide matching loans or grants. Such national funding can also be designed to leverage private sector financing. There are certain conditions that need to be put in place to attract and capture private sector investments. The three main conditions are (i) markets for green urban investment projects, (ii) good return on investment, and (iii) limited risk.

Cities and countries differ with respect to these conditions; as such, some of these instruments could be more appropriate for cities in industrialized and medium-income countries than lower-income developing countries, for which grants, loans, and other development finance instruments could be more relevant. There are several existing financial instruments that cities have applied to attract private finance for urban green infrastructure, including (i) private sector involvement in urban green infrastructure taking the form of PPPs, in which the long-term risk is transferred to the private sector; (ii) using an alternative instrument, tax increment financing, or future tax revenues to attract private finance; (iii) real estate developers paying for the infrastructure needed to connect their new development to existing infrastructure in the form of development charges (impact fees) and value capture (taxes that capture the value increases of real estate due to new infrastructure development nearby); (iv) loans, bonds, and carbon finance instruments used to attract private finance in well-functioning capital markets (Merk et al. 2012).

The Government of the United States recently passed the Water Infrastructure Finance and Innovation Act, which makes low-interest loans available to water utilities or local governments for capital improvements (Box 6.5). Countries can also design similar financing facilities that prioritize green infrastructure projects, such as storage reservoirs for stormwater to reduce the risk of flooding or facilities for the collection and treatment of rainwater. Such a financing mechanism therefore serves the double function of mobilizing additional sources of funding and prioritizing infrastructure investments with high and positive environmental impacts.

International Financing Mechanisms

This need for urban infrastructure financing is further compounded by the adverse impacts of climate change. If the challenges of climate change and reduced greenhouse gas (GHG) emissions are to be addressed, it is essential to reduce energy demand in cities and to build their resilience to climate change events. New investments are needed to change the city form, building design and development density, and logistics. Infrastructure needs to be "hardened" against climate change impacts. Urban management systems must be made more efficient and effective. Financing these investments will be a considerable challenge.

Box 6.5: Water Infrastructure Finance and Innovation Act, United States

The Water Infrastructure Finance and Innovation Act in the United States (US), passed in 2014, creates a low-interest loan facility for partial financing of public–private partnership water supply and wastewater projects. It covers new works as well as upgrades and renovations. Local governments or water utilities that have structured with private investors and/or operators can access a federal government loan to cover up to half of the project costs. The intention is to use the federal funds to leverage private investment. The terms are favorable: interest rates tied to long-term US Treasury rates and loan terms of up to 35 years. This law builds on the Transport Infrastructure Finance and Innovation Act, which has a strong track record in providing low-cost financing on similar terms for public transport projects in US cities.

Source: United States Environmental Protection Agency. 2015. Water Infrastructure Finance and Innovation Act. http://water.epa.gov/grants_funding/cwsrf/wifia.cfm

International financing mechanisms are needed to provide the support for those investments in the face of pressing developmental needs confronting urban managers in many areas. For this purpose, the existing $6.1 billion Strategic Climate Fund provided to multilateral development banks is too limited in scale, although it has piloted effective funding approaches (Climate Investment Funds 2015). The GCF (2015) could provide significant incentives if its funds are leveraged. But these financial mechanisms, while necessary, are not sufficient and need to be supported with appropriate national mechanisms to identify, formulate, and finance Green City investments on a systemic basis.

Of particular promise are the rapidly developing capital markets of Asia. Asian governments in general, and particularly Indonesia, Malaysia, and Thailand in their Association of Southeast Asian Nations (ASEAN) Green Cities Program, recognize that there is a need for a more systemic approach. If the appropriate enabling framework is in place, significant local investment funds, potentially augmented by institutional funds from the developed world, could be mobilized. The total amount of developing Asia's institutional funds (pension funds and life insurance) is $2.5 trillion and growing at approximately 5% per year (Towers Watson 2014). Banks, while constrained by Basel III requirements, have significant funds. In some countries, debt and equity funds have been successfully launched, also with support or in cooperation with international financing institutions as modeled in the India Infrastructure Project Financing Facility (ADB 2007b, 2009a, 2013a).[23] The problem, from the point of view of mobilizing these funds for infrastructure, is that the structures of local capital markets often severely constrain the provision of longer-term "patient capital" needed for infrastructure provision, and particularly for green infrastructure.[24] Credit enhancement mechanisms tailored to the needs of such green projects are required to provide credit

---

[23] The India Infrastructure Project Financing Facility was designed to support the Government of India's infrastructure development agenda by increasing private sector participation in infrastructure investments. The original ADB loan of $500 million was intended to catalyze investment of $2.5 billion–$3.5 billion from the private sector via public–private partnerships.

[24] In this case, both climate change-related mitigation and adaptation infrastructure and infrastructure designed to counter environmental pollution.

Philippines
The PINAI Fund

ADB Asian Development Bank
FIGHTING POVERTY IN ASIA AND THE PACIFIC
WWW.ADB.ORG

The Philippine Investment Alliance for Infrastructure Fund, or PINAI, is a private equity fund that will invest in core infrastructure assets in the Philippines. It's the largest and the first of its kind in the country, and is well-timed to capitalize on various public-private partnership opportunities.

HOW THE FUND WORKS

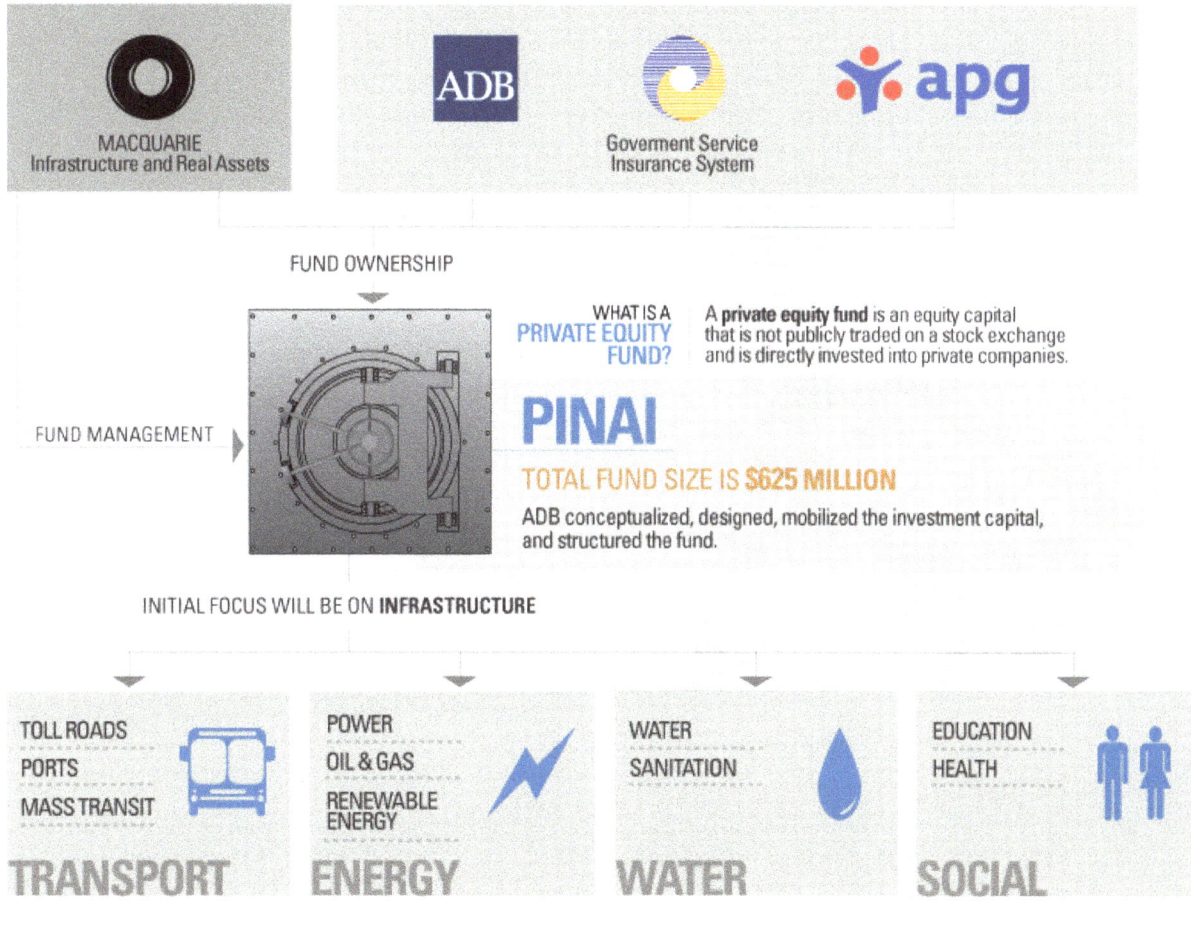

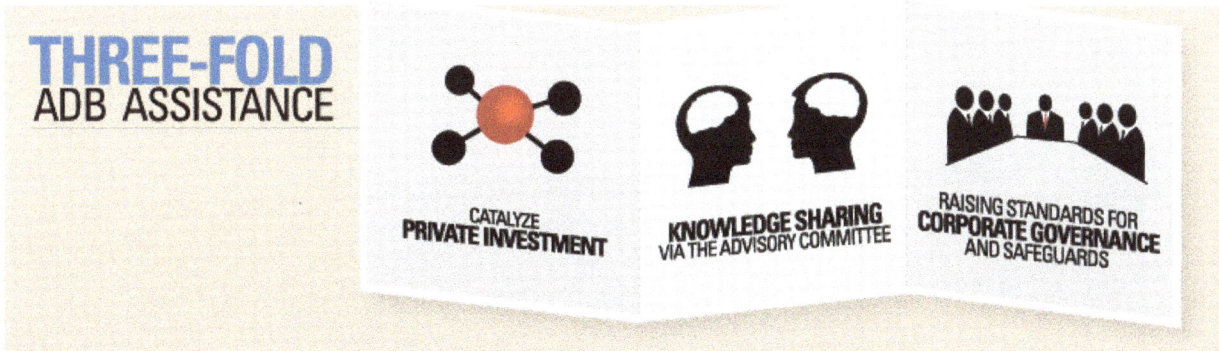

MACQUARIE
Infrastructure and Real Assets

ADB

Goverment Service
Insurance System

apg

FUND OWNERSHIP

WHAT IS A
**PRIVATE EQUITY
FUND?**

A **private equity fund** is an equity capital that is not publicly traded on a stock exchange and is directly invested into private companies.

FUND MANAGEMENT

PINAI

TOTAL FUND SIZE IS **$625 MILLION**

ADB conceptualized, designed, mobilized the investment capital, and structured the fund.

INITIAL FOCUS WILL BE ON **INFRASTRUCTURE**

TOLL ROADS
PORTS
MASS TRANSIT
TRANSPORT

POWER
OIL & GAS
RENEWABLE ENERGY
ENERGY

WATER
SANITATION
WATER

EDUCATION
HEALTH
SOCIAL

THREE-FOLD
ADB ASSISTANCE

CATALYZE
PRIVATE INVESTMENT

KNOWLEDGE SHARING
VIA THE ADVISORY COMMITTEE

RAISING STANDARDS FOR
CORPORATE GOVERNANCE
AND SAFEGUARDS

Photo Credit: ADB/Ralph Romero

Philippines: The Philippine Investment Alliance for Infrastructure (PINAI) Fund, a $625 million private equity fund, is the largest and first of its kind in the country and will invest in core infrastructure assets

ratings that can attract both local and international (i) project sponsor funds (such as Violia, on the one hand, and a local developer such as the Lippo Group in Indonesia, on the other) and (ii) institutional funds (such as Deutsche Bank Private Equity, on the one hand, and the Malaysian Employers Provident Fund, on the other, which generally require *investment grade* ratings).[25] The Philippine Investment Alliance for Infrastructure (PINAI) is an example of such a mechanism.[26]

Financing Mechanism for GrEEEn Cities

A mechanism for financing infrastructure for GrEEEn Cities is to develop a "twinned fund" with ADB as a catalyst for tapping global funds such as the CIF or GCF using existing financing facilities within ADB such as the Urban Financing Partnership Facility to catalyze GrEEEn Cities financing mechanisms at the national, provincial, or local level. Most such financing mechanisms would be multiwindow funds with local finance provided through national debt and/or equity markets, as appropriate, and with which international funding could either participate directly or in parallel. The principle, once established, of a multilateral development bank fund linked to local funds to finance grEEEn investments is revolutionary as it leverages large domestic sources of finance.

It also lays the basis of a mechanism through which the GCF can catalyze a transformational pipeline of investments it requires to fulfill its own mandate. Through such a mechanism, as demonstrated by PINAI, international institutional investors can be "crowded in"—in effect, such a mechanism is the only way that the GCF will be able to achieve the $100 billion transfers it is mandated to achieve.

---

[25]   These vary according to the regulatory context of the institution: "investment grade" to an Indian debt fund is not "investment grade" to a private equity fund based in the United Kingdom.

[26]   PINAI is a $625 million pool of resources in the Philippines from the Government Service Insurance System (GSIS), a unit of the Macquarie Group, APG Asset Management, and ADB. GSIS will contribute the most with $400 million, while ADB will provide $25 million. The two foreign firms will account for the rest (ADB 2012b).

Linking City Infrastructure Needs with Domestic Finance in Tamil Nadu, India

Introduction

In 1992, the Government of India passed the 74th Constitutional Amendment, which recognized that environmental infrastructure at the local level was best created by local governments, and that a framework was needed for municipalities to design, mobilize finance, create infrastructure, and pay for its use over time. The amendment responded to a need for a borrowing framework that can mobilize private long-term finance, thereby leveraging scarce budgetary sources.

For cities to mobilize private finance, they need to demonstrate clear revenue streams to service debt; hence, state-level actions are needed on the demand and supply sides. On the demand side, these include a rational and stable devolution framework, power over own source revenues, and a clear demarcation of functions. On the supply side of finance, the old practice of state government guarantee-backed financing of city infrastructure would need to be replaced by a borrowing framework so that cities can access domestic finance.

Since the mid-1990s, the Government of Tamil Nadu State had been attempting reforms to devolve greater authority to municipalities, reduce functional fragmentation, and provide a borrowing framework. These reforms included setting up the Tamil Nadu Urban Development Fund (TNUDF), an intermediary that would provide systemic access for smaller and medium-sized cities to longer-term sources of financing. The TNUDF was expected to pool small borrowing requirements and mobilize domestic finance for cities' financing needs.

This case study attempts to answer three questions: First, if the TNUDF experience is relevant for other situations, what are the reforms and/or enabling conditions that allow intermediation to perform its resource-raising functions for municipal infrastructure? Second, does efficient intermediation enable improved municipal performance in creating infrastructure and service delivery? Third, do reforms and intermediation need to go together?

State-Level Reforms and Enabling Conditions

Pre-1995

Prior to the 74th Amendment and associated reforms, infrastructure creation by municipalities was largely restricted to municipal roads, minor shopping complexes, and street lighting through ad hoc Tamil Nadu government grants and minor centrally sponsored schemes. In 1995, grants constituted 94% of municipal investments. Fiscal transfers to municipalities were low, ad hoc, lacking a clear trend, and with unsystematic inter se allocations. In 1996, the state's 102 municipalities carried a debt of Rs36.5 million on account of water supply and sewerage, with an own source revenue of Rs26 million. Decisions on accessing debt and competitiveness of its tenor and interest rate were made by the state and not municipalities. The loans, though a liability for the municipality, would be transferred from the state governments directly to the parastatals. Municipalities were neither involved in the design nor the implementation, and the delays in projects meant difficulties in collecting user charges, leading to a situation where cities became subsistence-level institutions with apathy to their financial performance and debt status.

The Municipal Urban Development Fund (MUDF, 1991–1996) provided direct financing for municipalities using a revolving fund and operated out of the housing departments of government. Unlike guarantee-backed financing, the MUDF established a direct relationship with municipalities and used modern appraisal techniques that required revenue improvements (as covenants) to finance its projects. The MUDF also provided grants for project preparation, which included a rigorous analysis of the municipal revenue system and debt-bearing status upon which loans were advanced. This criterion-based lending (as contrasted with guarantee-backed financing of parastatals) also resulted in high repayment rates of 95%, establishing the principle, that, however weak, municipalities could be credible borrowers, if loans are directly negotiated between the borrower and the lender and the responsibilities and rights are stipulated in a loan agreement.

In 1996, the MUDF performance encouraged the Tamil Nadu government to partner with the World Bank in broadening the scope of the MUDF, and position it as a financial intermediary, the TNUDF. The expectation was that with legal status, the TNUDF would be able to mobilize private capital for municipal investments and facilitate municipalities to invest in significant infrastructure, based on their demands and capacities to service debt.

Reform Actions: Post-1995
Following the passage of the 74th Amendment, the Tamil Nadu government enacted the corresponding legislation in 1995. After 23 years, municipalities were managed by an elected leadership. Key measures implemented in the coming years included rational devolution: 3.6% of the state's tax revenue was devolved to municipalities (with allocations based on population, per capita expenditure, and per capita revenue) and 15% set apart as an equalization-cum-incentive fund to reward performance and support weak and unviable cities. The expectation was that this would empower municipalities to assess local demands, create infrastructure, and improve service delivery.

On the supply side, the TNUDF was set up in partnership with private banks and a grant fund established (to be sustained from the Tamil Nadu government's share of profits from TNUDF lending) to improve the financial, technical, and managerial capacities of municipalities as well as to assist in bankable project preparation. Private sector involvement meant that scarce state and central government resources can be leveraged with private finance.

Tamil Nadu Urban Development Fund: Background, Structure, and Performance

The TNUDF was set up as a trust under the Indian Trust Act. The MUDF, which was previously located inside a government department, was restructured as a legal entity and expected to advance loans that would attract market finance. The TNUDF adopted lending policies and procedures that required borrowers to conform to viability and debt service ratios and opened up escrow accounts for loan repayments. TNUDF borrowings and lending were at fixed rates and in local currency, thereby avoiding currency and interest rate risks.

The fund disbursed around $100 million in its first 3 years to around 120 local governments for environmental and other infrastructure, with water and sanitation constituting a rising share of the portfolio. The TNUDF declared dividends to its shareholders and maintained a near 100% recovery rate. During 2001–2004, a period of fiscal stress at the state and municipal levels, the lending decreased, picking up during 2004–2007 when the fiscal situation improved. Over time, the TNUDF has maintained high asset quality, earnings, and capital adequacy that could be used to raise market finance for publicly owned infrastructure.

Mobilizing Private Finance through Intermediation

Leveraging its balance sheet, the TNUDF raised $35 million, 15 years tenor, in two bond offerings on the basis of an AA+ rating, at about 70 basis points above the state borrowing rate. The fund was also able to securitize its assets and raise market finance.

Recognizing the demand and need to lower costs for projects in the environment sector, the state government set up the Water and Sanitation Pooled Fund (WSPF) in 2003 as a trust with limited equity and eliminating dividend expectations. The WSPF, with little recourse to the capital, relied on credit enhancements of a debt service reserve fund and repayment from borrowers' taxes and fees. The average size of projects was $1 million (drinking water connections, pumping stations, etc.) and by pooling these demands, the WSPF raised $10 million through a bond issue (rated as AA with a spread of about 70 basis points over state government borrowing cost). A study of the bond issue of the WSPF demonstrated that domestic private debt can finance municipal infrastructure at low costs, if sufficient attention is given to the design of the intermediaries' capital structure, and security structures.

Institutional Impacts on Municipal Performance

At a macro level, the TNUDF/WSPF provided criteria based open access intermediation for smaller and medium-sized cities. Prior to these reforms and TNUDF presence, smaller and medium-sized cities depended on ad hoc state and national government grants for its own investments. Further, and perhaps most significant, municipalities took responsibility for larger environmental investments, such as water and sanitation and solid waste management, as compared with the majority of the investments going into shopping complexes and markets prior to the reforms. Implementation results show considerable savings in time and costs as compared with parastatal financing and implementation. Repayment rates were over 98% from these investments, as compared with 23% in state-guaranteed, parastatal-financed projects.

Systemic improvements, especially in the public space, are rarely on account of any single set of actions. The outcomes described are attributable to a collective institutional response, an active partnership with the World Bank, and an increasing sophistication of the Indian debt market. In this context, at least three major development impacts of the TNUDF can be identified: (i) the strengthening of municipal capacities to design, finance, and create infrastructure; (ii) the secular improvements in the management of subsidies, pricing, and service delivery; and (iii) the learning from below—the replication of successful financing by one city—to others and systemizing them at the state level.

Challenges and Lessons

The Tamil Nadu case demonstrates that the process of moving toward a sustainable financing system depends on devolving fiscal authority to local governments and reducing the fragmentation of markets. With elected local governments, the municipalities have all the incentives for ensuring the devolution of fiscal authority, but with little powers to effect this change. On the other hand, higher levels of government have all the powers to devolve, but few incentives. In this situation, the process of change can take time and is also likely to be subject to policy reversals (a key challenge in Tamil Nadu).

The first major lesson from the TNUDF experience is that intermediation is dependent on state-level reforms that free up municipal decision making. If municipalities are constrained in their basic functions—planning, design, and revenues—and in the absence of policy action to reduce functional and geographical fragmentation, intermediaries would be as constrained as the borrower. On the other hand, if local governments are transferred their share of taxes, they can be expected to leverage their finances and create infrastructure. In such a situation, an efficient intermediary makes the financing possible.

The second lesson is on the issues of ownership. Private ownership implies the need to service equity, and hence the higher costs of lending to the municipal sector. This question of returns is relevant, especially if the security mechanisms for debt service are the municipal cash flows themselves. As the WSPF example shows, if dividend expectations are removed, the costs of financing infrastructure would decrease. It is perhaps more appropriate for other states to design intermediation on the basis of the WSPF. The TNUDF or the commercial bank model needs continuous equity infusion and servicing, without any significant benefits over the flat equity structure of the WSPF. In retrospect, it would appear private ownership is neither a necessary nor sufficient condition for successful intermediation.

Opportunities

Given the small size of debt demands, relative to debt market norms, the benefits of reducing transaction costs through pooling and intermediation are obvious. International experience shows certain obvious commonalities on the demand and supply sides of financing small and medium-sized towns' environmental infrastructure: (i) the need for local, long-term debt to finance these investments; (ii) intermediation specifically designed by state policy, albeit in widely varying historical circumstances; (iii) support by all intermediaries to smaller local governments for project preparation; and (iv) varying cost of credit (as is to be expected), inversely with the strength of state support and the allowable security packages.

To begin with, two steps: a common agenda for reform and the identification of the borrowing framework. The reforms would be legal, technical, managerial, and financial steps that free up municipal decision making. Perhaps the time has come for more systemic reforms for linking municipal demand with domestic finance.

Note: This insert was prepared for ADB by K. Rajivan to provide an overview of a specific example for linking city infrastructure needs with domestic finance in the case of Tamil Nadu in India.

Source: K. Rajivan. 2014. Linking Cities With Domestic Markets: The Tamil Nadu Experience. Presentation at the ADB Enabling GrEEEn Cities Regional Conference, 13–14 May, Manila. http://www.scribd.com/doc/225208345/Tamil-Nadu-Urban-Development-Fund-TNUDF

Key Performance Indicators for GrEEEn Cities

Measuring Performance of Cities

The well-recognized aphorism "What you measure is only what you manage" has led to the establishment of indicators and associated indexes. These are measures of the effectiveness of management performance. In a city context, indicators are measures of a city's performance. Given that the city management involves a complex and integrated set of activities, it becomes necessary to prioritize those activities and the associated indicators as key performance indicators (KPIs). In other words, KPIs are selected indicators that are deemed to be relevant in measuring a city's performance in key activity areas and sectors.[27]

There are many initiatives under way to define what the KPIs in a city context should be. For instance, the Siemens (2015a) Green City Index assessed only the environmental performance of major cities in different world regions (e.g., Asia) by looking at the performance across different categories: energy and carbon dioxide, transport, water, land use and buildings, and waste and sanitation. In each of these categories, some indicators were identified, which eventually became the KPIs used to benchmark this index. Indicators were categorized as either qualitative or quantitative and weightages assigned to each indicator. Following a relative performance rating, cities were ranked against each other.

Similarly, there are other initiatives, which provide useful benchmarking information—based on KPIs—about how one city compares with other cities. This information is for the city's use to drive performance improvements (Box 6.6). While there are a number of KPI frameworks for intercity comparisons, there are also intracity ones to compare the city's own performance over the course of time. These identify KPIs across categories of environmental or other sustainability issues. All of these KPIs tend to be outcome indicators, which reveal how well the city has performed in the context of that category.

Some indexes have been developed that combine indicators (and even indexes) from existing sources (Centre for Sustainable Asian Cities, n.d.). These then form comprehensive indexes—measuring indicators under an overall framework or theme, as for instance quality of life (Mercer 2015), green growth (OECD 2014), or sustainability (Box 6.7).

KPIs Applied in the GrEEEn Cities Operational Framework

In the GrEEEn Cities Operational Framework (GCOF), KPIs are not solely measures for determining the effectiveness or performance levels of cities. By themselves, they are inherently tools to improve actual performance. KPIs are not restricted to outcomes across categories or groups. KPIs are also associated with processes. Broadly, KPIs include city livability indicators as well as process indicators. The city livability indicators are about status and condition, and are outcome-based. These are akin to how KPIs are generally used. In addition, some KPIs are also process indicators, which can be further divided into management process indicators (MPIs) and operational process indicators (OPIs). MPIs measure the management commitment, whereas OPIs measure the effectiveness of their implementation. In other words, the GCOF suggests to move away from only looking at

The GrEEEn Cities Operational Framework provides a platform that enables the identification of a combination of management and operational outcome-based key performance indicators for measuring and managing livability in cities.

---

[27] The following key indicator facilities were considered in developing the indicator approach in GrEEEn Cities: OECD (2014), Economist Intelligence Unit (2011), Global Cities Institute (2014), Green Growth Knowledge Platform (2013), ISO (2013), and ASEAN (2015).

Box 6.6: Global City Indicators Facility and ISO 37120

"The Global City Indicators Facility provides an established set of city indicators with a globally standardized methodology that allows for global comparability of city performance and knowledge sharing. This website serves all cities that become members to measure and report on a core set of indicators through this web-based relational database."

The Global City Indicators Facility (GCIF) has more than 250 member cities across the globe and various sponsoring partners, such as Cities Alliance or Philips, as well as institutional partners, such as UN-Habitat or Clean Air Asia. The GCIF provides a set of indicators, which are grouped in three types: There are profile indicators covering the categories people, housing, economy, government, geography, and climate. Performance indicators are sorted into two groups: (i) *city services* categories concern education, fire and emergency response, health, recreation, safety, solid waste, transport, wastewater, water, energy, finance, governance, and urban planning; and (ii) *quality of life* categories concern civic engagement, culture, economy, environment, shelter, social equity, technology, and innovation. Examples of future indexes, which are under development, are a social capital index, creativity index, or the urban accessibility index.

In May 2014 during the Global Cities Summit, the World Council on City Data and ISO 37120 (Sustainable Development of Communities – Indicators for City Services and Quality of Life) were launched to aim at open source data on cities that is consistent across the globe and can be compared through standardized metrics. Based on the GCIF's work, ISO 37120 is the first international standard to establish a set of such standardized indicators by providing a definition and methodologies for a set of indicators on cities' performance regarding services and quality of life. ISO 37120 can be applied to cities of any scale and stage of development. It enables comparisons and monitoring across time and place, thus contributing to improved urban management, better understanding of a city's progress, and lessons from cases of cities developing differently or similarly.

Sources: Global City Indicators Facility. 2015. Global City Indicators Facility. www.cityindicators.org/ International Organization for Standardization (ISO). 2014. How Does Your City Compare to Others? New ISO Standard to Measure Up. News article. 14 May. http://www.iso.org/iso/home/news_index/news_archive/news.htm?Refid=Ref1848; R. Teipelke. 2012. Global City Indicators Facility. http://blog.inpolis.com/2012/08/30/global-city-indicators-facility/

the livability or outcome-related aspects. It is also required to include KPIs related to the processes of achieving such livability. Drawing a parallel, solving a pollution problem cannot solely be achieved through end-of-the-pipe pollution control (treatment and proper disposal). Considering top-of-the-pipe and through-the-pipe solutions, which are similar to what will be achieved when looking at processes within the city as a whole, are needed.

Applied to the GCOF, MPIs and OPIs relate to integrated urban planning, economic competitiveness, the environment, and equity. Further, MPIs and OPIs can be defined for enablers (policies, strategies, sector plans, regulations, finance, governance, institutions, civil society, and the private sector), action plans, and Urban Management Partnerships (UMPs). These MPIs and OPIs complement outcome-focused livability indicators, which cover the economic, environmental, and equity dimensions as well. Under the framework, it will be clearly recognized that the city needs to measure its effectiveness across each of the different elements of the GCOF as well as the outcome. The interconnectedness between the elements, enablers, outputs, and outcomes will be captured in the KPIs.

Box 6.7: ARCADIS Sustainable Cities Index

The ARCADIS Sustainable Cities Index takes a broad perspective on the concept of sustainability, comparing 50 cities from 31 countries across the globe to analyze in how far these cities provide a livable environment for their residents, while not putting an undue burden on nature or future generations' livability. In order to include the multiple aspects within this broad perspective, the index uses a composition of various indexes from other multilateral organizations (e.g., World Bank World Development Indicators), the private sector (e.g., Siemens Green City Index), and academe (e.g., Globalization and World Cities Research Network).

The index has three broad subcategories: (i) people—measuring the social performance of cities, also regarding quality of life aspects; (ii) planet—capturing the environmental performance of cities; (iii) profit—assessing the economic performance of cities, including business-related factors of investment, production, and consumption.

The index shows many Western European cities ranking high, while not a single North American city ranks among the top due to their poor performance in the environmental category. Asian cities show a huge diversity from well-performing cities such as Seoul and Singapore to highly unsustainable cities such as Wuhan and Manila. Middle Eastern cities exemplify the possible trade-offs between concerns for environmental sustainability in relation to economic growth aspects. Overall, the diminishing affordability of business and finance hubs in the world has increasingly become a problem to be addressed.

Although the index compares and ranks cities, the corresponding report with some highlighted case studies underscores how each city has a unique set of strengths and weaknesses, opportunities, and challenges—with geographical features and historical–cultural characteristics forming a specific place identity, which requires a tailor-made urban development approach for each individual city.

Source: ARCADIS. 2015. Sustainable Cities Index 2015. http://www.sustainablecitiesindex.com/whitepaper/

In order to keep the application of KPIs in local contexts feasible, the GCOF envisions a selected number of KPIs instead of an endless list of indicators. The conventional approach toward the use of KPIs is to have as many indicators as there are categories or activities. Given the complexity of managing a city, KPIs under the GCOF will instead include one leading and one lagging indicator as representative KPIs for different elements. For instance, there will be two process KPIs each (leading and lagging) for integrated planning, economic competitiveness, the environment, equity, enablers, action plans, and UMPs. The leading KPI will be representative of aspects where the city is doing reasonably well. The lagging KPI will be representative of where the city is falling behind. The decision whether these should be MPIs or OPIs will depend on what is chosen as representative. For instance, if political commitment on equity issues is identified as a concern, it will be represented with a lagging MPI. On the other hand, if a lack of stakeholder access to equity programs is a problem, it will be represented with a lagging OPI.

As generally done with indicator use, KPIs under the GCOF will be declared and reported publicly. By doing so, the use of public monitoring to perform in relation to the KPIs will serve as a driving force to usher city management to follow up swiftly on required tasks.

Photo Credits: Renard Teipelke (right); ADB/Daro Sulakauri (bottom left); ADB/Lester Ledesma (top left)

Be it the progress of construction projects, the provision of social infrastructure, or the management of natural resources, key performance indicators help cities in monitoring and improving performance by focusing on key action areas that are conducive to improving its livability

Selecting KPIs for Improved Monitoring and Management

Not all indicators a city might measure fall within the KPIs. Depending on a city's capacities, a broader monitoring set with subindexes may be useful to closely track performance in various activity areas. However, for the performance tracking within the implementation of a GCAP, a city would strategically select a limited number of KPIs. This recognizes the need to keep KPIs manageable so that its usefulness in improving urban management is retained. In the past, many attempts to use indicators to drive performance improvements have been less effective due to a wide set of various KPIs, which required extensive data collection, analysis, and monitoring. Instead, cities should aim for KPIs that are easy to measure and to manage. Once performance in the corresponding areas has excelled, a city government can aim higher.

In that sense, monitoring KPIs will guide the city management on where the focus should be. Review of the results- or outcome-based livability KPIs will indicate where a city needs to improve. These will be linked to the performance against the MPIs and OPIs, which provide city managers with insight into how processes have to be adjusted to bring about enhanced livability. Furthermore, MPIs and OPIs can also identify whether it is the management or operational aspects that need to be strengthened to bring about an improvement in the livability of a city.

Every city management decision may have an impact on the KPIs. Therefore, these should be carefully analyzed to identify possible repercussions on a city's performance in a key performance area. Identified negative impacts might require an adjustment to city management decisions to keep repercussions minimal. This is in line with the GCOF of integrated urban development, where all city management decisions are aligned with the overall vision of a city and its GCAP. The monitoring and management along KPIs can be a useful guidance in this regard.

The GCOF does not suggest a fixed set of KPIs, as each city's context is unique and requires a tailor-made set of indicators. With an abundance of indexes available, cities can choose from a wide range of such indicator sets. More recently, attempts have materialized to build an international standard for city performance indicators. These initiatives can help cities in designing their own monitoring system following established methodologies. Furthermore, they enable city managers to compare their city's performance with other cities that share similarities. One takeaway from these recent developments in relation to the GCOF is that indicators and indexes should reflect the complexity of a city by having a multisector perspective, with indicators aligned to a broader vision of the city.

Decision Support Systems for City Planning and Management

GrEEEn Cities use decision support systems (DSS) to integrate urban development with environmental planning for achieving livability. They are tools and mechanisms to structure, improve, and integrate the planning, design, implementation, and O&M of urban projects and places. Enabled by technological change, including increased computing capacity, DSS are being more widely utilized in the urban development field.

DSS can be used at different stages of the GCAP process, and particularly for developing urban profiles and as a tool for integrated planning, design, implementation, and the operations stage. Selected applications of DSS applications that contributed in practice to goals such as conserving resources, lowering greenhouse gas (GHG) emissions, and improving the cost–benefit ratio of urban investments will be discussed.

The DSS tools presented here should be seen as enablers that support decision making rather as a replacement for political discussion and decision making. DSS in a particular context should be within a city's government approximate capacities and should not be seen as a one-time external technical input in the form of a complicated or overly sophisticated planning tool. They will realize their full potential if technical staff of city governments are actively engaged in understanding, scrutinizing, and applying particular tools, and if key variables and results are understood by other local stakeholders. Ultimately, DSS are only as good as the information and analysis they are based on, so they must be time-bound and regularly updated, and integrated into a city's planning and policy-making processes.

Assessment Tools

At an early stage of planning, DSS can be used to develop a profile of an urban area, to understand and analyze a city's status quo and/or its condition in particular sectors. Some of these assessment tools include a scenario perspective of planned urban development projects and their likely impact on a city. For example, the Tool for the Rapid Assessment of Urban Mobility (TRAM), prepared by Clean Air Asia and UN-Habitat, aims to benchmark a

Upstream deployment of the appropriate decision support systems for prioritizing issues, analyzing data, and designing green solutions for livability is enabled by the GrEEEn Cities Operational Framework through the GrEEEn City Action Plan process.

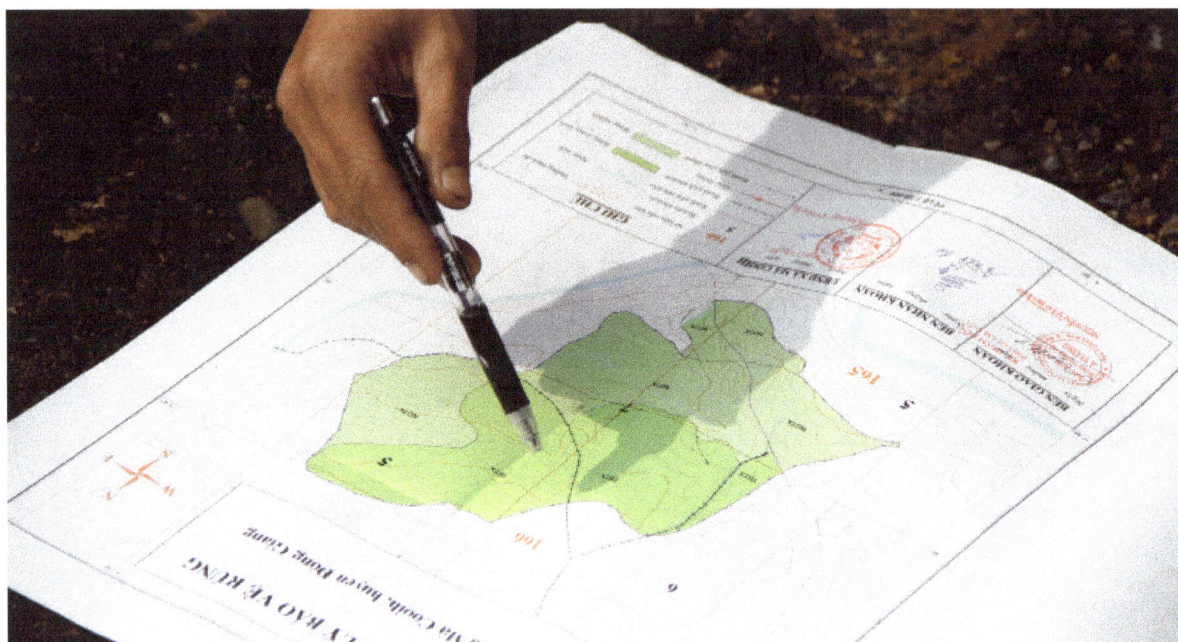

Photo Credit: ADB/Lester Ledesma

Decision support systems come in many ways, ideally adapted to the local context and capacities to assist in improving the whole project cycle from planning, design, and implementation to operation, maintenance, and monitoring

city's mobility situation through both participatory and analytical components (UN-Habitat, ITDP, and CAI 2013). In contrast to traditional tools for transport assessments, TRAM is less resource-intensive and can be applied in settings where data are scarce. Instead of solely assessing the mobility status quo in a city, TRAM can be used to focus on specific areas within a city or on its most disadvantaged residents. It also includes other tools, such as the Transport Emissions Evaluation Model for Projects – City (TEEMP City), to guide city managers from the assessment to the planning stage, where a mobility plan or concrete interventions are discussed and designed.

GHG inventories can also serve as effective DSS-style tools to develop an urban profile. The process of compiling a GHG inventory for a city entails estimating contributions of GHG emissions from multiple projects and sectors, and documenting these as part of a comprehensive inventory. Because of this, GHG inventories can serve as platforms for cross-sector planning and decision making, enabling cities to explore results-specific solutions with respect to environmental sustainability and climate change. Recent case studies provide evidence that GHG emission estimates establish valuable baselines for cities, allowing for credible, analysis-based determinations of the magnitudes of carbon-related impacts of urban projects, while also enabling cities to drive green investments, leverage and access climate financing, and raise public awareness (Sandhu and Kamal 2015).

Another type of DSS can help cities become more resilient to impacts from climate and disaster risks on the natural and built assets and a city's residents. Tools such as (geographic information system [GIS]-based) thematic maps or hydrological and hydraulic models enable decision makers to adjust urban development to prevent, control, and mitigate the negative impacts of floods.

A recent application of flood management DSS in Panama (Box 6.8) demonstrates how such systems can be used to identify climate-vulnerable urban areas, analyze how existing infrastructure systems exacerbate or mitigate related risks, and assess possible hard- and soft-side measures to increase climate resilience. In addition to analyzing a city's water system on both a hydrological scale (basin) and hydraulic scale (city), possible development paths and future scenarios in and around the urban area have also been analyzed. This includes answering questions such as: Where will the city grow? What infrastructure will be needed? How will these changes interact with the environment and the water system in particular? Which areas are particularly vulnerable to flooding now and in the future? Answers to these questions will point at different packages of hard- and soft-side measures. These can be used together with the scenarios to model potential future developments and climate vulnerabilities of a city.

It has to be underscored here that flood management DSS are not solely technical tools for a few engineering experts within a city government. Flood management is as much about physical solutions as it is about people's awareness and actions, which means that active engagement of stakeholders as well as capturing local knowledge about previous flood events, characteristics of neighborhoods, successful coping mechanisms, and vulnerabilities of certain groups are essential.

Such an approach would form the basis of a cost–benefit analysis that would assess how far the financial expenditures of various hard- and soft-side measures relate to their physical impact, sustainability, potential social impacts, and contribution to making a city more climate resilient. Such an approach is, for instance, applied by the Commonwealth Scientific and Industrial Research Organisation (CSIRO) in the National Climate Adaptation Flagship Project Sustainable Cities and Coasts, which focuses on integrated urban development and intelligent infrastructure design (Wang 2014).

Prioritization Tools

DSS for investment management systems address a traditional problem in urban development: there is a missing connection between an overall urban development strategy or plan, individual investment projects, and the annual budgeting process. Investment management DSS aim at interlinking these three elements to foster integrated urban development, which makes best use of available (and often limited) financial resources. Such systems can have a varying degree of complexity, although the principle remains the same: a city aligns its annual planning with an overall development strategy. This strategy can be derived from an urban master plan and would, ideally, be articulated in a GCAP, which translates the long-term development objectives of a master plan into prioritized, feasible, and time-bound actions (see Chapter 3).

Based on an urban development strategy, criteria can be defined about what makes an individual investment project worth financing. A GCAP of a city would, for instance, point at the 3Es of economic competitiveness, the environment, and equity, as well as their cross-sector benefits as reference for the formulation of criteria. These criteria are applied in the city government (typically by the planning department) to assess suggested individual investment projects from the various departments. Out of a long list, only those investments having the strongest contribution to realizing a city's development goals will be prioritized.

Box 6.8: Urban Water Drainage and Wastewater Master Plan of Colon, Panama

In 2011, Panama launched the 5-year Metro Water and Sanitation Improvement Project to increase quality, coverage, and efficiency of urban water distribution and wastewater services for several low-income communities. Component 2 of the project focused on modernizing water distribution and wastewater systems and had a cornerstone in the formulation of the Urban Water and Wastewater Management Master Plan for Colon District.

The master plan aimed to provide practical solutions to frequent flood problems occurring in six subdivisions, where a high population growth and a lack of water infrastructure planning posed major challenges. The formulation of the plan consisted of two phases: The first phase (planning) comprised (i) information compilation and analysis; (ii) multi-criteria diagnosis of existing infrastructures taking into account technical, social, environmental, economic, financial, and institutional issues; (iii) development of hydraulic models to simulate the current performance of urban drainage and wastewater infrastructures, as well as to define and analyze alternative solutions; (iv) assessment of discrete projected scenarios for a 20-year horizon by river basins and subbasins; (v) development and implementation of a methodology to evaluate alternative solutions (in the short-, mid-, and long-term) with a multi-criteria approach; and (vi) selection of the optimal solution and drafting of the plan itself. The second phase (basic design) focused on preparing detailed designs and costs for the selected solution(s).

Current and future scenarios were simulated with the help of hydraulic models, taking into account climate change. Major deficiencies were identified, and several short-, mid-, and long-term intervention measures, both structural (pumping stations, sewer improvement, river embankments, retention ponds, and other green infrastructure) and nonstructural (urban planning, flood forecasting and early warning systems, emergency plans, and operation and maintenance plans) were proposed. A hydraulic model was implemented to assess the performance of the six subdivisions under several flood scenarios (return periods). A fairly accurate digital elevation model was used to build the hydraulic model, and boundary conditions were determined based on a previous hydrological study on a river basin scale. Model outputs were flow water depth and velocity grids. With the help of this hydraulic model and an urban asset vulnerability analysis, a flood risk assessment was conducted and flood risk maps were produced. Further "green" structural measures, such as earth river embankments or retention ponds, were proposed and included in the plan when feasible.

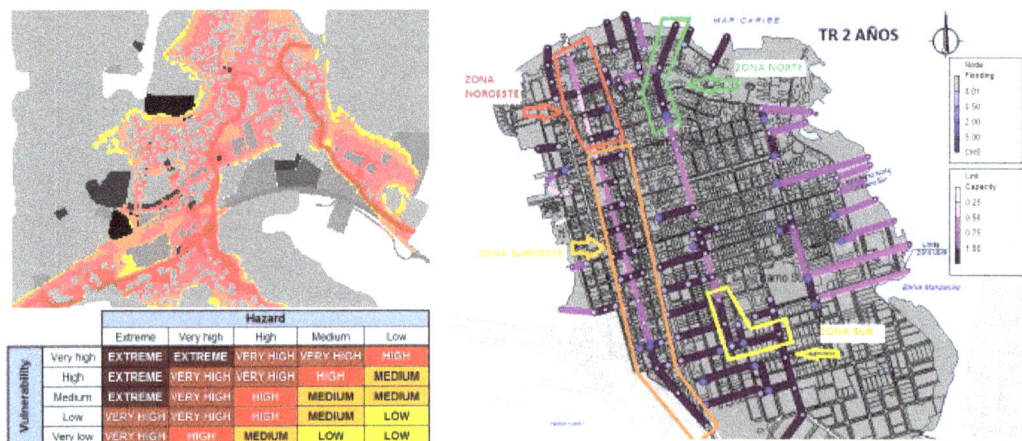

Note: The first two images (*left*) show an analysis of the flooding problems in Colon District, Panama, with the help of the two-dimensional hydraulic simulation model GUAD-2D. The third figure (*right*) shows an analysis of the proposed measures supported by hydraulic simulation models.

Source: P. Garcia de Mendoza and O.I. Rozados. 2015. DSS as a Tool to Implement the GrEEEn Cities Operational Framework from a Flood Protection Approach. Background write-up.

As the GCOF fosters integrated solutions, corresponding criteria would give additional credit to projects with multisector positive impacts and are coordinated between different departments.

The prioritized list of investment projects can be provided to the budgeting committee, which will have to discuss annual funding allocations to various departments. With a widely agreed urban development strategy in place, the budget discussions will evolve around high-priority activity areas, instead of debating small details of each proposed investment project. The Cities Development Initiative for Asia (CDIA) City Infrastructure Investment Programming and Prioritization (CIIPP) Toolkit has taken the initial stage of this process forward by providing a DSS tool to help decision makers at the prefeasibility phase of investment planning to prioritize a city's investments in light of limited budgets and capacities (Box 6.9).

In a more advanced version of investment management DSS, tools are GIS-based and, thus, connect strategic urban development objectives with a spatial dimension of where investments are proposed in a city (Box 6.10). The corresponding quality of such a joint database depends on the provision and updating of data from different departments. Such DSS require city departments to engage in interdepartmental consultations throughout the year to align their individual propositions with each other to design integrated projects, which will best meet the articulated criteria for the investment project assessment. This ensures an enhanced, more comprehensive understanding by sector experts of the overall development challenges of their city and promotes a cross-sector perspective on investment planning and design.

Approaching investment prioritization from the grassroots level, low-income neighborhoods have developed their own tools, some of them surprisingly low-tech. Children in Indian slums have carried out visioning exercises for upgrading their neighborhoods, including the prioritization of capital improvements, using hand-drawn maps (see the Humara Bachpan initiative discussed in Chapter 4). In Nairobi's Mathare Valley, local residents map their

---

Box 6.9: Application of the City Infrastructure Investment Programming and Prioritization Toolkit

The Vietnamese cities of Ha Giang, Hue, and Vinh Yen applied the Cities Development Initiative for Asia (CDIA) City Infrastructure Investment Programming and Prioritization (CIIPP) Toolkit during the preparation of their GrEEEn City Action Plans. The tool kit defines a process for prioritizing project wish lists into short lists. One team of technical experts was formed in each city to apply the 40 standardized criteria to each of the projects on the wish lists, thereby facilitating rational and systematic evaluations and rankings. Criteria included the strategic impact of the investment project at the city level (not just the neighborhood level), as well as a major role for the urban local authority as project owner and (at least) partial financier. The rigorous Excel spreadsheet-based process was used in these cities to whittle down a long list of investment projects included in master plans and other documents into a prioritized short list of projects that are critical to the implementation of the GrEEEn City Action Plans. Many of the projects are now being prepared under the Secondary Cities Development Program (Green Cities) financed by the Asian Development Bank.

Source: CDIA. 2015. CIIPP Toolkit. http://cdia.asia/resources/toolkit/

Box 6.10: Strategic Spatial Planning Linked to Infrastructure Investment
in Johannesburg, South Africa

In response to significant economic, demographic, and spatial growth, Metro Johannesburg began to explore flexible approaches for strategic urban planning, so that urban development strategies could be linked to investments into actual infrastructure. As a result, a growth management strategy was developed in 2008 and accompanied by a capital investment management system (CIMS).

The growth management strategy identifies infrastructure priorities across Metro Johannesburg, incorporating findings from stakeholder workshops and from across departments and semiautonomous municipality-owned enterprises. A geographic information system (GIS) database reflects these inputs, together with information on current capacities and development needs in different areas of Metro Johannesburg.

To translate the growth management strategy priorities into actual development, the GIS-based CIMS is used. The strategic planning team within the Department of Development Planning and Urban Management engages in consultations with each department to discuss proposed projects. These proposals are evaluated in the CIMS with regard to their alignment with the growth management strategy priorities and overall urban development strategies. The annual capital budgeting process is then informed by findings from the regular discussions between the planning department and other departments, based on the CIMS evaluation of proposed projects. This approach establishes a single, common platform for decision making on a single budget, which (ideally) allocates the limited fiscal resources to the high-scoring urban development projects. Extensive discussions with departments improve the coordination, understanding, and acceptance of different actors' needs and priorities. Use of the CIMS leads the department to adapt their projects to growth management strategy priorities, align with other sectors' projects, and cater to less advantaged areas.

However, Metro Johannesburg's development plans have been partly countered by competing interests of neighboring municipalities and development plans of the Government of Gauteng Province. In addition, the different investment horizons of the public and private sector can result in a partial investment mismatch (temporal and/or spatial), particularly with regard to less favorable development areas. Furthermore, there is a need to improve the monitoring of the CIMS, as departments have used loopholes to reallocate money in the course of the fiscal year from CIMS-prioritized projects to other investments.

Sources: City of Johannesburg. 2013. Growth Management Strategy. http://www.joburg.org.za/index.php?option=com_content&task=view&id=4030&Itemid=114; R. Teipelke. 2015. *Urban NEXUS Tools and Case Studies*. Sector Project Sustainable Development of Metropolitan Regions. Eschborn: Deutsche Gesellschaft für Internationale Zusammenarbeit; A. Todes. 2012. New Directions in Spatial Planning? Linking Strategic Spatial Planning and Infrastructure Development. *Journal of Planning Education and Research*. 32 (4). pp. 400–414.

slums using a handheld global positioning system (GPS). They record the location of streets without streetlights, uncollected piles of solid waste, and broken manholes. As in India, the maps are used to bring the most urgent problems to the attention of the authorities. Some streetlights in Mathare Valley have been installed recently as a result (Warner 2013).

What these examples underscore is that DSS for the prioritization of urban development improvements range from low- to high-tech, as well as from bottom–up approaches to institutionalized approaches and systems. The important key questions for the choice of a fitting DSS tool in this area are the following: What are the expected achievements of applying an investment prioritization DSS tool? What style and complexity of a DSS tool fits the application setting?

Decision support systems and Smart City tools bear tangible results, as is apparent in the transport sector examples of Jakarta's bus rapid transit system, Indonesia, and Singapore's electronic road pricing system

Integrated Planning Tools

Integrated urban development does not only require cross-sector solutions, but also a multidimensional understanding of the status quo of a city—that is, the complexity of interrelations between different sectors, actors, and levels across space and time. DSS tools, which aim at realizing sustainability in an urban system, address this setting by acknowledging the interdependencies and putting them to use in creating urban development paths that realize cobenefits and synergies that can enable economic growth in balance with environmental and social aspects. These systems are also able to compare urban development options against aspects such as asset management and financial feasibility (Box 6.11).

In particular, integrated planning DSS start with a systems analysis. A city's status quo in the different sectors (e.g., energy, water, transport, waste, and housing) is assessed, with a focus on the relationship between the different sectors. This perspective is widened by also including in the analysis other factors such as institutional setups, cultural characteristics, and interpersonal relationships. This understanding is connected with the urban development plan, strategy, goals, or indicators of a city. In how far does the current status quo meet formulated objectives toward a livable city? What are the different ways forward to improve performance in various fields? Integrated planning DSS tools can model different scenarios (both in space and in time) to provide insights into the future development paths of a city.

With a number of scenarios at hand, assessment criteria are developed to compare the different scenarios. Such criteria could focus on, for example, high energy efficiency and reduced water consumption, or effective land use and enhanced low-carbon mobility. Such a comparison leads to insights about critical points for a city to adjust its current practices and development patterns, and also about corresponding principles or guidelines for specific sectors which would help to achieve overall urban system sustainability. These DSS provide not only a snapshot of development options at one point in time, but also a perspective of how various options would play out over the short, medium, and long term (i.e., life-cycle costs). Such a systems analysis can also help develop key indicators to enable city managers to monitor their city's development.

Box 6.11: AECOM's Sustainable Systems Integration Model

AECOM's Sustainable Systems Integration Model (SSIM) is a decision support systems tool for an integrated, whole-systems approach to urban planning, design, and engineering. With a key focus on cost–benefit analysis, the SSIM analyzes the environmental, social, and economic impacts of existing cities and proposed urban development plans. The SSIM first projects, at a high level, the results of alternative urban layouts, then drills down into each subsystem (water, transport, energy, ecology, and sociocultural) to look at ways to improve performance, and then combines the subsystems and the layouts in an Excel-based optimization exercise to maximize the cost–benefit ratio. This analysis can support the decision-making process, also by adjusting the weight of different sustainability targets in evaluating development options and pathways. Following from the assessment, implementation guidelines can be developed to ensure that measures in various areas (for instance building, landscaping, and energy) are following predefined criteria.

Source: J. Bachmann. 2014. Sustainable System Integration Model (SSIM). Presentation at the ADB Enabling GrEEEn Cities Regional Conference, 13–14 May, Manila. http://www.scribd.com/doc/226085436/Sustainable-System-Integration-Model-SSIM

Smart Cities and Information and Communication Technology

The previously presented examples of DSS point at the importance data has in enabling effective urban development. Planning, design, implementation, operation and management, as well monitoring and evaluation can be improved through better data. In the past few years, the attention of both private sector service providers and public sector institutions has been directed toward the Smart City. While this concept is debated and various definitions make the Smart City refer to and include a multitude of activity areas and sectors, the overall direction seems to be clear (Vogl 2012). Focusing on information and communication technology (ICT) aspects and data systems for improved urban management, Smart City solutions can be applied in the management of cities to

- enable a more efficient use of resources;
- improve equitable access to infrastructure and services;
- facilitate the interaction of people and businesses;
- enhance the physical and virtual flow of goods, capital, information, resources, and people;
- strengthen capacity building and knowledge sharing;
- boast urban resilience;
- make government and governance more transparent and accountable; and
- improve the overall livability of cities.

Examples of the above could be integrated through e-governance applications (Table 6.1), which are used in a variety of city management areas (Figure 6.2).

The proliferation of smartphones creates the opportunity for people to interact more with their city governments. They can obtain information, contribute to planning efforts, and participate in feedback (Box 6.12). People can pay for infrastructure services online and file complaints for service disruptions. At the same time, technologies used in smartphones and other devices, such as Wi-Fi, GPS, or Bluetooth, provide a wide range of data that

Table 6.1: Smart Applications of Information and Communication Technology for Cities

Action Areas	Interventions	Applications
Public management	Engagement	Complaints management
		Access to civic information
		e-Municipality
		Social media
		Geographic information system technologies
		Smart judiciary
Industry		Incubators for entrepreneurs
		e-commerce facilities
		Business centers
Integrated city management	Urban innovation	Intelligent transport systems
		Smart grid solutions
		Smart water management
People apps	Public service delivery	e-health
		Smart campus
		Tourism applications
		Civic helpline
		Disaster management applications
		Community scorecards

Source: Adapted from A. Ramamurthy. 2015. Innovations in Urban Management Using ICT in SEUW. Presentation at Southeast Asia Urban Development and Water Division Meeting, 21 April, Manila.

Figure 6.2: e-Governance Application Areas in City Management

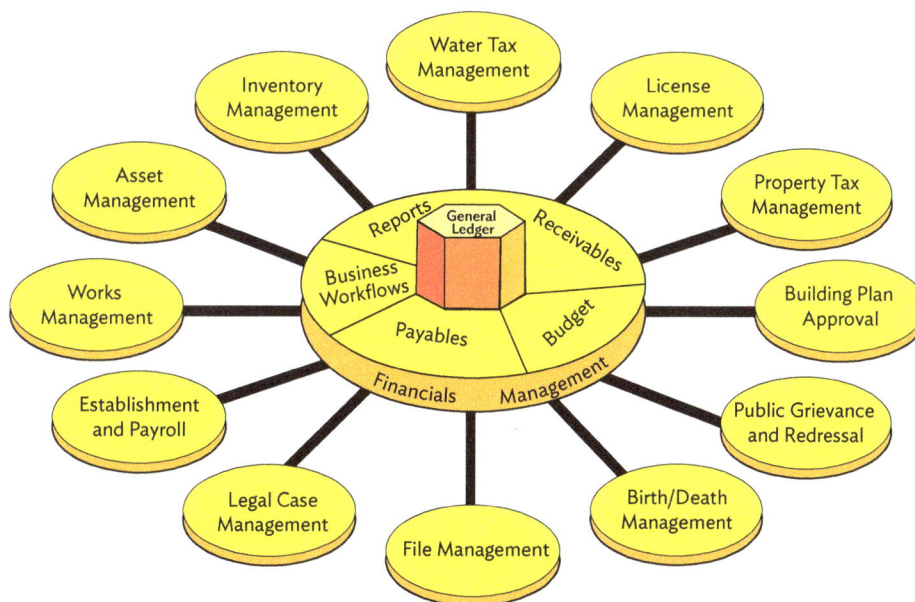

Source: S. Nadhamuni and K. Rupanagunta. n.d. Municipal eGovernance Systems for Urban Local Bodies in India. eGovernments Foundation. http://www.egovernments.org/docs/casestudies/municipal-egovernance%20systems%20for%20local%20bodiles.pdf

Box 6.12: Walkability in Asian Cities

In order to promote better walkability and pedestrian safety in Asian cities, Clean Air Asia has initiated the Walkability Asia project. Together with partners, it conducted walkability surveys in 27 cities across the region and scored their pedestrian-related policies and infrastructure against criteria for improved walkability. Findings and further material to good practices are captured on the project website (http://walkabilityasia.org), where progress of cities with regard to pedestrian-oriented solutions can be traced as well. As a next step, Clean Air Asia developed a walkability app. This smartphone app can be used to survey streets in a city, providing pedestrians an "audit tool" to make their voices heard in urban development pertaining to pedestrian facilities and services. This benchmarking of streets provides useful feedback to city governments to improve their performance in comparison to other cities.

Source: WalkabilityAsia. 2014. Walkability App a Finalist in the mBillionth Award. 26 July. http://walkabilityasia.org/2014/07/26/walkability-app-a-finalist-in-the-mbillionth-award/; WalkabilityAsia. 2012. About Walkability Asia. 23 July. http://walkabilityasia.org/2012/07/23/1286/

can inform urban planning. Even though it is still an emerging field, practical applications of such technologies have shown that they can provide a better understanding of human behavior, for example, with regard to mobility in complex formal and informal transport systems. Information about activity patterns, transportation modes, and location tracking can support traffic demand modeling, the design of spatial layouts of public areas, as well as the monitoring of such patterns of uses and behavior on the environment in relation to noise and air quality. Although promising in its technical potential, the use of private user data has to meet high standards of user privacy and data security (Seer 2015).

The application of technologies to arrive at better informed urban planning also includes the use of satellite earth observation. This can help to tackle the often scarce availability and/or low quality of useful data in urban planning. Combining satellite imagery with ancillary data from, for instance, Google Street View, Openstreetmap, and national statistical offices, can further strengthen data quality and interpretation and allow for a more fine-grained analysis of urban spaces. In developing member countries in Asia and the Pacific, ADB, together with its partners, piloted these technologies in a number of case studies to obtain information on the spatial distribution of transportation assets, producing detailed transport inventories, tracking spatial change over time, developing estimations of population densities, and mapping the land use of related spaces. The strength of the application of these technologies is that they do not only inform the spatial planning stage, but cover the whole range of a project cycle, also including strategic planning, detailed design of infrastructure, management of urban spaces, and monitoring of infrastructure systems (Grandoni 2015, ADB 2011d).[28]

Taking one example from the field of climate change and disaster resilience, ICT applications and DSS can strengthen not only a city's planning system to prevent disasters, but also support its mitigation of disaster impacts. One group of such tools addresses disaster preparedness and response. For instance, unified messaging systems offer a holistic and scalable early warning system to cities to increase risk awareness, to strengthen communication through a variety of channels, and to build capacities for both first responders to disasters and affected

---

[28]   Also see related projects under the cluster technical assistance (ADB 2011d).

Philippines: Dr. Yanga's Colleges Inc. students and FELTA Multi-Media Inc. at the ADB Enabling GrEEEn Cities Regional Conference, 13–14 May 2014, Manila. The students presented their Nature's Fury All-around Homing Operative of Nature (AHON) advanced early warning system and their All-around Goods Assistance Processor (AGAP) for autonomous repacking and distribution of relief goods and first-aid kits—an innovation, with which they successfully participated in the Third FLL Philippines Robotics competition, as well as the FLL World Festival in St. Louis, United Stated, in 2014

populations (Menon 2014). In this way, the role of DSS is drilled down to the lifesaving aspect of enabling prioritized communication between a variety of actors for improved decision making in extreme situations of systems congestion or even failure.

Practical examples for databases, tools, platforms, and systems, etc. are still evolving. Some cities have moved ahead to become "smarter" (Arup 2010). Companies have started to offer services to improve urban management, infrastructure planning, and human–technical interaction (IBM 2015). The research sector has also made significant innovative contributions in better understanding and applying these facilitating technological systems to make cities better places to live (MIT Cities 2015). In a similar vein, international organizations have used data in combination with web-based platforms to make information readily available to the broader public: The recent examples of UN-Habitat's (2015b) newly launched Urban Data platform, the European Environment Agency's (2011) Urban Atlas, and World Bank's (2015b) interactive mapVIETNAM show two key aspects in putting the available information to use: The first is the collection of data in an effective, organized, and rigorous way to actually make it into information. The second is to provide this information in a way that enables people to easily access, understand, and use it. Eventually, an intelligent integration of data with ICT systems can form the foundation for better-informed integrated urban development.[29] DSS enhance this process by providing the support tools to analyze complex urban settings and to develop proper solutions to urban development challenges. In addition, the use of KPIs can ensure that more effective planning approaches (enabled through DSS) are integrated into urban management processes.

---

[29] Also see Asin (2015).

7

Toward Livable Cities

Over time, citizens' demands for urban infrastructure and services have increased exponentially. These demands have exceeded the carrying capacity of cities due to the overconsumption of natural resources (TED-Ed 2013). Reconciling demands and needs of people that make up the urban ecosystem, within defined resource limits, and confronting environment and climate externalities is a major challenge faced by city managers, urban practitioners, and the academe (Salzman et al. 2014). Decision makers recognize the potential of green growth and the need to move toward livable cities, but only a limited number of cities have implemented green growth strategies and the results vary widely (LSE Cities, ICLEI, and Global Green Growth Institute 2013). This publication suggests a way to improve the quality of life for all and shares key insights and learning for "doing things differently" through the following six takeaway lessons:

1. Learn from Current Conditions and Approaches

The implications of almost irreversible environmental degradation and rapid urbanization have had a severe impact on today's cities, especially those in the developing world. This is exacerbated by increasing risks from natural disasters and the impact of climate change-induced risks on economic growth and environmental sustainability.

Historically, the urban space was framed by singular and unilateral approaches for service provision—a strong focus on physical infrastructure. Persistent and rigid imprints of past practices induced an inertia to change within the prevalent, fragmented institutional structures. Traditional master plans were too rigid and lacked flexibility to dynamic changes that are so characteristic for urban spaces. Strategic or structural plans were seen as substitutes, and, although they approached the problem in an integrated manner, they lacked the necessary linkages with investment plans as well as with project identification and structuring. Limitations remained in the translation from planning to engineering design, implementation, and operations. This often resulted in skewed project prioritization and unbalanced urban development. Further, such planning reflected only the views of government stakeholders, rather than those of citizens and businesses. The lack of consultation and meaningful participation meant unpopular and unresponsive decisions that neither made strategic sense nor reflected the priorities of the private sector and civil society.

2. Unbundle the 3Es at the City–Region Level to Internalize Risks and Capture Opportunities

The 3Es—economy, environment, and equity—form the building blocks for grEEEn projects and programs (Table 7.1). The challenge is to balance and prioritize dimensions of sustainability, since these differ among projects, programs, and cities.

Table 7.1: Building Blocks of the 3E Pillars

Economy	Environment	Equity
Economic competitiveness	Environmental sustainability	Social equity
• Identifying the economic drivers necessary for urban services that lead to increased productivity but place demands on the urban ecosystem • Promoting sustainable energy systems for improved efficiency • Telecommunications for fast and better connectivity • Supporting innovation hubs and value-adding economic clusters to maximize on external and internal knowledge • Applying latest technologies and well-proven practices for more efficient service delivery • Maximizing financing from a city's own revenue sources • Leveraging financing from a variety of sources through partnerships • Monetizing cobenefits by internalizing environmental and social values, as well as life-cycle costs • Recognizing the potential of green business and building skills through technical and vocational education and training • Streamlining the regulatory regime for investment and development to ensure appropriate incentives • Developing indicators for monitoring revenue gains for financial sustainability of infrastructure and services	• Enhancing environmental conditions and ecological assets through green design • Reducing greenhouse gas emissions through policy reform and low-carbon technologies for enhanced climate mitigation • Analyzing interconnections of projects and the ecosystem to enhance its efficiency and minimize environmental risk • Cascading resource flows for natural resource optimization through low-impact urban infrastructure design • Looping of resources between conjunctive uses for enhancing the circular economy • Prioritizing compact and efficient design to optimize space constraints and increase densities • Integrating climate adaptation to build a city's resilience, protect lives, assets, land, and essential services • Internalizing the pollution management hierarchy of avoidance, reduction, recycling and recovery, treatment, and disposal • Minimizing environmental and social risks through safeguard policies • Monitoring environmental quality for land, air, and water	• Designing affordable, accessible, and resilient investments for poor and vulnerable groups • Enhancing rural–urban interlinkages for access to markets and livelihood opportunities • Activating urban spaces with universal design principles for a diversity of uses by different groups • Strengthening human resource skills and assets • Enabling citizens' ownership through a transparent and accessible process of consultation, communication, involvement, and accountability • Defining and strengthening the accountability chain for improved links between government, service providers, and customers • Prioritizing pro-poor interventions based on citizens' feedback • Minimizing conflicts during resettlement and land acquisition through inclusive resettlement • Developing indicators to monitor access to services, employment, and quality of life.

3E = economy, environment, and equity.

Source: Authors.

3. Recognize the Fourth E: Enablers—Harnessing the Power of Partnerships

Cooperation increases the knowledge, skills, and resource base—including finance—for achieving development goals and provides benefits in the management or implementation of any plan, initiative, or project. Successful partnerships allow each organization to achieve an attractive mix of benefits and costs, thereby generating value added for all involved. Partnerships can leverage combined influence to increase political and community acceptance and approval as well as provide access to finance by pooling government budgets and/or partnering with external agencies, the private sector, or local community groups. Urban Management Partnerships (UMPs) are a conduit and avenue for engaging local stakeholders. Through city-to-city peer learning and knowledge sharing, UMPs are designed to make use of demonstration impact to improve skills and competencies in integrated urban development, environmental planning, and project management within government, civil society, and the private sector. The flexible and scalable approach is based on the idea that, through collaboration and delineation of responsibilities, government and nongovernment agencies and the private sector can more effectively achieve their mutually dependent development goals through UMPs. Using UMPs enables the core implementing agencies to establish the appropriate level of collaboration for implementing GrEEEn City Action Plan (GCAP) actions.

4. Use Decision Support Systems for Informed Decisions

Feasible solutions for GrEEEn City development can be developed through the use of decision support system (DSS) tools such as urban simulation, investment prioritization, hydrological modeling, and sustainability benchmarking. These contribute to conserving resources, lowering greenhouse gas emissions, improving the cost-benefit ratio of urban investments, and creating more livable urban communities. DSS, as enabling tools, model current circumstances and future development through scenarios to achieve long-term urban development goals. For this, there are several tools available to cater to different needs, capacities, and resources.

For instance, climate and disaster resilience DSS help cities increase their resilience against climate and disaster risks by preventing, controlling, and mitigating negative impacts through various modeling tools that can inform decision makers at all stages. Investment management systems establish or strengthen the link between urban development planning, project identification and design, and budgeting to align a city's investments with its overall vision and development goals and targets. Smart Cities and information and communication technology (ICT) provide better information to make complex interlinkages manageable for improved urban management processes, thereby contributing to key performance indicators for improved urban infrastructure and services performance.

5. Promote Asset Management as a Platform for Sustainability and Resilience

The management of assets is a critical element in the achievement of sustainable and resilient development. The GrEEEn Cities Operational Framework (GCOF) is about building infrastructure assets and systems that will underpin a greener, more inclusive, and resilient economy. It involves the development of policy and planning systems applicable nationally and needs to ensure that city level systems are capable of constructing, maintaining, and funding investments at an operational level. Asset management systems are applicable at both levels, strategic and operational.

Effective asset management can be seen as an enabling tool for ensuring resilience of urban infrastructure. It enables preventive and timely corrective actions to be undertaken by cities so that poor infrastructure does not impair upon economic competitiveness, damages a city's cultural and historical heritage, or harms its natural environment or the life of its citizens. Financial savings result from extending the life of an existing asset, thus deferring the need for new investments. The GCOF enables improved asset management to be linked with enhanced livability and encourages a city to examine and manage its natural attributes as well as its cultural, built, and human resource assets through an asset management framework. Considering the capacity and resource constraints within city governments, the strengths of the private sector need to be leveraged with respect to access to finance, technology, and efficiency in operations.

6. Partner for Better Ways of Green Infrastructure Financing

It is imperative to address the shortfall of infrastructure financing in a timely manner. The public sector alone will not be able to finance a transformation toward livable cities. Repackaging available financing from the public sector, private sector, and international development assistance for investment needs is part of the solution. Innovative financing mechanisms, involving partnerships, need to be catalyzed across various revenue streams.

The GCOF provides a results-oriented mechanism for streamlining prioritized investments and matching these with the appropriate financing modality. The framework fosters partnerships of institutionally different actors, thereby distributing the risks and sharing the benefits of GrEEEn City development. A major intervention involves the development of finance mechanisms that mobilize financial resources by unlocking large domestic sources of finance and providing a platform for private sector financing for green infrastructure. Through such a mechanism, international institutional investors can be "crowded in" to raise sufficient funds for urban infrastructure needs.

From Green Growth to GrEEEn Cities

"Green growth" is widely recognized as a viable approach to offset compromises on economic development goals and increase resilience in communities, infrastructure, and service delivery. This is progressively evolving and has been downscaled to the urban context. Since 2010, sustainable urban development has been focused increasingly on internalizing climate change resilience. All of these initiatives and approaches recognize that the prevailing constraints of institutional and regulatory fragmentation in the urban planning and development processes are key barriers to their effective implementation.

Building on lessons learned from previous conceptual approaches and practical experiences from across the world, the GCOF demonstrates a new paradigm in decision making for urban transformation. This places livability at the core of an air, water, and land pyramid enabling city managers to identify critical natural parameters that impact the quality of life. A platform for synergistic planning is created for stakeholders to formulate and achieve a vision for their city on the 3E principles defining an exclusive triple bottom line. This innovative approach enables cities to commence smart and optimal planning from any point in their development journey to a sustainable path that will progressively deliver livable cities using GCAPs as road maps. These involve the following:

- An effective consensus-based, grEEEn vision, and an understanding of the citizens' aspirations for ownership at the community level that would transcend political changes.
- A situation and gap analysis that assesses the current state of the city's development journey, its business-as-usual path, and recognizes its competitive advantage. GCAPs will coexist with strategic development plans, city master plans, or city development strategies, and provide directional guidance for integration toward livability results.
- Programming a combination of time-based, result-oriented capital investments and initiatives to maximize their value effectiveness. These should be judiciously combined with enabling measures covering policy, governance reform, institutional capacity building, strategy formulation, sector planning, and financial incentives. They, with civil society and the private sector as well as DSS, will contribute to a road map with identified 3E benefits, prioritized to eventually realize the GrEEEn City vision. This will also identify the possible financing sources.
- Deriving innovative institutional mechanisms that view the city as "one system" with a variety of strongly interconnected subsystems under strong leadership, harnessing political will and multidisciplinary teams to break technical silos.
- Articulating collaborative UMPs among city administration, local stakeholders, and external organizations, including the private sector for enabling technological innovation, and out-of-the-box thinking for increasing development impact.
- Creating platforms for continuous citizens' feedback and transparency in the implementation of the GCAPs through effective documentation endorsement, disclosure, and monitoring and evaluation mechanisms to improve the response of city governments.

The demand for the GCOF is demonstrated by the participation of cities across Southeast Asia in preparing and piloting GCAPs since 2012. Pilot GCAPs have applied the GCOF to connect the dots within existing institutional frameworks, developed and operationalized strategies and visions, and prepared road maps that would lead to an improved quality of life. These are effectively translating into investment, project designs, and knowledge products for replication.

The value added of the GCOF is the mainstreaming of such integrated approaches for sustainable investment. Moving beyond the adoption of the Sustainable Development Goals in September 2015, it is now of great importance to customize the goals for sustainable development to regional, national, and local contexts. It is here where the GCOF is a conduit to help translate the global development commitments to urban-level actions to achieve livable cities.

References

ARCADIS. 2015. Sustainable Cities Index 2015. http://www.sustainablecitiesindex.com/whitepaper/

Arup. 2010. *Smart Cities: Transforming the 21st Century City via the Creative Use of Technology*. London.

_____. 2014. *City Resilience Framework*. London.

Asian Development Bank (ADB). 1997. *Economic Analysis of Projects*. Manila.

_____. 1998. *Guidelines for the Economic Analysis of Water Supply Projects*. Manila.

_____. 2000. *Handbook for the Economic Analysis of Health Sector Projects*. Manila.

_____. 2003a. *Infrastructure and Poverty Reduction – What Is the Connection?* Manila.

_____. 2003b. *Neighborhood Upgrading and Shelter Sector Project*. Manila (IDN 35143-013).

_____. 2007a. Good Practices for Estimating Reliable Willingness-to-Pay Values in the Water Supply and Sanitation Sector. *ERD Technical Note Series*. No. 23. Manila.

_____. 2007b. *India Infrastructure Project Financing Facility – Project 1*. Manila (IND 40655-033).

_____. 2007c. *Philippines: Local Government Financing and Budget Reform Program Cluster (Subprogram 1 and 2)*. Manila (Project No. 39516-013/023).

_____. 2007d. Tourism for Pro-Poor and Sustainable Growth: Economic Analysis of Tourism Projects. *ERD Technical Note Series*. No. 20. Manila.

_____. 2008. *Strategy 2020: The Long-Term Strategic Framework of the Asian Development Bank, 2008–2020*. Manila.

_____. 2009a. *India Infrastructure Project Financing Facility – Project 2*. Manila (IND 40655-043).

_____. 2009b. *Safeguard Policy Statement*. Manila.

_____. 2010a. *Sustainable Transport Initiative Operational Plan*. Manila.

_____. 2010b. *Technical Assistance for Public–Private Partnership Development in the Brunei Darussalam–Indonesia–Malaysia–Philippines East ASEAN Growth Area and Indonesia–Malaysia–Thailand Growth Triangle*. Manila (TA 7626-REG).

_____. 2011a. *Competitive Cities*. Manila.

_____. 2011b. *Green Cities*. Manila.

_____. 2011c. *Inclusive Cities*. Manila.

_____. 2011d. *Technical Assistance for Implementation of Sustainable Transport in Asia and the Pacific – Better Transport Data for Sustainable Transport Policies and Investment Planning (Subproject 1)*. Manila (TA 8046-REG).

_____. 2011e. *Water Operational Plan 2011–2020*. Manila.

_____. 2012a. *Key Indicators for Asia and the Pacific 2012: Green Urbanization in Asia*. Special chapter. Manila.

_____. 2012b. Philippines: The PINAI Fund. http://www.adb.org/news/infographics/philippines-pinai-fund

_____. 2012c. Skills Development for Inclusive and Sustainable Growth in Developing Asia-Pacific. *Technical and Vocational Education and Training: Issues, Concerns and Prospects*. Volume 19. Heidelberg: Springer. http://www.adb.org/sites/default/files/publication/30071/skills-development-inclusive-growth-asia-pacific.pdf

————. 2012d. *Technical Assistance for Capacity Building Support for Project Identification*. Manila (TA 8251-MYA).

————. 2012e. *Technical Assistance for Green Cities – A Sustainable Urban Future in Southeast Asia*. Manila (TA 8314-REG).

————. 2013a. *Accelerating Infrastructure Investment Facility in India*. Manila (IND 47083-001).

————. 2013b. *Cost–Benefit Analysis for Development: A Practical Guide*. Manila.

————. 2013c. *Environment Operational Directions 2013–2020*. Manila.

————. 2013d. Greening Asia's Cities. Video: 16 September 2013. http://www.adb.org/news/videos/greening-asias-cities

————. 2013e. *Knowledge Management Directions and Action Plan (2013–2015): Supporting "Finance ++" at the Asian Development Bank*. Manila.

————. 2013f. *Mongolia: Ulaanbaatar Urban Services and Ger Areas Development Investment Program*. Manila (Project No. 45007-003).

————. 2013g. *Technical Assistance for Sustainable Infrastructure Assistance Program – Green Cities: A Sustainable Urban Future in Indonesia (Subproject 4)*. Manila (Project No. 46380-005).

————. 2013h. Technical Assistance for Green Cities – A Sustainable Urban Future in Southeast Asia. GCAP Visioning and SWOT Analysis Workshop, 22 November, Hue, Viet Nam.

————. 2013i. *Urban Operational Plan 2012–2020*. Manila.

————. 2014a. *Coastal Towns Environmental Infrastructure Project*. Manila (BAN 44212-013).

————. 2014b. Diverse Views on the Green Cities Initiative. Video: 14 May 2014. http://www.adb.org/news/videos/diverse-views-green-cities-initiative

————. 2014c. Enabling GrEEEn Cities Regional Conference. 13–14 May, Manila. http://www.adb.org/news/events/enabling-greeen-cities-sustainable-urban-future-southeast-asia

————. 2014d. Green Cities. http://www.adb.org/green-cities/index.html#intro

————. 2014e. Green Cities Are an Imperative for Asia's Future. Video: 14 May 2014. http://www.adb.org/news/videos/green-cities-are-imperative-asias-future

————. 2014f. *Green City Action Plan Melaka, Malaysia*. Final report of the Technical Assistance for Master Plan on ASEAN Connectivity Implementation. Manila (TA 8040-REG).

————. 2014g. *Guidance Note: Poverty and Social Dimensions of Urban Projects*. Manila.

————. 2014h. Local Community Helps Keep Manila River Clean. Video: 16 December 2014. http://www.adb.org/news/videos/local-community-helps-keep-manila-river-clean

————. 2014i. *Midterm Review of Strategy 2020: Meeting the Challenges of a Transforming Asia and Pacific*. Manila.

————. 2014j. *Neighborhood Upgrading and Shelter Project (Phase 2)*. Manila (IDN 46094-001).

————. 2014k. *Operational Plan for Integrated Disaster Risk Management 2014–2020*. Manila.

————. 2014l. *Project Preparatory Technical Assistance for Secondary Cities Development Program – Green Cities*. Manila (TA 8671).

————. 2014m. Secondary Cities Development Program (Green Cities): Project Data Sheet. http://adb.org/projects/details?page=details&proj_id=47274-001

————. 2014n. *Toward a Green Mandalay*. Final report for the Scoping Study of a Strategic Development Plan for Mandalay. Manila (TA 8251).

————. 2014o. *Unflooding Asia: The Green Cities Way*. Manila.

————. 2014p. Water Operators Partnerships: Twinning Utilities for Better Services. Brochure, 2 July. http://www.adb.org/sites/default/files/publication/42702/twinning-utilities-better-services.pdf

————. 2015a. *Addressing Disaster Risk through Improved Indicators and Land Use Management*. Manila.

————. 2015b. *Enabling GrEEEn Cities: Hue GrEEEn City Action Plan*. Manila.

————. 2015c. *Enabling GrEEEn Cities: Vinh Yen GrEEEn City Action Plan*. Manila.

_____. 2015d. *GrEEEn City Action Plan for Songkhla and Hat Yai Municipalities*. Manila.

_____. 2015e. *Green City Development Tool Kit*. Manila.

_____. 2015f. *Making Money Work: Financing a Sustainable Future in Asia and the Pacific*. Manila.

_____. 2015g. *Proposed Loan for the People's Republic of China: Jiangxi Pingxiang Integrated Rural–Urban Infrastructure Development*. Manila (Project 47030-002).

_____. Forthcoming in 2016. Guidance Notes on Reducing Disaster Risk in Urban Areas through Land Use Management. Manila.

_____. Forthcoming in 2016. Ha Giang GrEEEn City Action Plan. Final report of the Preparatory Technical Assistance to the Socialist Republic of Viet Nam for the Secondary Cities Development Program (Green Cities). Manila (TA 8671-VIE).

_____. Forthcoming in 2016. Proposed Results-Based Loan for Viet Nam: Secondary Cities Development Program – Green Cities. Manila.

Asian Development Bank and GIZ. 2011. *Changing Course in Urban Transport: An Illustrated Guide*. Manila: Asian Development Bank.

Asin, A. 2015. Smart Cities 2.0: What Works Today. 3 November. Meeting of the Minds – Urban Sustainability Blog. http://cityminded.org/smart-cities-2-0-what-works-today-14314

Association of Southeast Asian Nations (ASEAN). 2015. ASEAN Cooperation on Environmentally Sustainable City. http://environment.asean.org/asean-working-group-on-environmentally-sustainable-cities/

Bachmann, J. 2014. Sustainable System Integration Model (SSIM). Presentation at the ADB Enabling GrEEEn Cities Regional Conference, 13–14 May, Manila. https://www.scribd.com/doc/226085436/Sustainable-System-Integration-Model-SSIM

Banerjee, B. 1999. Security of Tenure: Integrated Approach in Vishakhapatnam. *Shelter*. 2 (3/4).

Beauchamp, B., J. Adamowski, and J. Beausejour. 2015. A Water-Centric Approach to Develop Green Infrastructure. Background write-up.

Belgian Development Agency. 2014. Urban Upgrading in Ho Chi Minh City. Reflection paper. January 2014/002. http://www.btcctb.org/files/web/publication/002_Urban%20upgrading%20in%20Ho%20Chi%20Minh%20City_Tan_Hoa_Lo_Gom_Canal_EN.pdf

Bhattacharyay, B. 2010. Financing Asia's Infrastructure: Modes of Development and Integration of Asian Financial Markets. *ADBI Working Paper Series*. No. 229. Tokyo: Asian Development Bank Institute.

Birch, E. 2009. *The Urban and Regional Planning Reader*. New York: Routledge.

Biswas, A.K., and C. Tortajada. 2010. Water Supply of Phnom Penh: An Example of Good Governance. *International Journal of Water Resources Development*. 26 (2).pp. 157–172.

Brosio, G.. 2014. Decentralization and Public Service Delivery in Asia. *ADB Economics Working Paper Series*. No. 389. Manila: Asian Development Bank.

Brown, R., N. Keath, and T. Wong. 2009. Urban Water Management in Cities: Historical, Current and Future Regimes. *Water Science and Technology*. 59 (5). pp. 847–855.

Cardama, M. 2015. Inextricably Interlinked: The Urban SDG and the New Development Agenda—A Framework of 17 Interconnected Stories. Citiscope, 18 September. http://citiscope.org/habitatIII/commentary/2015/09/inextricably-interlinked-urban-sdg-and-new-development-agenda

Central Park Water. 2015. A Sustainable Water Community. http://centralparkwater.com.au/

Centre for Liveable Cities. 2013. *10 Principles for Liveable High-Density Cities: Lessons from Singapore*. Singapore: Urban Land Institute and Centre for Liveable Cities. http://uli.org/wp-content/uploads/ULI-Documents/10PrinciplesSingapore.pdf

_____. 2014. How to Make Cities Livable. Screened at the World Cities Summit (http://www.clc.gov.sg). Video: 2 June 2014. https://www.youtube.com/watch?v=u-S5TWkLeyk

Centre for Sustainable Asian Cities. n.d. *An Assessment Framework for Monitoring Cities' Sustainability*. Singapore: National University of Singapore.

Cities Alliance. 2014. City Development Strategies (CDS). http://www.citiesalliance.org/cds

Cities Development Initiative for Asia (CDIA). 2014 and 2015. *City Infrastructure Investment Programming and Prioritisation Toolkit*. Manila.

Cities of Melbourne, Port Phillip, Stonnington, Yarra, and Maribyrnong. 2009. *Inner Melbourne Action Plan*. Melbourne.

City Council of Kansas City, Missouri. 2014. *Citywide Business Plan 2014–2019*. Kansas City: Department of Finance.

City Council of Pasadena. 2006. *Green City Action Plan*. Pasadena. cityofpasadena.net/WorkArea/DownloadAsset.aspx?id=6442458275

City of Hamburg. 2011. Hamburg – European Green Capital 2011. Video: 13 September 2013. https://www.youtube.com/watch?v=oB4orXsmUx4

City of Johannesburg. 2013. Growth Management Strategy. http://www.joburg.org.za/index.php?option=com_content&task=view&id=4030&Itemid=114

City of Montreal. 2015. Community Gardens. http://ville.montreal.qc.ca/portal/page?_pageid=5977,68887600&_dad=portal&_schema=PORTAL

City of Vancouver. 2011a. *Greenest City 2020 Action Plan*. Vancouver.

_____. 2011b. Greenest City Draft Action Plan Introductory Video. Video: 13 January 2011. https://www.youtube.com/watch?v=wZCV-JFvuZo

_____. 2014. *Greenest City 2020 Action Plan: 2013–2014 Implementation Update*. Vancouver.

_____. 2015. *2015 Corporate Business Plan*. Vancouver.

City of Vienna. 2011. *Smart City Wien: Vision 2050, Roadmap for 2020 and Beyond, Action Plan for 2012–15*. Vienna.

City of West Melbourne. 2010. Intergovernmental Coordination Element Goals, Objectives, and Policies. Horizon 2030 Comprehensive Plan. http://www.westmelbourne.org/DocumentCenter/Home/View/937

The City Project. 2015. The City Project: Equal Justice, Democracy, and Livability for All. http://www.cityprojectca.org/about/index.html

The Climate Group. 2012. *Lighting the Clean Revolution: The Rise of LEDs and What It Means for Cities*. London.

Climate Investment Funds. 2015. Strategic Climate Fund. http://www.climateinvestmentfunds.org/cif/node/3

Coutts, A.M., and R. Harris. 2013. *A Multi-Scale Assessment of Urban Heating in Melbourne during an Extreme Heat Event and Policy Approaches for Adaptation*. Technical report. Melbourne: Victorian Centre for Climate Change and Adaptation Research.

Crowdicity. 2015. UK Water Industry Use Crowdsourcing to Gain Insight into Important Issues. http://crowdicity.com/en/news/uk-water-industry-use-crowdsourcing-to-gain-insight-into-important-issues/

Crowhurst Lennard, S.H., and H.L. Lennard. 1995. *Livable Cities Observed*. Carmel, CA: Gondolier Press.

Dahiya, B. 2012. Cities in Asia, 2012: Demographics, Economics, Poverty, Environment and Governance. *Cities*. 29 (2). pp. S44–S61.

De Urbanisten. 2015. Water Squares. http://www.urbanisten.nl/wp/?portfolio=waterpleinen

Desouza, K.C., and T.H. Flanery. 2013. Designing, Planning, and Managing Resilient Cities: A Conceptual Framework. *Cities*. 35. pp. 89–99.

Development Finance International. 2014. *LED Road Lighting Design Manual*. Manila.

Development Finance International and Philips Lighting. 2015. GrEEEn Cities Energy-Efficient Lighting Plan. Background write-up.

Dr Nik and Associates. 2015. Iskandar Malaysia Corridor and City Transformation Programme. Segget River Flood Mitigation and Rehabilitation Study. Project summary.

Duany, A., J. Speck, and M. Lydon. 2010. *The Smart Growth Manual*. New York: McGraw-Hill Professional.

Dutch Water Authorities. 2015. *Water Governance: The Dutch Water Authority Model.* The Hague.

Economist Intelligence Unit. 2011. *Asian Green City Index: Assessing the Environmental Performance of Asia's Major Cities.* Munich: Siemens.

EuroFoundationCentre. 2013. Jan Gehl on Changing Mindsets about Urban Planning and Living. Video: 4 June 2013. https://www.youtube.com/watch?v=Lid9ELzzT8Y

European Environment Agency. 2011. Urban Atlas for Europe. http://www.eea.europa.eu/data-and-maps/explore-interactive-maps/urban-atlas-for-europe

Florida, R. 2005. *Cities and the Creative Class.* New York and London: Routledge.

Flow Systems. 2015. Energy: Unlocking Benefits. http://flowsystems.com.au/energy/water-energy/unlocking-benefits/

Garcia de Mendoza, P., and O.I. Rozados. 2015. DSS as a Tool to Implement the GrEEEn Cities Operational Framework from a Flood Protection Approach. Background write-up.

Georgia Tech. 2014. Crowdsourcing Could Lead to Better Water in Rural India. http://www.news.gatech.edu/2014/09/17/crowdsourcing-could-lead-better-water-rural-india

Gerding Edlen. 2015. South Waterfront Central District. http://www.gerdingedlen.com/properties/single/c/p/name/south-waterfront-central-district/

GIZ and ICLEI (Local Governments for Sustainability). 2014. *Operationalizing the Urban NEXUS: Toward Resource Efficient and Integrated Cities and Metropolitan Regions.* Eschborn: GIZ.

GIZonlineTV. 2015. Energy Efficiency in Public Buildings in Rural Mongolia. Video: 11 February 2015. https://www.youtube.com/watch?v=LVuZCDKBjQI

Global Cities Institute. 2014 and 2015. Global City Indicators Facility. http://www.cityindicators.org/

Global Commission on the Economy and Climate. 2014. *New Climate Economy.* Washington, DC: World Resources Institute. Chapter 2: Cities – Engines of National and Global Growth. http://2014.newclimateeconomy.report/cities/

Göktug, G., L. Hoyt, J. W. Meek, and U. Zimmermann. 2008. *Business Improvement Districts: Research, Theories, and Controversies.* Boca Raton: Auerbach Publications (Taylor and Francis Group).

Government of Japan, Ministry of the Environment. 2009. *Manual for Quantitative Evaluation of the Co-Benefits Approach to Climate Change Projects.* https://www.env.go.jp/en/earth/cc/manual_qecba.pdf

Government of Ontario (Canada), Ministry of Infrastructure. 2012. *Building Together: Guide for Municipal Asset Management Plans.* Toronto.

Government of Saskatchewan (Canada), Ministry of Government Relations. 2012. Ch. 2 – Asset Management Principles, Municipal Asset Management and Saskatchewan. Video: 24 January 2012. https://www.youtube.com/watch?v=anE1jRHtSjo

Grandoni, D. 2015. Satellite and GIS Technologies: What Can Be Done. Case Study from Baku, Peshawar, Karachi, Fiji, Micronesia. Presentation at the ADB Transport Sector Group and Urban Sector Group Joint Knowledge Sharing Event on How to Use Technology to Understand Urban Infrastructure and Human Mobility: A Hands-On Guide, 17 September, Manila.

Greater London Authority. 2015. *The London Plan: The Spatial Development Strategy for London Consolidated with Alterations since 2011.* London.

Green Climate Fund (GCF). 2015. Background. http://www.gcfund.org/about/the-fund.html

Green Growth Best Practice Initiative (GGBP). 2014. *Green Growth in Practice: Lessons from Country Experiences.* Seoul: GGBP and Global Green Growth Institute.

Green Growth Knowledge Platform. 2013. Moving toward a Common Approach on Green Growth Indicators. A Green Growth Knowledge Platform Scoping Paper. Paris. http://www.unep.org/greeneconomy/Portals/88/documents/partnerships/GGKP%20Moving%20toward%20a%20Common%20Approach%20on%20Green%20Growth%20Indicators.pdf

Green Infrastructure Valuation Network (GIVan). 2013. *Building Natural Value for Sustainable Economic Development: The Green Infrastructure Valuation Toolkit User Guide.* http://www.greeninfrastructurenw.co.uk/resources/Green_Infrastructure_Valuation_Toolkit_UserGuide.pdf http://www.greengrowth.org/?q=publication/green-infrastructure-valuation-tool-kit-user-guide

Habitat for Humanity. 2012. Recovery and Resilience in Vietnam.* 24 April. http://www.habitatforhumanity.org.uk/page.aspx?pid=1108

Hammer, S., L. Kamal-Chaoui, A. Robert, and M. Plouin. 2011. Cities and Green Growth: A Conceptual Framework. *OECD Regional Development Working Papers.* 8/2011. Paris: OECD.

Hashimoto, T. 2014. Urban Challenge and City Level International Technical Cooperation of Yokohama with Cebu. Presentation at the ADB Enabling GrEEEn Cities Regional Conference, 13–14 May, Manila. http://www.scribd.com/doc/226081893/City-to-City-Learning

Houstoun, L.O. Jr. 2003. *Business Improvement Districts.* 2nd edition. Washington, DC: Urban Land Institute.

Humara Bachpan. 2014. About the Campaign. http://www.humarabachpan.org/aboutus_campaign.php

IBM. 2013. IBM Harnesses Power of Big Data to Improve Dutch Flood Control and Water Management Systems. https://www-03.ibm.com/press/us/en/pressrelease/41385.wss

IBM. 2015. Smarter Cities. http://www.ibm.com/smarterplanet/sg/en/smarter_cities/overview/

ICLEI (Local Governments for Sustainability). 2015. GreenClimateCities Program: A Pathway to Urban Low-Carbon Development. http://www.iclei.org/our-activities/our-agendas/low-carbon-city/gcc.html

ICLEI (Local Governments for Sustainability) and Rockefeller Foundation. 2015. *ICLEI ACCCRN Process: Building Urban Climate Change Resilience: A Toolkit for Local Governments.* New Delhi: ICLEI South Asia.

In Asia. 2015. Seoul & Ulaanbaatar Mayors: Cooperation Vital to Global Green Development. 7 October. http://asiafoundation.org/in-asia/2015/10/07/seoul-ulaanbaatar-mayors-cooperation-vital-to-global-green-development/

Indonesia–Malaysia–Thailand Growth Triangle (IMT-GT). 2011. Director's Message. http://www.imtgt.org/director_msg_feb2011.htm

Institute of Asset Management. 2015. What Is Asset Management? https://theiam.org/what-asset-management

International Centre for Environmental Management (ICEM). 2015. *Nature Based Solutions for Sustainable and Resilient Mekong Towns.* Ha Noi: Asian Development Bank, Nordic Development Fund, and ICEM.

International Organization for Standardization (ISO). 2013. ISO 14031:2013, Environmental Management – Environmental Performance Evaluation – Guidelines. http://www.iso.org/iso/home/store/catalogue_ics/catalogue_detail_ics.htm?csnumber=52297

———. 2014. How Does Your City Compare to Others? New ISO Standard to Measure Up. 14 May. http://www.iso.org/iso/home/news_index/news_archive/news.htm?Refid=Ref1848

International Research Initiative on Adaptation to Climate Change. 2015. Coastal Cities at Risk. http://coastalcitiesatrisk.org/wordpress/

International Technical Cooperation Division, City of Yokohama. 2011. Y-PORT Brochure.

International Telecommunication Union, Telecommunication Development Sector (ITU-D). 2015. ITU Statistics: Aggregate 2005–2015 ICT Data. http://www.itu.int/en/ITU-D/Statistics/Pages/stat/default.aspx

International Water Centre Alumni Network (IWCAN). 2014. Public–Private Partnership for Urban Water Management (Australia). http://iwcan.org/public-private-partnership-australia/

* ADB recognizes "Vietnam" as Viet Nam.

Jagannathan, S., and D. Geronimo. 2013. Skills for Competitiveness, Jobs, and Employability in Developing Asia-Pacific. *ADB Briefs.* No. 18, November. Manila: Asian Development Bank. http://www.adb.org/sites/default/files/publication/31139/skills-competitiveness-jobs-employability.pdf

Jamer, M. 2015. Infrastructure Asset Management: Can the Canadian Municipal Experience Help Inform Better Practices in Southeast Asia? *The Governance Brief.* Issue 21. Manila: Asian Development Bank. http://www.adb.org/sites/default/files/publication/152995/governance-brief-21-infrastructure-asset-management.pdf

Kamal, S. A. 2015. The GrEEEn Cities Operational Framework Applied to Urban Water Systems. Background write-up.

Kang, S-B.C. 2014. Green Technology-Transfer Cases and Future Direction: ADB-GTC-K Cooperation Perspective. Presentation at ADB, 2 April, Manila.

Kavaratzis, M. 2004. From City Marketing to City Branding: Toward a Theoretical Framework for Developing City Brands. *Place Branding.* 1. pp. 58–73.

Kavaratzis, M., G. Warnaby, and G. Ashworth. 2015. *Rethinking Place Branding: Comprehensive Brand Development for Cities and Regions.* Cham: Springer.

K-Water. 2015. SWMI. http://english.kwater.or.kr/eng/busi/SWMIPage.do?s_mid=1552

Lee, C.W., M. McQuarrie, and E.T. Walker. 2015. *Democratizing Inequalities: Dilemmas of the New Public Participation.* New York City: New York University Press.

LSE Cities, ICLEI, and Global Green Growth Institute. 2013. *Going Green: How Cities Are Leading the Next Economy.* London: London School of Economics and Political Science.

m2ocity. 2015. Introduction. http://www.m2ocity.com/presentation/introduction.html

Mahadevia, D. 2002. Sustainable Urban Development in India: An Inclusive Perspective. In United Nations Research Institute for Social Development (UNRISD), ed. *Development and Cities.* Chapter 2. Oxford: UNRISD. http://peoplebuildingbettercities.org/wp-content/uploads/2013/04/Mahadevia-2002-.pdf

Marsden Jacob Associates. 2006. Securing Australia's Urban Water Supplies: Opportunities and Impediments. A Discussion paper prepared for the Department of Prime Minister and Cabinet. Camberwell. http://www.environment.gov.au/system/files/resources/a4c27c83-6edd-4fc5-84a2-70e38b183fc4/files/urban-water-report.pdf

Menon, S. 2014. Early Warning Systems (EWS) for Safer Cities. Presentation at the ADB Enabling GrEEEn Cities Regional Conference, 13–14 May, Manila.

Mercer. 2015. Quality of Living City Rankings. http://www.imercer.com/content/quality-of-living.aspx

Merk, O., S. Saussier, C. Staropoli, E. Slack, and J-H. Kim. 2012. Financing Green Urban Infrastructure. *OECD Regional Development Working Papers.* 2012/10. Paris: OECD Publishing. http://dc.doi.org/10.1787/5k92p0c6j6r0-en

Metropolitan Area Planning Council and Lincoln Institute of Land Policy. 2011. Land Pooling: A Possible Alternative to Eminent Domain and Tool for Equitable Urban Redevelopment. Presentation at the Land Pooling Symposium, 11 May, Boston, MA, United States. http://www.mapc.org/sites/default/files/FINAL_MAPC%20Presentation%20-%20Land%20Pooling%20Symposium%20-%205%2011%202011.pdf

MIT Cities. 2015. City Science. http://cities.media.mit.edu/

Modak, P. 2015. Guiding Document for the Implementation of Melaka Green City Action Plan. Final report for the Technical Assistance for Public–Private Partnership Development in Brunei Darussalam–Indonesia–Malaysia–Philippines East ASEAN Growth Area and Indonesia–Malaysia–Thailand Growth Triangle. Manila (TA-7626 REG).

Nadhamuni, S., and K. Rupanagunta. n.d. Municipal eGovernance Systems for Urban Local Bodies in India. eGovernments Foundation. http://www.egovernments.org/docs/casestudies/municipal-egovernance%20systems%20for%20local%20bodiles.pdf

Naik Singru, R. 2015. Regional Balanced Urbanization for Inclusive Cities Development: Urban–Rural Poverty Linkages in Secondary Cities Development in Southeast Asia. *Southeast Asia Working Paper Series*. No. 11. Manila: Asian Development Bank.

Naik Singru, R., and M. Lindfield. Forthcoming in 2015. *Enabling Inclusive Cities: Tool Kit for Inclusive Urban Development Projects*. Manila: Asian Development Bank.

———. Forthcoming in 2016. *Manual for Undertaking National Urban Assessments*. Manila: Asian Development Bank.

Naik Singru, R., S. Vaideeswaran, M. Popesco, and J. Salukvadze. Forthcoming in 2015. Georgia: National Urban Assessment. Manila: Asian Development Bank.

National Research Council (NRC), Committee to Review the New York City Watershed Management Strategy. 2000. *Watershed Management for Potable Water Supply: Assessing the New York City Strategy*. Washington, DC: National Academy Press.

Natural England. 2009. Green Infrastructure Guidance. www.naturalengland.org.uk/publications

Nexthamburg. 2015. www.nexthamburg.de/en/

Noda, Y. 2014. Building Cities and Infrastructure of the Future. Presentation at the ADB Enabling GrEEEn Cities Regional Conference, 13–14 May, Manila. https://www.scribd.com/doc/226085547/Building-Cities-and-Infrastructure-of-the-Future

Orange Business Services. 2011. Veolia Water and Orange Launch m2o city, a Smart Metering Operator. http://www.orange-business.com/en/press/veolia-water-and-orange-launch-m2o-city-a-smart-metering-operator

Organisation for Economic Co-operation and Development (OECD). 2006. Applying Strategic Environmental Assessment: Good Practice Guidance for Development Co-Operation. *DAC Guidelines and Reference Series*. Paris.

———. 2009. Focus on Citizens: Public Engagement for Better Policy and Services. *OECD Studies on Public Engagement*. Paris. http://www.oecd-ilibrary.org/governance/focus-on-citizens_9789264048874-en;jsessionid=10pkqk4u34xgs.x-oecd-live-03

———. 2010. SMEs and Green Growth: Promoting Sustainable Manufacturing and Eco-Innovation in Small Firms. OECD Working Party on SMEs and Entrepreneurship: Bologna+10 High-Level Meeting on Lessons from the Global Crisis and the Way Forward to Job Creation and Growth, 17–18 November, Paris. Issue Paper. No. 3. http://www.oecd.org/cfe/smes/46404383.pdf

———. 2013. Green Growth in Cities. Paris. http://www.oecd.org/regional/green-growth-in-cities.htm

———. 2014. *Green Growth Indicators 2014*. Paris. http://www.oecd-ilibrary.org/environment/green-growth-indicators-2013_9789264202030-en

———. 2015. *Water and Cities: Ensuring Sustainable Futures*. Paris. http://www.oecd.org/fr/regional/water-and-cities-9789264230149-en.htm

Pareek, S. 2015. His Traditional Rainwater Harvesting Techniques Are Helping a Parched Rajasthan Conserve Water. 28 July. http://www.thebetterindia.com/17159/jethu-singh-reviving-traditional-methods-rain-water-harvesting/

PBL. 2009. Co-benefits of Climate Policy. *PBL Report*. No. 500116005. http://www.pbl.nl/en/publications/2009/Co-benefits-of-climate-policy

Pieterse, E. 2000. Participatory Urban Governance: Practical Approaches, Regional Trends and UMP Experiences. Research paper prepared for the Urban Management Program of the United Nations Development Programme, United Nations Centre for Human Settlements, and the World Bank. http://isandla.org.za/publications/72/

Porter, M.E. 1990. *The Competitive Advantage of Nations*. New York: Free Press.

Portland Development Commission. 2011. Portland: We Build Green Cities. Video: 31 October 2011. https://vimeo.com/31402984

Puppim de Oliveira, J., C.N.H. Doll, and A. Suwa. 2013. Urban Development with Climate Co-Benefits: Aligning Climate, Environmental and Other Development Goals in Cities. *UNU-IAS Policy Report*. Yokohama: UNU-IAS. pp. 5—8. http://archive.ias.unu.edu/resource_centre/urban_development_with_climate_cobenefits-e.pdf

Rajivan, K. 2014. Linking Cities With Domestic Markets: The Tamil Nadu Experience. Presentation at the ADB Enabling GrEEEn Cities Regional Conference, 13–14 May, Manila. http://www.scribd.com/doc/225208345/Tamil-Nadu-Urban-Development-Fund-TNUDF

Ramamurthy, A. 2015. Innovations in Urban Management Using ICT in SEUW, Presentation at Southeast Asia Urban Development and Water Division Meeting, ADB, 21 April, Manila.

Reid, L., and D. Spector. 2014. Quantifying Sustainability Performance to Support Investment. Presentation at the ADB Enabling GrEEEn Cities Regional Conference, 13–14 May, Manila. https://www.scribd.com/doc/226085436/Sustainable-System-Integration-Model-SSIM

Revkin, A.C. 2009. Peeling Back Pavement to Expose Watery Havens. *The New York Times*. 17 July.

Roberts, B.H. 2015. *Toolkit for Rapid Economic Assessment, Planning, and Development of Cities in Asia*. Manila: Asian Development Bank.

Robinson, J. 2008. Developing Ordinary Cities: City Visioning Processes in Durban and Johannesburg. *Environment and Planning A*. 40 (1). pp. 74–87.

The Rockefeller Foundation. 2015a. *100 Resilient Cities*. http://www.100resilientcities.org/
_____. 2015b. *Resilience*. http://www.rockefellerfoundation.org/our-work/topics/resilience

Rouse, D.C., and I. Bunster-Ossa. 2013. *Green Infrastructure: A Landscape Approach*. Chicago and Washington, DC: APA Planning Advisory Services.

Rytter, H. 2014. Retrofitting Public Buildings for Melaka. Presentation at the ADB Enabling GrEEEn Cities Regional Conference, 13–14 May, Manila. https://www.scribd.com/doc/226085678/Retrofitting-Public-Buildings-for-Melaka-Cities-Henrik-Jensen

Salzman, J., C.A. Arnold, R. Garcia, K. Hirokawa, K. Jowers, J. LeJava, M. Pelosa, and L. Olander. 2014. The Most Important Current Research Questions in Urban Ecosystem Services. *Duke Environmental Law & Policy Forum*. XXV (1). pp. 1–47.

San Francisco Water Power Sewer. 2015. High Quality, Efficient and Reliable Water, Power and Sewer Services. http://sfwater.org/index.aspx?page=161

Sandhu, S., and S.A. Kamal. 2015. *Greenhouse Gas Inventories for Urban Operations in Southeast Asia: Challenges and Opportunities*. Manila: Asian Development Bank.

Sandhu, S., and R. Naik Singru. 2014. Enabling GrEEEn Cities: An Operational Framework for Integrated Urban Development in Southeast Asia. *Southeast Asia Working Paper Series*. No. 9. Manila: Asian Development Bank.

Santucci, L., I. Puhl, A.H. Md. Maqsood Sinha, I. Enayetullah, and W.K. Agyemang-Bonsu. 2015. *Valuing the Sustainable Development Co-Benefits of Climate Change Mitigation Actions*. Bangkok: United Nations Economic and Social Commission for Asia and the Pacific.

The School of Life. 2015: How to Make an Attractive City. Video: 26 January 2015. https://www.youtube.com/watch?v=Hy4QjmKzF1c

Seer, S. 2015. How to Use Technology to Understand Human Mobility in Cities? Presentation at the ADB Transport Sector Group and Urban Sector Group Joint Knowledge Sharing Event on How to Use Technology to Understand Urban Infrastructure and Human Mobility: A Hands-On Guide, 17 September, Manila.

Sharrocks, M. 2015. Urban Design Sustainability and Liveability Principles. Background write-up.

Sheikh, K. 2011. Establishing Social Accountability Mechanisms to Improve Municipal Service Delivery. Policy Brief. No. 2. New Delhi: Action Learning Initiatives of PRIA (Society for Participatory Research in Asia). http://indiagovernance.gov.in/files/Social%20Accountability_policy%20brief.pdf

Siemens. 2015a. Green City Index. http://www.siemens.com/entry/cc/en/greencityindex.htm

_____. 2015b. Resilience Cities: Infographics – Water Management System. http://w3.siemens.com/topics/global/en/sustainable-cities/resilience/pages/home.aspx#w2gHTM-900x725-/topics/global/en/sustainable-cities/resilience/Documents/resilience-appetizer/index.html?tab=tab1_4

Sood, P., M. Mays, and M. Lindfield. 2012. Subnational Finance for Infrastructure: Potential Roles and Opportunities for ADB. *Sustainable Development Working Paper Series*. No. 20. Manila: Asian Development Bank.

Steinberg, F., and M. Lindfield. 2012. Spatial Development and Technologies for Green Cities. In M. Lindfield and F. Steinberg, eds. *Green Cities*. Manila: Asian Development Bank. pp. 23–107.

Sturgis, S. 2015. Kids in India Are Sparking Urban Planning Changes by Mapping Slums. Citylab. 19 February. http://www.citylab.com/tech/2015/02/kids-are-sparking-urban-planning-changes-by-mapping-their-slums/385636/?utm_source=SFFB

TED-Ed. 2013. Urbanization and the Evolution of Cities across 10,000 Years – Vance Kite. Video: 12 September 2013. http://ed.ted.com/lessons/urbanization-and-the-future-of-cities-vance-kite

Teipelke, R. 2012. *Global City Indicators Facility*. http://blog.inpolis.com/2012/08/30/global-city-indicators-facility/

_____. 2015. *Urban NEXUS Tools and Case Studies*. Sector Project Sustainable Development of Metropolitan Regions. Eschborn: GIZ.

Tetteroo-Bueno, F. 2014. Green Innovation and Products. Presentation at the ADB Enabling GrEEEn Cities Regional Conference, 13–14 May, Manila. https://www.scribd.com/doc/226084841/Green-Innovations-and-Products

Todes, A. 2012. New Directions in Spatial Planning? Linking Strategic Spatial Planning and Infrastructure Development. *Journal of Planning Education and Research*. 32 (4). pp. 400–414.

Towers Watson. 2014. *Top Pension Fund Assets Hit $15 Trillion*. 2 September. https://www.towerswatson.com/en/Press/2014/09/Top-pension-fund-assets-hit-15-trillion-US-dollars

UK Water Industry Research. 2015. Water Talkers. https://watertalkers.crowdicity.com/

United Cities and Local Governments (UCLG). 2011. A Very Civil Partnership. *United Cities*. March. pp. 44–46. http://www.citiesalliance.org/sites/citiesalliance.org/files/CA_Images/MENTORING%20article%20in%20united%20cities.pdf

_____. 2014. Why We Need an #UrbanSDG - 1st World Cities Day. Video: 30 October 2014. https://www.youtube.com/watch?v=EIQByFfVJ28

United Nations Department of Economic and Social Affairs (UNDESA). 2014. Open Working Group proposal for Sustainable Development Goals. https://sustainabledevelopment.un.org/sdgsproposal

_____. 2015a. Sustainable Development Goals. https://sustainabledevelopment.un.org/topics

_____. 2015b. Sustainable Development Knowledge Platform. https://sustainabledevelopment.un.org/

United Nations Development Programme (UNDP). 2013. Sustainable and Livable Cities: Toward Ecological Civilization. China National Human Development Report 2013.* http://hdr.undp.org/en/content/sustainable-and-liveable-cities-toward-ecological-civilization

United Nations Economic and Social Commission for Asia and the Pacific (UNESCAP). 2015a. Green Growth. http://www.greengrowth.org/

_____. 2015b. *Water and Green Growth: Case Studies from Asia and the Pacific*. Bangkok.

United Nations Environment Programme (UNEP). 2008. *Green Jobs: Toward Decent Work in a Sustainable, Low-Carbon World*. Washington, DC: Worldwatch Institute. http://www.unep.org/PDF/UNEPGreenjobs_report08.pdf

* ADB recognizes "China" as the People's Republic of China.

_____. 2011. *Toward a Green Economy: Pathways to Sustainable Development and Poverty Eradication—A Synthesis for Policy Makers*. Paris. www.unep.org/greeneconomy

United Nations Human Settlements Programme (UN-Habitat). 2000. Global Campaign on Good Urban Governance. Concept paper. Nairobi.

_____. 2009a. *Innovative Approaches for Involuntary Resettlement: Lunawa Environmental Improvement and Community Development Project*. Nairobi.

_____. 2009b. *Planning Sustainable Cities: Global Report on Human Settlements 2009*. London and Sterling: Earthscan. http://cn.unhabitat.org/downloads/docs/GRHS2009/GRHS.2009.pdf

_____. 2012. Better Cities for Kosovo – Visioning as Participatory Planning Tool – Learning from Kosovo Practices. Chapter 3: Visioning Toolkit. Nairobi. pp. 24–33. http://unhabitat-kosovo.org/repository/docs/UN-Habitat_visioning_toolkit-c_205245.pdf

_____. 2013a. PSUP Introduction Video. Video: 2 December 2013. https://vimeo.com/80786019#at=276

_____. 2013b. *State of the World's Cities 2012/2013: Prosperity of Cities*. New York: Routledge. http://unhabitat.org/books/prosperity-of-cities-state-of-the-worlds-cities-20122013/.

_____. 2014. Paper City – An Urban Story. Video: 9 October 2014. https://www.youtube.com/watch?v=-Bqx2BuFjik

_____. 2015a. Climate Change. http://unhabitat.org/urban-themes/climate-change/

_____. 2015b. UN-Habitat Urban Data. http://urbandata.unhabitat.org/

United Nations Human Settlements Programme (UN-Habitat), Institute for Transportation and Development Policy (ITDP), and Clean Air Initiative (CAI). 2013. *The Tool for the Rapid Assessment of Urban Mobility in Cities with Data Scarcity (TRAM)*. Nairobi: UN-Habitat. http://mirror.unhabitat.org/downloads/docs/The_%20tool_for_rapid_assessment_of_Urban_Mobility_in_Cities_with_Data_Scarcity.pdf

United States Environmental Protection Agency (US EPA). 2015a. Pollution Prevention (P2) and TRI. http://www2.epa.gov/toxics-release-inventory-tri-program/pollution-prevention-p2-and-tri

_____. 2015b. Water Infrastructure Finance and Innovation Act. http://water.epa.gov/grants_funding/cwsrf/wifia.cfm

_____. 2015c. *What Is Green Infrastructure?* http://water.epa.gov/infrastructure/greeninfrastructure/gi_what.cfm

Urban Climate Change Research Network (UCCRN), Center for Climate Systems Research, Earth Institute, Columbia University. 2011. *Climate Change and Cities: First Assessment Report of the Urban Climate Change Research Network*. Cambridge: Cambridge University Press.

Urban Gateway. 2015. Urban Gardening Builds Cohesive Communities. http://www.urbangateway.org/news/urban-gardening-builds-cohesive-communities

Van Averbeke, W. 2007. Urban Farming in the Informal Settlements of Atteridgeville, Pretoria, South Africa. *Water South Africa*. 33 (3). pp. 337–342.

Van Etten, J. 2014. Prioritizing City Infrastructure Investments. Presentation at the ADB Enabling GrEEEn Cities Regional Conference, 13–14 May, Manila. https://www.scribd.com/doc/226085277/City-Infrastructure-Investment-Programming-and-Prioritization-CIIPP-Toolkit

Vanier, D. J., and S. Rahman. 2004. *MIIP Report: A Primer on Municipal Infrastructure Asset Management*. Montreal: National Research Council Canada. http://nparc.cisti-icist.nrc-cnrc.gc.ca/npsi/ctrl?action=shwart&index=an&req=20377283&lang=en

Vogl, A. 2012. Smart Concepts for Greener Cities. In M. Lindfield and F. Steinberg, eds. *Green Cities*. Manila: Asian Development Bank. pp. 373–405.

Vojinovic, Z., and J. Huang. 2014. *Unflooding Asia the Green Cities Way*. London: IWA Publishing for Asian Development Bank. http://www.adb.org/sites/default/files/publication/149304/unflooding-asia.pdf

WalkabilityAsia. 2012. About Walkability Asia. 23 July. http://walkabilityasia.org/2012/07/23/1286/

——. 2014. Walkability App a Finalist in the mBillionth Award. 26 July. http://walkabilityasia.org/2014/07/26/walkability-app-a-finalist-in-the-mbillionth-award/

Wamsler, C., E. Brink, and C. Rivera. 2013. Planning for Climate Change in Urban Areas: From Theory to Practice. *Journal of Cleaner Production*. 50. pp. 68–81.

Wang, X. 2014. Design and Management for the Built Environment in Response to Climate Change. Presentation at the ADB Enabling GrEEEn Cities Regional Conference, 13–14 May, Manila. www.scribd.com/doc/226076393/Design-Management-for-the-Built-Environment-in-Response-to-Climate-Change

Warner, G. 2013. In Kenya, Using Tech to Put an "Invisible" Slum on the Map. National Public Radio: 17 July. http://www.npr.org/blogs/parallels/2013/07/17/202656235/in-kenya-using-tech-to-put-an-invisible-slum-on-the-map

Water Integrity Network. 2013. Citizen Monitoring of Public Finances for Water Projects. http://www.waterintegritynetwork.net/2013/07/17/instilling-water-integrity-in-sibagat-the-philippines/

World Bank. 2010a. *Demand for Good Governance in the World Bank: Conceptual Evolution, Frameworks and Activities*. Washington, DC. http://siteresources.worldbank.org/EXTSOCIALDEVELOPMENT/Resources/244362-1193949504055/DFGG_WB_Conceptual_Evolution.pdf

——. 2010b. *Eco2Cities: Ecological Cities as Economic Cities*. Washington, DC.

——. 2013. Energizing Green Cities in Southeast Asia: Applying Sustainable Urban Energy and Emissions Planning. Washington, DC.

——. 2014. *Result-Based Northern Mountains Urban Program Project for Viet Nam*. Washington, DC. (P143596).

——. 2015a. Improving Environmental Sanitation in Coastal Cities in Vietnam.* 27 July. http://www.worldbank.org/en/results/2015/07/27/improve-environmental-sanitation-in-coastal-cities-in-vietnam

——. 2015b. mapVIETNAM. http://www.worldbank.org/mapvietnam/

World Economic Forum and Boston Consulting Group. 2014. *Strategic Infrastructure: Steps to Operate and Maintain Infrastructure Efficiently and Effectively*. Geneva. http://www3.weforum.org/docs/WEF_IU_StrategicInfrastructureSteps_Report_2014.pdf

World Vision. 2014. *Just Cities for Children: Voices from Urban Slums*. Surabaya. http://www.wvi.org/urban-programming/publication/just-cities-children-voices-urban-slums

Zhou, X., and M. Parves Rana. 2012. Social Benefits of Urban Green Space: A Conceptual Framework of Valuation and Accessibility Measurements. *Management of Environmental Quality: An International Journal*. 2 (23). pp. 173–189.

About the Authors and Contributors

Authors

Sonia Chand Sandhu

Senior Advisor to the Vice-President for Knowledge Management
and Sustainable Development, Asian Development Bank

Sonia Chand Sandhu, an environment engineer, climate resilience and sustainability specialist, is Senior Advisor to ADB's Vice-President for Knowledge Management and Sustainable Development. She has 23 years of international development experience in environmental sustainability, resilience, and integrated institutional solutions for management of multisector infrastructure operations at ADB, the World Bank (South Asia and Africa), and in the private sector. In her 17 years at the World Bank, she provided technical expertise to the design of complex operations such as the national urban sector improvement program in Kenya, co-managed India's first integrated coastal zone management program and country environmental analysis, led the environment reform through policy lending in Himachal Pradesh, and played a key role in establishing the environment management division at the India Office. At ADB, she led the GrEEEn Cities Initiative for secondary cities in Southeast Asia for balanced urban transformation and developed innovative knowledge solutions for climate resilience in the Greater Mekong Subregion. She was presented with the Innovation Award in 2013, the Knowledge Sharing Achieving Results/Impact (Innovation) award by the Vice-President and Southeast Asia Department in 2014, and the "One ADB" Integrated Initiative in Urban Development Award by the Urban Community of Practice in 2014. She holds a master's degree in environmental engineering from the University of Maryland at College Park in the United States, a bachelor's degree in architecture from Chandigarh University in India, and an executive diploma in urban management tools for climate change from the Institute for Housing and Urban Development Studies at Erasmus University Rotterdam in the Netherlands.

Ramola Naik Singru

Urban Development Specialist, Urban Development and Water Division,
Central and West Asia Department, Asian Development Bank

Ramola Naik Singru is an architect, urban designer, and planner with over 16 years of international experience in integrated urban development spanning project management, technical advisory services, research, knowledge management, and capacity building. She has worked as a consultant to ADB, the UN-Habitat, the Cities Development Initiative for Asia (CDIA), think tanks, and in the private sector. She was an adjunct faculty member of the Asian Institute of Management (AIM) and the program director for the CDIA–AIM urban management program. She has designed operational and analytical products and delivered urban management training programs for government officials, development practitioners, and urban managers from over 18 countries in Asia and the Pacific. At ADB, she jointly led the

GrEEEn Cities Initiative for secondary cities in Southeast Asia, the formulation of national urban assessments, and the Enabling Inclusive Cities tool kit under ADB's Urban Operational Plan 2012–2020. She was presented the Urban Community of Practice Chair's Award for Excellent Contribution and the "One ADB" Integrated Initiative in Urban Development Award, as well as the Knowledge Sharing Award by the ADB Vice-President for the East Asia, Southeast Asia, and Pacific Departments in 2014. She has authored and co-authored numerous publications and papers. She holds a master's degree in city design and social science from the London School of Economics and Political Science in the United Kingdom and a bachelor's degree in architecture from the University of Mumbai in India.

John Bachmann
Director at AECOM

An architect and urban planner, John Bachmann has led the preparation of development plans and strategies for more than 20 cities worldwide. His expert understanding of the spatial planning, land management, and infrastructure dimensions of city development has been built up through the preparation of urban infrastructure investment programs comprising over $4 billion in roads, water supply, sewerage, stormwater drainage, and district heating improvements. He has extensive experience in stakeholder consultation and institutional reform at the local government level. Mr. Bachmann recently led a multidisciplinary team to develop GrEEEn City Action Plans for the cities of Hue and Vinh Yen in Viet Nam, and has served as team leader for the ADB study "Addressing Disaster Risk through Improved Indicators and Land Use Management."

Vaideeswaran (Vaideesh) Sankaran
Environment, Climate Change, and Sustainable Solutions Consultant

Vaideeswaran (Vaideesh) Sankaran is a trained engineer and economist with about 25 years of work experience in the public and private sectors. Vaideesh has worked both in developed (United States, United Kingdom, and Singapore) and developing countries (India, Bangladesh, Nepal, Sri Lanka, the Maldives, Malaysia, Myanmar, Viet Nam, and in Africa). He is regularly engaged in assignments with bilateral and multilateral agencies, particularly the Asian Development Bank and the World Bank. Having worked with different types of organizations (government, private sector, and civil society organizations), Vaideesh brings with him an eclectic mix of knowledge, skills, and perspectives that enables him to provide unique, out-of-the-box, and integrated solutions.

Pierre Arnoux
Social Development Specialist (Consultant)

With a background in education, human geography, and urban planning, Pierre Arnoux has garnered extensive experience in resettlement and social development through his involvement in various projects in Southeast Asia funded by the Asian Development Bank, the World Bank, the Canadian International Development Agency, and other international donors. His expertise lies in the social dimensions of projects (resettlement, livelihood restoration, social inclusion, and stakeholder consultation). In his projects, he aims to address the interests of citizens and other stakeholders by considering them as development partners. For the last 22 years, he has worked mainly in Southeast Asia and is now permanently based in Ho Chi Minh City, Viet Nam.

Project Coordinators and Contributors

Renard Teipelke
Urban Development Specialist (Consultant), Southeast Asia Urban Development
and Water Division, Southeast Asia Department, Asian Development Bank

Renard Teipelke is the urban development specialist and project coordinator for ADB's project preparatory technical assistance for the Secondary Cities Development Program (Green Cities) in Viet Nam. As a seconded urban development specialist at ADB, he has contributed to the regional technical assistance on GrEEEn Cities. For GIZ and UN-Habitat, he has been working on the sustainable development of metropolitan regions and urban climate resilience. He also was a Mercator Fellow for International Affairs, focusing on rapid urbanization in peri-urban areas. As a team member of the Typhoon Yolanda Reconstruction Assistance and the GrEEEn Cities Initiative, he was awarded the Achieving Results/Impact Award (2013) and the Knowledge Sharing Award (2014) by the ADB vice-president for the East Asia, Southeast Asia, and the Pacific departments. He holds a master's degree in urban and economic geography and studied at the Free University of Berlin and Goethe University Frankfurt (Germany), as well as the University of California in San Diego (United States).

Sameer A. Kamal
Urban Development Specialist, Urban Development and Water Division,
Southeast Asia Department, Asian Development Bank

An environmental engineer by training, Sameer A. Kamal has over 8 years of experience in the water, environment, and urban sectors. At ADB, his work focuses on urban, water, and sanitation projects in Southeast Asia. Prior to joining ADB in 2014, he spent 5 years at the World Bank Group, where he worked on the design, development, implementation, and evaluation of water and environment projects in East and West Africa. This included a multiphase water security program in Kenya, technical assistance in the Nile and Niger river basins, and coauthoring the World Bank's water strategy for Uganda. Previously, he worked as an environmental specialist for an environmental consulting firm in the United States and as a researcher for a development consulting firm in Pakistan. He has two graduate degrees (master's of engineering and engineer's degree) in environmental engineering from the Massachusetts Institute of Technology and a bachelor's degree in chemical engineering from the University of Texas at Austin. Mr. Kamal contributed Insert C "The GrEEEn Cities Operational Framework Applied to Urban Water Systems" to Chapter 4 and supported the team in restructuring the publication.

Phuong Nguyen
Environmental Specialist, Viet Nam Country Office, World Bank

Phuong Nguyen has been the research analyst and national coordinator for ADB's regional technical assistance for Green Cities: A Sustainable Urban Future in Southeast Asia. She holds a doctorate in sustainability, a master's degree in engineering for sustainable development (from the United Kingdom), and a bachelor's degree in environmental engineering. She has worked in both developed and developing countries, now mainly in Viet Nam as an independent consultant and researcher on sustainable development, climate change, and environmental management for development projects funded by ADB, the World

Bank, Japan International Cooperation Agency, United Nations Industrial Development Organization, United Nations Environment Programme, and other international agencies. Ms. Nguyen has a strong network and substantial experience working with the Government of Viet Nam (central and local) at both the policy and operational and technical levels.

Contributors
In alphabetical order

Balamurugan Ratha Krishnan
Deputy Director, Economic Cooperation and Integration Division, Center for IMT-GT Subregional Cooperation (CIMT)

Balamurugan Ratha Krishnan was attached with the Economic Planning Unit, a Malaysian government agency, for 7 years. He commenced his career back in 2006 as an assistant director for the Regional Development Section under the Economic Planning Unit for the Prime Minister's Department and was appointed principal assistant director in 2012 and 2013. Since 2013, he has been at the Center for IMT-GT Subregional Cooperation (CIMT), an international organization based in Malaysia. He is Deputy Director for the Economic Cooperation and Integration Division, in charge of projects that serve the vision of CIMT for improving the quality of life in the subregion by establishing collaborative relationships globally and executing projects for the betterment of people's lives. He earned a bachelor's degree in computer science in 2004. In 2007, he received his public management diploma (with distinction). Mr. Balamurugan contributed good practices from the IMT-GT Subregional Cooperation experience.

Pierre Beauchamp
Municipal, Civil, and Environment Engineer (Consultant), Urban Development and Water Division, Southeast Asia Department, Asian Development Bank

Founder and senior member of exp, Pierre Beauchamp offers 40 years of experience in engineering and management. He completed his studies in art at Laval University in 1967 and received a bachelor's degree applied science from the University of Sherbrooke in 1973, a certificate in management from the University of Quebec in 1977, and a master's degree in science (bioresource engineering) from McGill University in 2014 (Canada). He has managed over 60 projects related to filtration and wastewater treatment plants, including their respective pipe networks. As a team leader, he has also conducted more than 100 project missions in the People's Republic of China and Viet Nam in the last 20 years. Today, he specializes in green infrastructure. Mr. Beauchamp developed an integrated framework to assist engineering organizations in planning the startup of new projects in the context of greening and sustainability related to stormwater, water supply, and wastewater. He is a member of the Quebec and Ontario Orders of Engineers. Mr. Beauchamp contributed to the application of the GrEEEn Cities Operational Framework to green infrastructure and low-carbon technology in Chapter 4.

Royston A.C. Brockman
Team Leader and Urban Planner, Secondary Cities Development Program (Green Cities),
Urban Development and Water Division, Southeast Asia Department,
Asian Development Bank

Royston Brockman has had more than 40 years of professional experience working in the infrastructure and urban development sectors of the developing and developed world for both the private and public sectors. He has extensive country experience throughout Asia and the Pacific, Africa, and Europe, and has advised national and local governments and the private sector on infrastructure project finance, public–private partnerships, strategic urban development, urban renewal, affordable housing, and service delivery improvement. He has been working as a consultant for ADB and the World Bank, preparing and structuring urban development, shelter, and infrastructure projects for financing, and has been engaged in institutional strengthening and capacity development programs. Recent assignments have included projects in Mongolia, the Philippines, and Viet Nam. Mr. Brockman has coauthored several major publications including ADB's *Managing Asian Cities and City Development Strategies to Reduce Poverty*. He contributed to the application of the GrEEEn Cities Operational Framework to asset management in Chapter 6 and provided comments on the Executive Summary and Chapter 7.

Pedro García de Mendoza
Specialist in Hydrology, Flood Protection and DSS (Consultant), Urban Development
and Water Division, Southeast Asia Department, Asian Development Bank

Pedro García de Mendoza is a senior consultant in the water sector, with a strong focus in hydrology, river environment planning, and hydraulic control, under multidisciplinary approaches. His background is built upon 23 years of professional experience in key managerial positions in TYPSA (as director of hydraulic planning and control, and science, technology and innovation, and as regional head of water engineering) and later in the INCLAM Group (as head of the hydrology and hydraulics department). In Southeast Asia and in ADB-funded projects, he has been engaged in the Design of a Project Demonstration Activity to Improve Environmental Conditions of Estero de Paco in Metro Manila (Philippines) and in the ongoing Secondary Cities Development Program (Green Cities) in Viet Nam. He holds a master's degree in civil engineering (Polytechnical University of Catalonia, Spain), and a certificate from the Management Development Programme from the IESE Business School in Barcelona (Spain). Mr. Mendoza contributed to the application of the GrEEEn Cities Operational Framework to decision support systems in Chapter 6.

Sushma Kotagiri
Social Development Specialist, Transport and Communications Division,
East Asia Department, Asian Development Bank

Sushma Kotagiri, a sociologist with development experience of over 12 years at ADB, Oxfam GB, Eldis UK, Lepra Society, and Mahila Samakhya, has been focusing on various social dimensions and sustainability solutions including monitoring and evaluation across a diverse sector portfolio of urban and municipal infrastructure, health, transport, education, child labor, forestry, and natural resources management. She currently leads social inclusiveness and accountability applications for project operations and policy across Cambodia, Indonesia, the Lao People's Democratic Republic, Myanmar, the Philippines, and Viet Nam. In the past, she led the assessment and preparation of social development and safeguards feasibility for public–private partnership projects across a multisector portfolio in 10 cities across five major states in India. She holds a master's degree in gender and development studies from the Institute of Development Studies, University of Sussex (United Kingdom). Ms. Kotagiri contributed to the application of the GrEEEn Cities Operational Framework to resettlement in Chapter 4.

Michael R. Lindfield
Institutional Specialist, Secondary Cities Development Program (Green Cities),
Urban Development and Water Division, Southeast Asia Department,
Asian Development Bank

Michael Lindfield is an economist and financial analyst with over 30 years experience in international sustainable urban development policy formulation and in designing the institutional and financial mechanisms to implement urban development and infrastructure policy. He is a senior advisor to the SMART Infrastructure Facility. Previously, he was lead urban development specialist and chair of the Urban Community of Practice at ADB, as well as program manager for the Cities Development Initiative for Asia. He has also served as department head of the Institute for Housing and Urban Development Studies in the Netherlands and as deputy director and senior research fellow in the Australian Housing and Urban Research Institute (Queensland University of Technology). He has worked as a consultant for the World Bank, ADB, and the United Nations, as well as for private sector and government agencies. He has a bachelor's degree in architecture (Sydney University), a master's degree in commerce (University of New South Wales in Australia), and a doctorate in economics (Erasmus University in the Netherlands). Mr. Lindfield contributed to GrEEEn City financing in Chapter 6.

Rajivan Krishnaswamy
Consultant; former Managing Director and CEO, Tamil Nadu Urban Development Fund

Rajivan Krishnaswamy has a master's degree and doctorate in economics from the University of Southern California, Los Angeles. He has worked for the Government of India (1979–1996) at various levels, starting from city level administration to the prime minister's office. Subsequently, he worked in the private sector, as the CEO and managing director of the Tamil Nadu Urban Development Fund (1996–2003), and later as senior urban finance specialist at the World Bank in Washington, DC (2003–2008). Currently, he is an independent consultant based in Chennai, working in the People's Republic of China, Ghana, Indonesia, Nepal, and Viet Nam. Mr. Rajivan contributed Insert D "Linking City Infrastructure Needs with Domestic Finance in Tamil Nadu, India" in Chapter 6.

Savita Mullapudi Narasimhan
Consultant, Strategy and Policy Department, Asian Development Bank

Savita Mullapudi Narasimhan is a development policy expert trained in law and economics with over 12 years of experience in international trade, law, innovation systems, and interconnections in health, agriculture, environment, and education sector imbalances, and how sustainable livelihoods (urban and rural) are impacted through cross-sector linkages. She has contributed to technical assistance and capacity development in over 52 developing countries. She has worked for the World Bank in Washington, DC, the United Nations Development Programme in New York, and is currently with ADB in Manila. She holds a bachelor's degree in economics (merit recipient) and a bachelor's degree in law from

Bombay University, as well as a master's degree in law from George Washington University, Washington, DC. She is currently with the Strategy and Policy Department at ADB working on the global sustainable development agenda 2030 and assisting in building an ADB-wide strategic response to Financing for Development, the Sustainable Development Goals, and the upcoming climate change deal. Ms. Narasimhan contributed inputs on linkages of the Sustainable Development Goals and Financing for Development in Chapter 2.

Joji I. Reyes
Economist, Secondary Cities Development Program (Green Cities),
Urban Development and Water Division, Southeast Asia Department,
Asian Development Bank

Joji I. Reyes, president of the US-based GlobalWorks International Corporation, is an economist with over 30 years of experience in policy analysis and reform, program and project design and implementation, and economic and financial appraisal in Asia and the Pacific. She has worked with the World Bank, ADB, Department for International Development of the United Kingdom, United States Agency for International Development, other donors, public financial institutions, and private sector groups in the areas of urban development and housing, water supply and sanitation, agribusiness development, microfinance and enterprise development, public sector governance, and public–private partnerships. Ms. Reyes holds a master's degree in business administration from the University of the Philippines at Diliman and a doctorate in economics from the University of Hawaii. She is also an alumna of the Hawaii-based East–West Center (EWC), an internationally recognized organization that promotes better understanding among the people and nations of the United States, Asia, and the Pacific through cooperative study, research, and dialogue. Ms. Reyes contributed to the economic and financial analysis and cobenefits of the 3Es in Chapter 4 and to the GrEEEn City financing section in Chapter 6.

Mike Sharrocks
Urban Designer, Secondary Cities Development Program (Green Cities), Urban
Development and Water Division, Southeast Asia Department, Asian Development Bank

Mike Sharrocks is a director of a consultancy practicing in urban and regional planning, urban design, and sustainable tourism planning. He has 35 years of experience in development planning projects in North America; Europe; the Middle East; and South, East, and Southeast Asia, as well as the South Pacific. This work has included the preparation of urban master plans and development frameworks, area-based development strategies, sustainable development and infrastructure projects, tourism strategies at the national and regional level, as well as sustainable land management and environmental improvement schemes. He has carried out projects for a range of multilateral and national donor agencies, private sector companies, as well as national and local government agencies. He has a bachelor's degree in urban and regional planning and a postgraduate diploma in urban design from Oxford Polytechnic. Mr. Sharrocks has worked on a number of ADB-funded projects including as an urban designer on the Secondary Cities Development Program (Green Cities) in Viet Nam. Mr. Sharrocks contributed Insert A "Integrated Urban Design Principles" in Chapter 4.

Niels Van Dijk

Water Operators Partnerships Program Team Leader (Consultant),
Sector Advisory Service Division, Sustainable Development
and Climate Change Department, Asian Development Bank

Niels Van Dijk is a senior urban management specialist with over 20 years of professional experience in urban infrastructure development in Asia. He has been senior advisor and team leader (consultant) of ADB's Water Operators Partnerships (WOP) program since 2010. This highly successful regional technical assistance program focuses on replicating best practices in utility operations. He also advises ADB on establishing a similar program for supporting implementation of Green City Action Plans through Urban Management Partnerships. Mr. Van Dijk lives in Dubai from where he manages the international business of Otak, Inc., a United States-based multidisciplinary urban design firm, and the Middle East business of HanmiGlobal, a Project and Construction Management consulting firm based in the Republic of Korea. Mr. Van Dijk, with John Sutton (Water Management Specialist at Urban Solutions), contributed to Chapter 5.

Viet Nam: Secondary Cities Development Project – Green Cities team of consultants and ADB specialists on field mission

Photo Credit: Ramola Naik Singru

Index

Boxes, figures, notes, and tables are indicated by b, f, n, and t following page numbers. Italicized page numbers indicate photographs.

Glimpses of the
First Regional Conference on Enabling GrEEEn Cities

13–14 May 2014 • ADB headquarters, Manila

A Paradigm Shift:
Doing things Differently

Photo Credit: ADB/Edsel Roman

MAKING
GREEEN
Cities
A REALITY

Join Our Live Online Chat | 29 May 2014, 0600-0730 GMT

We have to work hand in hand across sectors and with different levels of government. For this, we have to strengthen our GrEEEn governance structure. And I want to congratulate ADB and the GrEEEn Cities Initiative for partnering with us and other cities across the region to foster a more sustainable, participatory, and integrated urban development. We are together on this journey, whose achievements and challenges are so well captured in this book. I sincerely hope to see more governments join this effort to make our future grEEEner and a better place to live.

Datuk Seri Ir. Hj. Idris bin Hj. Haron
(Chief Minister, State of Melaka, Malaysia)

This book provides a wide range of actual and useful cases of grEEEn urban solutions for policy makers and practitioners in Asia and the Pacific to follow and adopt. Our city, Yokohama, also took a clear path of putting environment considerations up front in our urban development and management and turning them into opportunity for economic growth and equitable society already. Alongside ADB, we will continue to collaborate with and provide grEEEn solutions to enhance sustainable developments for cities in Asia and the Pacific through our urban partnership program "Y-PORT."

Fumiko Hayashi
(Mayor, City of Yokohama, Japan)

Instead of asking if our cities can become grEEEn, citizens more and more often are asking what they can actually do to contribute to this clear pathway toward livability. This book resembles that understanding of achieving more sustainable cities through a joint effort at the local, national, and international levels. The book's message links integrated urban development with the global development agenda, with cities making a difference by reducing greenhouse gas emissions and promoting green technology and businesses, as reflected in the numerous practice examples presented and discussed in this book.

Raymond Louie
(Councillor and Acting Mayor, City of Vancouver; and President, Federation of Canadian Municipalities, Canada)

A local approach to sustainability has proven to be a success. But the apparent silo-thinking in local governments underscores the need for a paradigm shift in urban development toward integrated solutions, as this book argues. It is a challenge city leaders have to tackle together with civil society, the private sector, and international organizations such as ADB and ICLEI. And this book proposes possible pathways for such cooperation through the Urban Management Partnerships toward achieving livable cities.

Gino Van Begin
(Secretary General,
ICLEI—Local Governments for Sustainability)

This is an incredibly important piece of work, and it comes at precisely the right moment. The authors are building their arguments and insights based on urban praxis rather than yet more theoretical perspectives. They have managed to put together an impressive review and catalogue of the urban green growth literature and relevant praxis tools. This will certainly be of great value far beyond the Asian focus.

Philipp Rode
(Executive Director, Urban Age, LSE Cities,
London School of Economics and Political Science)

About the Authors

Sonia Chand Sandhu is the senior advisor to the Vice-President for Knowledge Management and Sustainable Development, Asian Development Bank.

Ramola Naik Singru is an urban development specialist with the Urban Development and Water Division, Central and West Asia Department, Asian Development Bank.

John Bachmann is a director at AECOM.

Vaideeswaran Sankaran is an environment, climate change, and sustainable solutions consultant.

Pierre Arnoux is a social development specialist.

Dedicated to the future generation

Roshni, Vivek, Deryek, Vishal, Shreya
Ishaan, Sana
Rachel, Kaden, Kai
Sanan, Sanjula
Guillaume, Étienne, Philippe